THE BASIS FOR CHRISTIAN ETHICS

THE BASIS FOR CHRISTIAN ETHICS

JOHN GALLAGHER, C.S.B.

PAULIST PRESS
New York/Mahwah

Copyright © 1985
by John Gallagher

Library of Congress
Catalog Card Number: 84-62560

ISBN: 0-8091-2690-7

Published by Paulist Press
997 Macarthur Boulevard
Mahwah, New Jersey 07430

Printed and bound in the
United States of America

CONTENTS

III.   Practical Moral Judgment

IV.   Individual Conscience
and the Church

ACKNOWLEDGEMENTS

This book is the product of a long process of thought, and I wish to acknowledge the contribution to that process of the two families to which I am fortunate to belong. I thank God for the deep faith, integrity and understanding of Mary Alberta and the late Fergal Gallagher, my parents and first teachers of morality. If my academic reflections maintain some contact with everyday experience, much credit must go to my three sisters and four brothers, who from time to time have been known to express an opinion or two, and whose opinions I respect. To my second family, the Basilian Fathers, I am grateful for support and encouragement, and for a religious and academic training which I cherish. I wish to mention especially the late Fr. Elliot Allen, C.S.B., who gave generously of his time, wit and wisdom to me as to many others, and Fr. Leo Walsh, C.S.B., whose patience and insight in reviewing a monotonous series of drafts has saved this work from numerous oversights and lapses in logic or grammar. It is stretching the notion of familial debts only slightly to include among them what I owe to those Redemptorist Fathers and Brothers of the Christian Schools who have been so important in my education.

INTRODUCTION

The title "The Basis for Christian Ethics" gives only a general indication of the contents of this book. Some explanation of the meaning of that title will give a more precise indication of what to expect in the following pages.

The term "ethics" is explained by reference to the term "moral." We speak of certain actions as moral actions. This accountant who embezzles a tidy sum and flees to Rio de Janeiro does something morally bad. His neighbor who gives an honest day's work in return for his pay is doing something morally good. A man who is temporarily insane burns down his friend's garage. We would not consider his a moral action at all. By "ethics" we mean the study of moral life, or the study of actions and persons insofar as they are moral.

Having explained "ethics" by reference to "moral," one might be expected next to define "moral." That is no simple matter, however. Ethicists differ in the meanings they give or imply for this term. One can justify a particular definition of the term only after one has proceeded some way in elaborating one's ethical theory. For the time being, therefore, we will depend on people knowing more or less what we mean when we use the term "moral." Thorough analysis of its meaning will come later.

Ethics, we have said, is a study of moral life. However, not every study of moral life is ethics. An anthropologist describing the moral behavior of a Papuan tribe is not necessarily doing ethics. What kind of study of moral life is called ethics? For the purposes of this book, ethics is defined as a general study of moral life which deals with two types of question, one critically normative and the other theoretical.

What is a critically normative question? First, what is a moral norm? It is a standard by reference to which a particular action can be judged morally good or bad. A certain individual with educated fingers picks your pocket on payday. We judge that his action, though technically pro-

1

ficient, is morally bad because stealing is morally bad. His particular action is judged by reference to the general norm that stealing is morally bad. Ethics not only studies these moral norms. It studies them critically. That is, it does not simply list or describe various norms which people use. It attempts to show that certain norms are correct or incorrect.

The ethicist is confronted not only by questions about norms, but also by other questions such as: What is it that makes an action to be a moral action? By what sort of thought processes does one use general norms in making moral judgments about particular cases? The study of such questions and their solutions is not a normative but a theoretical study. In popular usage if we say that something is theoretical we may mean that it is hypothetical, or abstract, or perhaps unreal. By calling this part of ethics theoretical we do not mean any of those things. We mean that in these matters the ethicist strives to explain what is, not what ought to be. For example, an ethicist may explain that in a moral action there are two elements, a judgment and a choice. Here he is not stating a norm concerning what ought to be. He is stating what is in fact the case.

One could divide ethics into two disciplines. One, ethics proper, would be critically normative. The other, to which we might give a separate name, would deal with theoretical questions. Most books on ethics, however, do not clearly and systematically separate the two parts, and some considerable difficulties arise when one attempts to do so. In this book no clear and systematic separation is attempted. Here ethics is treated as one discipline which deals with two types of questions, one critically normative and the other concerned with the theoretical material which provides the proper context for the critically normative study.

Ethics is a *general* study. What this means may be explained by comparing ethics with medicine. Medicine deals both with particular realities and with generalities. A physician prescribes this particular treatment for this particular patient who has this particular case of pneumonia. A medical textbook, on the other hand, makes statements which apply not merely to one particular case of pneumonia but to a whole class of cases. If the textbook focused only on what is unique about a particular case it would not help the physician recognize and treat other cases of pneumonia when he meets them later. Accordingly in medicine there are two levels on which people function. On the level of the *practice* of medicine the physician uses general truths but he focuses on something particular—the particular person who has a particular ailment requiring a particular treatment. On the level of *general study* (the science of medicine), conversely, one studies particular cases but one focuses on the general statements which apply to whole classes of cases.

In moral matters too people function on two different levels. On the level of *practice* one pays a debt or refuses to pay a debt, having first made a judgment about whether refusal to pay the debt in this case is morally good or bad. The individual may use general principles in making this judgment but he focuses on something particular, the action of paying this debt, performed by this particular individual in this particular set of circumstances. On the level of general study (ethics), conversely, one may study particular cases but one focuses on general statements which hold true for whole classes of cases. If ethics focused only on what is unique about a particular case of paying a debt it would give no help in making judgments in other cases of paying of debts.

To sum up: just as in medicine there is a level of practice and a level of the general study or science of medicine, so in moral life there is a level of moral practice and a level of general study which we call ethics.

Having discussed the nature of ethics, we can ask what it means that this is a book on *Christian* ethics. Contemporary scholars argue about the very notion of Christian ethics. Temporarily setting aside these disputes we will define Christian ethics as that ethics which should serve as guide to Christian moral life. Later we will discuss such disputed questions as whether there is a specifically Christian ethics, and, if there is, how it is related to philosophical ethics.

The term ''moral theology'' can be used interchangeably with ''Christian ethics.''

This book is concerned with the *basis* for Christian ethics. One can distinguish two sorts of basis for ethics, one normative and the other theoretical.

To illustrate what is meant by a normative basis, let us consider the norm that it is morally wrong to steal. Why is it morally wrong to steal? One line of argument could be that if stealing is allowed then people will have no adequate incentive to produce those things necessary or useful for life because it would be more profitable to spend one's time stealing and protecting one's property against theft. In this way one supports the norm against stealing by appealing to the principle that it is good to produce certain things. Next one may ask why one should accept this latter principle. In answer one may appeal to still other principles.

There are two alternatives concerning the outcome of this process. One is that it is endless, each principle being justified by appeal to another principle which in turn requires justification by appeal to still another principle. If this is the case the whole process is fruitless, because one is no closer to a basis for ethics after participating in the reasoning process than one was before. For reasons which become clear in the course of this book, I have rejected this first alternative.

The other alternative is that, in some cases at least, the process of showing that moral norms are correct can eventually arrive at first principles. A first principle for a particular thinker is a principle which he accepts as evident in itself and not because it is demonstrated by an appeal to something else. (Whether what one ethicist accepts as a first principle will be accepted by everyone as a first principle is an issue to be clarified later.) Those first principles which can be used to demonstrate the correctness of moral norms constitute the *normative basis* for ethics.

We noted earlier that ethics deals not only with normative but also with theoretical questions. What is it that makes an action to be a moral action? By what sort of intellectual processes does one use general norms to come to sound moral judgments in particular cases? In pursuing such questions we will not always reach exhaustive explanations which leave no further questions to ask. However, we can realistically hope for explanations sufficiently clear and convincing that they deserve at least tentative assent. The effort to pursue these questions to as satisfactory an explanation as possible is to seek to give the *theoretical basis* for ethics.

This book is concerned with both the normative and the theoretical basis for Christian ethics. In the pursuit of answers it is often cumbersome and difficult to separate rigorously the normative from the theoretical elements in ethics, and this book makes no effort to do so.

To explain the word "the" in our title may seem to be carrying thoroughness too far. However, "The Basis for Christian Ethics" may sound presumptuous, suggesting that the truth of the matter is to be found here and that all differing explanations are wrong. "A Basis for Christian Ethics" would suggest, more modestly, that there may be several appropriate ways of dealing with the subject and that this is a tentative and imperfect effort to give one such way.

Why then the definite rather than the indefinite article in the title? I believe that there is one correct basis for Christian ethics. Any explanation of the basis for Christian ethics is inadequate insofar as it fails to set forth fully this one basis.[1] This book, of course, gives one of those inadequate explanations, a characteristic that I presume it shares with ethical writings generally. ''The'' in our title indicates that this work is an attempt to discuss this one basis for Christian ethics. It does not imply the belief that this basis has been fully and adequately explained in these pages.

This book contains four parts. The first two parts deal with the criteria for deciding what is morally good or morally bad. Part One discusses that topic from the point of view of human reason and experience without using Sacred Scripture. Part Two discusses the same topic using Sacred Scripture. Part Three examines how one makes moral judgments in particular cases while making proper use of general moral norms. Part Four deals with the role of the Church community in helping the individual to make correct moral judgments.

There are certain Christian ethicists, those who reject natural law in ethics, who hold that human reason is corrupted or at least gravely distorted by sin. They point out that reason by itself cannot know either the true goal of human life or the way to that goal provided by Jesus Christ. Therefore, they conclude, human reason without Sacred Scripture is not a reliable guide for Christian moral life.[2] Such thinkers might well object to the inclusion of Part One in a work which claims to be Christian ethics.

However, by beginning this work with the non-scriptural treatment in Part One I am not deciding the question of what role human reason should play in Christian ethics. That question will be discussed later, after the scriptural data and the human experience of morality have been analyzed. In Sacred Scripture God speaks to us in human terms. In order to understand what Scripture may say about morality it is useful first to analyze the human experience of morality and the terms we use to discuss it. It is for that reason that I begin with the analysis of moral experience in Part One.

It might be objected that by beginning with a philosophical analysis in Part One I risk distorting the message of Scripture by forcing it into preconceived categories. I recognize the risk. However, it is a risk also for those who refuse to analyze the experience and the terms used to interpret Scripture. Scholarly method and the believing community provide several means for minimizing such distortion. Naiveté about terms is not one of them.

Other readers will find Part One unsatisfactory for quite a different reason. For them this part will seem to ignore the very essence of morality. It will appear to fall into the naturalist fallacy, reducing the analysis of norms (what ought to be) to an analysis of nature (what is). At this point I can answer only that I believe that much of modern ethical speculation is based on a misunderstanding or mystification whose sources can be traced back at least as far as the voluntarism in certain theological schools of thirteenth and fourteenth century Europe. I hope that at the end of Part One it may be clearer to these readers why I reject certain notions that are accepted as obvious by many modern ethicists. To sort out the historical details would require an extensive history of ethics.

This book is intended especially for students who have finished a first university degree and are beginning a concentrated study of theology. I hope that it will be useful also to undergraduate students and to the educated public generally. It presupposes no previous courses in ethics or theology. I have tried to explain terms and concepts as they are introduced. However, readers with no previous courses in ethics may find some passages rather heavy reading. This is not a popularization. It tries not to gloss over the principal difficulties inherent in the subject matter. On the other hand, it does not elaborate on the alternative positions of different thinkers on particular points and the reasons for or against such positions. Such a procedure might be satisfying for advanced scholars specializing in Christian ethics, but it would make this work too long or too difficult for other readers.

My understanding of ethics is dominated by what I have learned from Thomas Aquinas. I have not, however, set out to write a Thomistic work. I am not an expert on Aquinas. On many points in the following pages I have not confined myself to the ideas of Aquinas. Nor do I wish to draw fire from those to whom "Thomist" suggests an attempt to breathe life into outdated ideas. This book then should be allowed to stand or fall on its own.

This book was written by a Roman Catholic, and some of its ideas will find readier acceptance or understanding among Roman Catholics than among other Christians. Yet I have hesitated to call it a work on Roman Catholic ethics. I have tried to take account of certain insights, questions and objections of non-Catholic Christians. Much more ecumenical work remains to be done in Christian ethics, of course. At this point I cannot hope to satisfy Christians generally. I hope, however, that Anglican, Protestant and Orthodox readers may find this book more interesting than it would have been had I discussed only more narrowly Roman Catholic interests.

A number of aspects of moral life have been treated separately in the following chapters. It is important, however, that each distinct aspect be understood not in isolation but in relation to the others. Part One understood without Part Two might give the false impression that human reason is presented as a source of ethics independently of Sacred Scripture. To read Parts One and Two without Part Three is to stop at the level of abstract generalities without investigating how these are to be related to practice. The omission of Part Four might give the disastrous misconception that the reader is being sent out, armed with this book, to discover moral values in an individualistic way. No part of this work can be properly understood or applied apart from the whole.

This book omits several topics which might properly have been included in a work such as this. For example, I have presumed that the moral agent is a free and responsible agent, but I have not discussed what that means. As a result, this book is an incomplete treatment of the basis for Christian ethics. It focuses on how one can judge correctly what is morally good or bad, and does not discuss the freedom and responsibility with which the moral agent follows or fails to follow that judgment. However, had freedom and responsibility been discussed, still further topics would remain untreated. One must draw the line somewhere. Freedom and responsibility are topics whose importance and difficulty merit book-length treatment. I hope eventually to deal with them in a companion volume to this one.

PART ONE

The Criteria for Moral Judgment:
Human Reason and Experience

A physician decides not to inform a particular patient that his illness is grave. Along with the medical judgment the physician also judges that this is the morally good thing to do in the circumstances. Another person interested in the case disagrees, claiming that the physician has a moral obligation in this case to let the patient know the true gravity of his illness. In response the physician gives reasons why it is morally good to withhold that information. Such reasons used to argue in favor of a moral judgment we will call the criteria for moral judgment.

Two people who disagree about a moral judgment may appeal to differing, even contradictory, criteria. This raises the question: How can we discover which criteria are correct? That is the question addressed in Parts One and Two of this book.

Part One discusses this question on the basis of human reason and experience without using Sacred Scripture.

Chapter One

ELEMENTS OF
THE MORAL ACT

Using the example just given we can distinguish three factors in a moral act. One factor is judgment. The physician judges that in this case it is morally good to withhold the information from the patient. The judgment of what is morally good or bad in a particular case we will call the judgment of conscience.

Another factor in a moral act is choice. The physician chooses to withhold the information. The choice is something distinct from the judgment of conscience. The physician could make the same judgment of conscience but then choose to act against this judgment by giving the information to the patient.

The third factor involves what we will call the objective elements of the moral act. These objective elements include the act itself and those realities which are affected by the act and which should be considered in deciding whether the act is morally good or bad. In the above example the objective elements would include the patient, his illness, the act of telling the patient, the likely effect that knowing his condition will have on his recovery, and also the possibility of his death, his proper preparation for death, and the effect on this preparation of his knowing the gravity of his illness. The objective elements may also include other persons insofar as they are affected by what the physician does in the situation.[1]

An act may have an indefinite number of effects. A word to one's friend affects his action, which changes a situation, which influences someone else, and so on perhaps to the end of human history. One cannot consider every effect of an act. One can be obliged to consider only those effects which are foreseeable and morally significant to some degree which we will not try to specify here. By the objective elements of a moral act we mean those realities affected by the act insofar as the effects are to some extent foreseeable and morally significant.

An act can be called morally good in either of two quite different senses, as the following example illustrates.

A family has a pet deer. A relatively poor man goes hunting, hoping to get some venison to contribute to his family's food supply. He sees the pet deer. Through no fault of his own he mistakes it for a wild deer and he kills it. His judgment of conscience is that what he does is morally good.

In one sense at least the hunter has performed a morally good act. His choice, to shoot the deer, was in accord with his judgment as to what was morally good. He followed his conscience. There is something good and praiseworthy about doing what you think is good, even if it is actually bad. This goodness which consists in choosing in accord with one's judgment of conscience we will call goodness of choice or subjective moral goodness.

Most people would claim that in spite of the subjective goodness in the hunter's act, there was also something about it which was bad. It had a bad effect. They would say that the hunter's judgment was wrong, because he didn't know that the deer was a pet belonging to a family. The good act in the circumstances would have been to refrain from shooting the deer. The hunter's action though subjectively good lacked objective goodness, or goodness of the objective elements.

A fully good moral act will have both kinds of goodness. First, one will judge correctly what is the objectively good thing to do. Then one will choose to act in accord with that judgment. Finally the objectively good thing will be done.

It is important that the judgment be right. If the judgment is wrong, then though the person acts in a subjectively good way yet the bad effect follows. The family has lost its pet deer even though the hunter thought he was doing something morally good.

The main concern of this book is objective goodness, not subjective goodness. Were the ethicist concerned only with discovering what is subjectively good his task would be easy. An act is subjectively good when choice conforms to the judgment of conscience. Having pronounced this truth the ethicist could return home to rest or take up some more remunerative occupation. People will be dissatisfied, however, perhaps even short-tempered, with ethicists who so easily dispose of their duties. Suppose that you are wondering whether you should pay for damage which you, through negligence, have caused to your neighbor's property. You ask an ethicist what is the morally good thing to do. He answers that your action will be subjectively morally good so long as you choose in accord with your judgment about what is morally good. The answer applies only if you have already made a judgment about what is right. You might be tempted to reply that if you had already made that judgment you would have had no need to consult with anyone.

This, then, is the task to which we must address ourselves: How can we discover the correct criteria for judging concerning the objective goodness of moral actions?

Chapter Two

ETHICAL RELATIVISM

This book does not attempt to explain the differing schools of ethics. At this point however, to help to formulate the problem before us, we will consider some elements from the school of ethics which is often called ethical relativism.[1] One can distinguish two forms of ethical relativism, one cultural and the other individualistic.

The general position of cultural ethical relativism[2] can be summarized in three propositions.

The first proposition is that all moral norms are products of particular cultures.

Culture here includes those beliefs, attitudes, and behavioral patterns which are common to a group of people and are learned because of membership in that group. Such learning may be formal and deliberate, as in school instruction. More often it is informal. It often takes place without participants being aware that they are either teaching or learning.

According to this first proposition, then, if I think that killing an innocent person is immoral, I so think because I happen to live with and learn from people in a cultural group in which that norm is accepted.

The second proposition of cultural ethical relativism is that, though some moral norms are accepted by many cultures, there are no moral norms which are accepted by all cultures.

The third proposition of cultural ethical relativism is that no moral norm can be proven to be correct absolutely. In seeking a basis for a moral norm one is confronted by the fact that the norm is accepted by some cultures and rejected by others. There is no basis for proving that in this respect some cultures are right and others wrong.

When I say that Napoleon Bonaparte died in 1821 I assert it as something that is true absolutely. ''True absolutely'' here does not mean that it is maintained with complete certitude. It means that it is not true only for me or for certain people. It is true whether or not people acknowledge it. Cultural ethical relativism holds that there is no way by which one can show that a moral norm is correct in this absolute sense.[3]

The cultural ethical relativist does not say that all arguments about the moral norms of a culture are fruitless. Suppose, for example, that people in culture X accept the moral norm that the wage scale for black workers should be the same as that for white workers. In culture Y the wage scale for blacks is lower than that for whites, and people do not consider this morally bad. However, investigation shows that in culture Y, just as in culture X, people accept the general moral norm that people should not be made to suffer because of their race. You might argue with someone in culture Y that if he accepts this latter norm, then he should agree that differentiation of wages on the basis of race is morally bad. If he is willing to think consistently rather than let other factors such as greed obscure his reasoning, then your argument will convince him.

This argument settles a difference between cultures by appealing to a norm initially accepted by both cultures. A cultural ethical relativist would admit the legitimacy of your argument. He would point out, however, that the norm initially accepted by both cultures cannot be shown to be absolutely correct. It can be used to resolve this particular difference between cultures only because it happens to be accepted by both cultures.

Cultural ethical relativists warn against judging people of one culture by the moral norms of another. In your culture adultery (or euthanasia, or theft, or homosexual activity, or polygamy) is considered morally bad in all or nearly all cases. In another culture people accept adultery as morally permissible in many situations. You may look down on this other culture as holding to an inferior moral code. The cultural ethical relativist would see your attitude as unwarranted cultural imperialism.

Certain findings of modern human sciences are used to support cultural ethical relativism. Anthropology has shown that many moral beliefs taken for granted for a long time in the Western world have little or no place among certain tribes. Sociologists argue that moral norms vary even from class to class within one nation, and that acceptance of moral norms is influenced by economic and other factors. Many psychologists hold that one's moral principles are learned at an early age. If I now believe that theft is morally wrong, might this not be because when I was a child my parents stressed that stealing is bad and so they caused me to feel guilty about it? Had they taught me something different, I would have different moral beliefs today.

The findings presented by the human sciences do not constitute the whole of the cultural ethical relativist position. They do, however, constitute important parts of that position and important reasons why it has gained a considerable number of adherents in this century.

Some critics have attacked the supposed factual basis of cultural ethical relativism. These critics claim that in fact there are some moral norms which are accepted by all cultures.[4] That is, they deny the second proposition of cultural ethical relativism.

Even if one holds that a refutation of cultural ethical relativism by this line of argument is possible, one should recognize that it is difficult. To show that a single particular norm is accepted by all cultures one must study a great number of cultures. Nor is it always easy to identify precisely the meaning of a moral norm accepted by a culture. Behavior patterns and concepts of one culture are easily misinterpreted by an observer from another culture. One may have to live with and study a people for a number of years in order to understand correctly its moral norms. Even if one accepts as beyond dispute the work that anthropologists have already done in this area, a great deal more remains to be done.

Cultural ethical relativism holds that there are no moral norms accepted by all cultures. If, eventually, you prove that there is one moral norm that is accepted by all cultures, you refute cultural ethical relativism in its most thoroughgoing form. However, it does not collapse totally from your single assault. The wily relativist will retreat to a modified form of his doctrine. Granted, there may be some moral norms which are accepted by all cultures. However, in many important areas of morality cultures differ greatly in their moral norms. These areas include property rights, sexual ethics, euthanasia, slavery, murder, and almost every important area of morality. What is more, few, if any, of these differences can be resolved by appealing to the one or two vague norms which you claim to have found in all cultures. The relativist will remain convinced that in all these important areas you cannot prove that a moral norm is correct absolutely.

If you continue to argue from the facts of cultural acceptance of moral norms, how can you refute this modified form of cultural ethical relativism? Before accepting any moral norm as correct absolutely you must first examine all cultures and discover either that they all accept that norm or, if they differ, that the differences can be resolved by appeal to other norms which all cultures accept.[5] My opinion is that by this method we can establish few, if any, moral norms as absolutely correct. Rather, I suspect, we will be forced to conclude that such things as the Nazi slaughter of the Jews was morally bad only in the sense that in some cultures it was and is considered morally bad; but in that case we should refrain from the cultural imperialism of judging Nazi actions by norms not accepted by the Nazi culture. Even should it prove possible to establish some norms as absolutely correct on the basis of a consensus of all cultures, the research to make this possible has not been done. The absolute correctness of all or nearly all moral norms is left in doubt.

These are the difficulties if we try to refute cultural ethical relativism by attacking its factual basis. This book follows a different line of criticism. Let us suppose, for a moment, that proposition two is true—that no moral norm is accepted by all cultures. Does it follow necessarily that proposition three is true—that no moral norm can be shown to be absolutely correct?[6] Suppose that there is another way of demonstrating the absolute correctness of a moral norm, a way which does not appeal to a consensus of all culture concerning moral norms. In that case proposition three would not follow from proposition two. On the contrary, proposition three would be proven false. The remaining chapters of Part One will discuss this other way of demonstrating the absolute correctness of moral norms.

Besides the cultural form, there is an individual form of ethical relativism. Put in a simple form, individual ethical relativism holds that the only rule one should follow is one's own desire.[7] To follow a norm which goes against one's desires is to miss out on something good. If the term "moral good" is used in this context it must refer to what an individual desires in a situation. What is good will vary as the desires of people vary. Today I want to steal, so theft for me is good. Next week in the same kind of situation my desire may be for the welfare of the owner of the property which might be stolen, and in that case theft for me would be bad. Often one and the same action appears good to one, bad to another. If I desire revenge against my neighbor and get it by harming his wife and children, my action appears good to me but bad to my neighbor and his family. For the individual ethical relativist there is no way of resolving this difference of opinion between my neighbor and me, no way of proving that my action is good or bad in itself or absolutely.

Our response to individual ethical relativism will be similar to our response to cultural ethical relativism. We will attempt to show a way of demonstrating the absolute correctness of moral norms, a correctness which does not depend on a consensus of cultures or of individuals.

Chapter Three

INTELLIGENT APPETITIVE ACTIVITY

In the next three chapters we will set aside the term ''moral'' and reflect in a more general way on human activity. In this chapter we will consider some implications of the fact that human activity involves appetite and intelligence.

A. The Appetitive and Intelligent Factors in Human Activity

According to a distinction commonly made in the intellectual tradition of the Western world, conscious acts[1] are of two general kinds, cognitive and appetitive. Cognitive acts are acts of knowing. There are, of course, many kinds of knowing. Feeling the coolness of a breeze, understanding the proof of a theorem in geometry, recognizing a familiar face, all of these are cognitive acts. In all of them we are aware in some way of some reality. An appetitive act is of such a nature as to be able to motivate or determine further activity. An appetitive act is not in itself cognitive but presupposes some cognitive act. To enjoy a sunset, to dislike hard work, to love one's spouse, to be afraid of falling off a roof, all of these are appetitive acts. Each presupposes some knowledge, some awareness of a reality. In each, along with this knowledge there is a reaction to the known reality, a reaction which is able to motivate or determine activity. This reaction is the appetitive act.

There are two main types of appetitive act. The first type, which we will call positive appetite, includes all those appetitive acts which are able to motivate one toward something, acts such as hunger for food, enjoying a symphony, or wishing to visit an old friend.

Every positive appetitive act involves an attraction toward something. We will refer to this element of attraction as *liking*. Some appetitive acts consist of liking and nothing else. Frequently, however, an appetitive act involves not only a liking but also some additional reaction to something in the situation. When a farmer hopes for rain for his crops, his hope is not only a liking for rain and what it will produce, but also a reaction of anxiety or urgency because the rain is a future good which may or may not occur on time to help the crops. This additional element makes his act of hoping for rain quite different from his rejoicing over the rain when it comes. Always, however, the element of liking is at the basis of all else in the positive appetitive act. If the farmer had no liking for the rain and what it would produce, there would be no act of hope. Liking is the basic positive appetite, the basic motivation toward things.

The second type of appetite, which we will call negative appetite, includes all appetitive acts which are able to motivate one to avoid certain things, acts such as fear of the pain from a dentist's drill or disapproval of the noise level at a neighbor's party. Every negative appetitive act contains an aversion from something. From here on we will refer to this element of aversion as *dislike*. Some appetitive acts consist of dislike alone. In other acts dislike is accompanied by other reactions to factors in the situation. As I walk along a dark street and hear footsteps following me, my fear of being mugged includes not only a dislike for the pain involved, but also a reaction to the fact that the danger might possibly be averted if I take immediate and vigorous evasive action. The dislike is at the basis of the other reactions. Had I no dislike of the effects of mugging I would have no motivation for the additional urge to flee. Dislike is the basic negative appetite, the basic motivation to avoid things.

Properly human acts involve not only appetite but also intelligence. Often, of course, human beings perform actions without exercising intelligence, digesting food, moving suddenly when startled, destroying property while "out of one's mind." These acts are not properly human acts because they do not have the properly human quality of intelligence.

A properly human act combines appetite with intelligence. On a particular Saturday morning a man considers several alternative ways of spending the day. He could play golf, or relax with a book, or fix up a few things around the house, or take his family for a drive to view the colorful autumn leaves. Each alternative has something attractive about it. Whatever he chooses, his course of action will be motivated by a liking for something. Had he no liking in any respect for a course of action he would have no motive to choose it, and his choice of it would be inexplicable. Along with this appetitive element, however, he uses his intelligence. He compares the alternatives and considers some of their consequences. Having decided to take his family for a drive, he then uses his intelligence to get things arranged in such a way as to make the drive possible.

Human activity is motivated by appetite, and guided by intelligence.

B. Definitions of Good and Evil

We are in a position now to define good and evil (bad). These are definitions not of specifically moral good and evil but of good and evil in general. Good we will define as the object of liking.[2] Evil we will define as the object of dislike.

According to these definitions the same object may be good and bad at the same time insofar as it is both liked and disliked. Taking this medicine helps me overcome an illness, and from that point of view I desire it and so it is good. The medicine has an unpleasant taste, however, so I dislike it, and from that point of view it is evil.

The same object may be good for one person and bad for another, according as people differ in their likes and dislikes. My neighbor plays a certain type of rock record at a volume to which he apparently has become accustomed. To my untrained ear this sound has approximately the same aesthetic quality as the sound of a freighter running aground on a reef. To my neighbor the sound is good. To me it is bad.[3]

Is this a correct way to define good and evil? That is not a question that can be answered simply. One could consult a dictionary to discover whether these definitions conform to commonly accepted usage. Dictionary definitions, however, are not always the most useful ones for a specialized study. Some room should be left for a writer to define key terms in his or her own way. To be useful, such definitions should fulfill certain requirements.

Definitions should be as clear and unambiguous as the subject matter allows. Our definitions seem to be relatively clear and unambiguous when compared to definitions implicit or explicit in other writings.

A definition should help to make clear what is significant for the question under discussion. The reader will be able to apply this criterion properly only after seeing how our definitions are used in this and the following chapters. Our definitions have this initial advantage in that they give an immediate explanation of the reasons for doing good and avoiding evil.

Definitions should not depart so radically from common usage as to confuse readers unnecessarily. The initial evidence on our definitions may appear ambiguous. To a certain extent at least they conform to common usage. Often we speak of things as good insofar as we like them and as bad insofar as we dislike them. To have a good time is to enjoy oneself. A good apple tree is one which has the desired effect of producing an abundance of tasty apples. A bad fall is a fall whose effects one dislikes. When I explain to someone that it is good for him to swim twenty lengths of the pool each day I am really trying to point out reasons for desiring to do so. On the other hand, there are numerous instances in which, at first sight at least, popular usage seems to go contrary to our definitions. Some motorists like to drive at speeds which are good neither for themselves nor for others. Many people like foods which are bad for them. Sadists apparently like to cause pain, behavior which most people would call evil.

Our position in this book is that our definitions of good and evil serve well to express what is significant in the matters under discussion, and that when the implications of our definitions are explained the difficulties just mentioned can be resolved. That this is so can be shown only as our investigation proceeds.

C. The First Rule of Human Activity

We are ready now to formulate the first rule of human activity. We will formulate it first in its simplest form. Later we will give a more elaborate formulation of the rule in order to take account of comparisons between goods and evils. In its simplest form the rule is this: seek the good (i.e., that which you like) and avoid evil (i.e., that which you dislike.)

This rule is not enforced on human activity from the outside. It expresses the inner reality of liking and disliking. To seek the good, that which you like, is to follow the tendency of liking, to do what liking demands to be done. To avoid evil, that which you dislike, is to follow the tendency of dislike.

If this rule is seen in relation to appetite only it is seen to operate automatically. One automatically seeks that which one likes and avoids that which one dislikes. Human activity, however, is not the product of appetite alone, but of appetite and intelligence. Human activity is moved by appetite and guided by intelligence. Once intelligence is a factor in activity then this first rule is no longer followed automatically, but it is followed. That is, even when activity is guided by intelligence it is still governed by the seeking of what is liked and the avoidance of what is disliked. If one does not like something in some way one has no motive to seek it, with or without intelligence. If one does not dislike something in some way there is no motive to avoid it.

This simple formulation of the first rule of human activity is very abstract. It would apply properly only if a person were choosing concerning a single good or evil in isolation. If I am confronted by one good, one thing that I like, and my options are to choose it or reject it, then the rule ''seek the good'' applies properly. Likewise, if I am confronted by a single evil and my options are to choose it or reject it, then the rule ''avoid evil'' applies properly.

Human situations in which choices are made are not usually so simple. If I am confronted by several incompatible goods I can choose only one and must reject the others. In this situation the rule ''seek the good'' does not provide much guidance. In another situation it may be inevitable that some evil will result and my only choice concerns which evil it will be. In this situation the rule ''avoid evil'' is hardly useful. In situations in which each alternative is a combination of several goods and evils, the simple formulation of the first rule of human activity will be hopelessly vague. What is needed is a formulation that takes account of the complex situations which make up real life. This will require the comparison of goods and evils.

First we will take account of the comparison between one good and another. Some things we like better than others. Suppose that my two alternatives on a particular evening are to read the evening paper or to attend a play by my favorite playwright featuring a gifted cast. At that particular time I like both alternatives but I like the second much more than the first. I have a greater liking for the second alternative and a lesser liking for the first. Consistent with our definition of the good are the following definitions of the greater good and the lesser good: a greater good (or that which is better) is that which is the object of a greater liking; a lesser good is that which is the object of a lesser liking.

Taking account of the comparison of goods we can now add to the first part of the first rule of human activity, so that it reads: Seek the good, and in choosing between goods seek the greater good.

This formulation is still very abstract. It abstracts from everything about the objects except that they are the objects of greater or lesser liking. In a particular situation I like both A and B but I like B more than A. B then is a greater good for me than is A. Abstracting from any other factors than these, then the choice of B over A is the only response which makes sense. To choose A over B would go against the very nature or meaning of liking. In this situation the rule "In choosing between goods, seek the greater good" is simply an expression of the nature of liking.

Just as we have greater and lesser likes so we have greater and lesser dislikes. Accordingly we will define a greater evil as that which is the object of a greater dislike, and a lesser evil as the object of a lesser dislike.

We have added to the part of the rule which says: "Seek the good." Similarly we must add to the part of the rule which says: "Avoid evil." The addition to the second part cannot be exactly parallel to the addition to the first part. It is not adequate to say: "In choosing between several evils, avoid the greatest evil." The point is to avoid all evils. A choice among evils makes sense only when some evil is inevitable and one can choose which evil it is to be. Accordingly we will add to the second part of the first rule of human activity as follows: "When it is inevitable that some evil will result, seek the lesser evil." This rule simply expresses the meaning of dislike, as the first part of the rule expresses the meaning of liking.

The second part of this reformulated rule directs that certain evils be sought, i.e., those lesser evils in situations in which some evil is inevitable. By implication the first part of the reformulated rule directs that certain goods are not to be sought, i.e., those which are incompatible with greater goods.

Lesser goods by the very fact of being lesser are in some respect bad insofar as they are incompatible with greater goods. The lesser good is an object of liking but insofar as it rules out a greater good it is an object of dislike. A farmer may like dry sunny weather but also dislike it because it is part of a drought which is ruining the crops on which he depends for a livelihood. A lesser evil by the very fact of being lesser is in some respects a good insofar as it is an alternative to a greater evil. Staying in a dark chilly room is an evil insofar as it is disliked. It may also be liked if it is the only alternative to being captured and tortured by the enemy.

Accordingly, when the first rule of human activity directs that a lesser evil be sought it is directing the seeking of something which is in some respect good. When it directs, by implication, the avoidance of certain goods, it is directing the avoidance of things which are in some respect bad.

In choosing between alternatives not only must one compare goods with goods and evils with evils, but one must often compare goods with evils. In certain cases a good outweighs an evil because the liking for the good is greater than the dislike for the evil. For example, I dislike studying a boring subject but I do it because it enables me to pass an examination which qualifies me to do work which I very much enjoy. My dislike for the boring work is outweighed by my liking for the enjoyable work. In other cases an evil outweighs a good because the dislike for the evil is greater than the liking for the good. For example, a person likes the taste of a certain kind of food. However, the food causes him acute indigestion. He avoids eating the food because his liking for the food is outweighed by his dislike of indigestion.

Frequently one or more of the alternatives which one may choose are combinations of goods and evils. It is not necessary to reformulate once again the first rule of human activity to take account of that fact. We will simply understand that when the rule dictates that one seek the greater good it means that, when goods and evils are mixed, one seeks the alternative which provides the greater preponderance of good over evil. When the first rule dictates that one seek the lesser evil it means that, when goods and evils are mixed, one seeks that alternative which provides for the lesser preponderance of evil over good.

The first rule of human activity in its full form is this: Seek the good, and in choosing between goods seek the greater good; avoid evil, and when it is inevitable that some evil will result, seek the lesser evil.[4]

This rule may conjure up the image of a lawless relativism, of people doing as they please and justifying it by saying that what they do is good because they like it. They are simply following the nature of like and dislike. To act otherwise would not make sense.[5] Does this "lawless" sort of relativism follow from the first rule of human activity? We will seek an answer in a further examination of human activity.

D. The Choice of Means

Some things we like for their own sakes. I like to lie in the sun and read P.G. Wodehouse, not because it accomplishes anything but because it is enjoyable in itself. This kind of good we call an end. Other things we like because they are useful to achieve an end. I like to jog not because I enjoy the jogging itself but because it helps to keep me fit and that makes me feel better. A good which is liked not for its own sake but because it is useful to achieve some desired end we call a means to an end.

A gourmet, far from his native France and dissatisfied with the local cuisine, chooses to dine at a restaurant whose French name suggests that it will provide something suitable to his palate. He is deceived. The *escalopes de veau Normande* are smothered in a tasteless cream sauce. The chocolate mousse has the vaguely gelatinous consistency of custard. He leaves the premises with uneasy feelings about a civilization which allows this sort of barbarism to be practiced openly. Later he has occasion to mention his misadventure to a friend. The latter is properly sympathetic, but adds that in fact there are a couple of quite adequate French restaurants in the city. To one of these recommended havens the gourmet repairs some days later. His friend was right. From the pâté, through the entrée, *coq au vin*, to the fresh strawberries in Grand Marnier and white wine, everything meets with his approval.

In his second attempt the gourmet achieved the good. In the first attempt he did not; rather, he made the mistake of choosing as a means to an end something which was unable to achieve that end. In this first attempt the gourmet in a sense did what he liked. He liked, in some sense, to go to this restaurant. However, he liked this not for its own sake but as a means to an end. Since a means is liked for the sake of an end, it is a mistake to like something as a means when it is unable to achieve the end.

Many human failures are, substantially, mistakes concerning means. A girl feels lonely and thinks that marriage to this young man will remedy the situation. Two years later she feels lonelier than ever. The prime minister of a politically volatile nation decides, as a means of stabilization, to use repressive measures against a relatively weak opposition. This alienates some of his potential allies and makes the situation even less stable.

The first rule of human activity tells us to seek what we like, the good. We have seen that, in the area of means at least, this does not at all mean a lawless relativism according to which the only rule is to do whatever pleases me. Rather, the very nature of the liking of a means to an end demands that, in order to achieve what I like I must know what means achieve particular ends. This involves me in matters which are absolutely true, that is, matters which are true whether I know it or not, matters which are true regardless of how I feel about them at a particular moment.

As in the pursuit of good, so in the avoidance of evil, correct evaluation of means requires correct knowledge of what effects follow from particular causes. Suppose, for example, that I avoid eating cabbage in order to avoid indigestion. I reject cabbage as an evil because I judge it to be a means of causing indigestion. This evaluation of eating cabbage as an evil in this situation is correct only if cabbage actually does cause me to have indigestion.

This discussion of choice of means may be summed up in a subordinate rule to accompany the first rule of human activity. This subordinate rule is: The proper seeking of means to desired ends and the proper avoidance of means to undesired results requires correct knowledge of the ability of means to produce particular effects.

E. Choice of Ends

We will consider now those goods which are liked for their own sakes (ends) and those evils which are disliked for their own sakes. Concerning these might it not be true that a sort of lawless relativism follows from the first rule of human activity? If the rule says to seek the good, or the greater good, might I not do anything I like and claim that it is good because I like it, or a greater good because I like it more? Might I not avoid any unpleasant duty on the grounds that to do it is evil because I dislike it?

Further examination shows that this first rule gives rise to at least two more subordinate rules which point in a direction contrary to lawless relativism. One such rule is that in order to maximize the achievement of what is liked and the avoidance of what is disliked one must choose not in accord with the likes and dislikes of which one is immediately aware but in accord with one's whole range of likes and dislikes. This subordinate rule can be illustrated.

A particular region is occupied by a foreign army which imposes a curfew. All citizens must be indoors after 8 P.M. under threat of severe penalties. A citizen journeying on foot through the region at night builds a small fire to warm himself. The fire allows the occupation troops to locate and apprehend him. He is severely tortured for breaking the curfew. Later the traveler can see that building the fire was a foolish risk to take. He should have known that he was likely to get caught if he lit a fire. At the time, however, he was not thinking of this. He was thinking only of his need to be warm.

The traveler acted in accord with the liking of which he was aware at the time of acting. Certain other likes and dislikes (e.g., a dislike of pain) were not operative in his decision, but became operative when certain consequences followed his decision. Had he considered the consequences these other likes and dislikes would have entered into his decision. His failure to consider the consequences led to a failure to maximize the achievement of what he liked and the avoidance of what he disliked.

This subordinate rule is concerned with the likes and dislikes of which one is capable at the time of making the decision. Of some of these likes and dislikes one may be aware at the time of the decision. Of others one may not be aware at that time. There is another subordinate rule, one which pushes concern beyond the likes and dislikes of which one is capable at the time of the decision. This second subordinate rule is that in order to maximize the achievement of that which one likes and the avoidance of that which one dislikes one must choose not in accord with the likes and dislikes of which one is capable at the time of choice but in accord with one's likes and dislikes during the whole time affected by the choice. A couple of examples will illustrate this rule and show some reasons why people often fail to follow it.

A university student has two offers of summer employment. The pay and the nature of the work are about equally attractive in either job. The difference in the attractiveness of the two jobs is this: If she takes the first job she will get no vacation during the first summer; during the second summer, however, this job will take her to Europe, where she will have time off to tour the continent; the other job would allow her time for a vacation during the first summer. From the point of view of the girl's likes and dislikes at the time of the decision, there is good reason to believe that the second job is most in accord with her likes and dislikes. From the point of view of her likes and dislikes over the entire period of time affected by the choice, the first job is more in accord with her likes and dislikes.

She chooses the second job because it offers her an immediate vacation. This is a mistake. She allows her liking for an immediate good to prevent her from choosing that which would have more completely satisfied her liking over the whole period of time affected by the choice.

Two men who have been close friends for a long time have a quarrel. While angry, one of them so insults the other that there is a serious break between the two. In a sense, to hurl the insult is what the angry man most likes to do at the moment. Nevertheless, it is a mistake. By following a momentary liking he causes something which he dislikes over a long period of time.

We will now summarize this chapter. We have set aside any explicit mention of specifically moral good and evil and have discussed good and evil in a more general sense. Good and evil have been discussed here in relation to human activity insofar as that activity is motivated by appetite and guided by intelligence. Good has been defined as the object of the appetite of liking. Evil has been defined as the object of dislike. The first rule of human activity arises as an expression of the nature of liking and dislike. That rule is: Seek the good, and in choosing between goods seek the greater good; avoid evil, and when it is inevitable that some evil will result, seek the lesser evil. This rule does not command an indiscriminate following of one's urges at a particular moment. In order to achieve the most of what one likes, the good, and to avoid as much as possible what one dislikes, evil, intelligence must guide human action according to certain rules. We have outlined three of these rules. These subordinate rules are not imposed on human activity from the outside. They arise from the nature of human beings as liking and disliking.

Chapter Four

HUMAN APPETITIVE POTENTIAL

The first rule of human activity does not mean that one should simply follow the likes and dislikes of the moment. Nonetheless, our analysis to this point still leaves a great deal of room for variation between different individuals in standards governing human activity. For example, Mr. A's desires are such that he seeks physical pleasure as his chief good. Mr. B has trained himself to find satisfaction in listening to classical music, studying philosophy, and engaging in intellectual discussions. Mr. C. is happiest when pursuing wealth and power. Mr. D is moved by compassion to help the unfortunate people in his neighborhood to get some joy out of life. These four men share some likes and dislikes, no doubt. However, their dominant likes and dislikes are different, so different that each finds his greatest satisfaction in a set of goods quite different from those which most satisfy any of the other three. It is not at all evident that their differences concerning what is good can be resolved by using the three subsidiary rules given in Chapter Three.

The problem can be summarized. Chapter Three has shown that the first rule of human activity does not lead to a lawless relativism. The three subsidiary rules show this. However, it is still clear that people differ markedly concerning what goods provide the greatest satisfaction. This means that they differ markedly concerning what each person finds to be his or her greatest goods. It is not evident that all these differences can be resolved by appealing to the three subsidiary rules. Therefore, while ruling out a lawless relativism, yet we must admit a great variation in evaluating what is good according as people's likes vary. Can one find any further criteria to determine whether people are right or wrong in evaluating what is good? Or must one simply admit that if your basic desires are different from mine, then what is good for you is different from what is good for me?

Some such criteria may be found if we consider potential (as distinct from actual) human appetites.

A. Human Appetitive Potential as Criterion for Good and Evil

Charlie is a normal six-year-old boy. His mother, thirty years of age, is considered by her friends to be a sensitive and mature woman. Charlie and his mother have quite different views on the relative merits of ice cream and friendship. This difference comes into play one day when Charlie comes into possession of a double portion of ice cream. His five-year-old friend, who shares Charlie's enthusiasm for ice cream, happens along before Charlie has consumed the object of their desire. His friend urges on Charlie the wisdom of sharing the ice cream. Charlie remains firm, however, and refuses. There follows an exchange of unfriendly words and a temporary estrangement between the two boys. Charlie's mother upon learning of the incident scolds her ungenerous son and tells him that he should have shared his ice cream.

Charlie, in refusing to share his ice cream, is acting in accord with his likes and dislikes. It is not that he is without any appreciation of friendship. Given a choice, he would prefer to be on good rather than bad terms with his five-year-old friend. However, he is quite content to suffer the temporary loss of his friend's good will in order to savor more fully the delights of ice cream. Because his mother appreciates friendship more than does Charlie, according to her likes and dislikes Charlie has made a mistake. The question arises: By what right can she impose her own likes and dislikes as guides for her son's action? Must we not admit that there is no absolute right and wrong here, that what is right from the point of view of Charlie's likes and dislikes is wrong from the point of view of those of his mother? The mother, being able to coerce her son, may ''resolve'' the issue by demanding that her son follow her judgment. In doing so, however, is she not imposing on him something that, though good from her point of view, is bad from his point of view?

A clue to the answer to that question appears if we examine a difference between the liking for ice cream and the liking for friendship.

The liking for ice cream normally occurs quite spontaneously, with little need for effort or learning. As a matter of fact, any effort to develop the appetite will have little effect, normally, in one's liking for ice cream. In the field of ice cream appreciation there are no giants or heroes who have achieved extraordinary status by means of years of dedication and training. Charlie at six years of age is probably close to his full potential as an aficionado of this food. The appreciation for friendship is quite different in this respect from the appreciation for ice cream. The liking for friendship may require effort and training, rather than occurring spontaneously. However, it shows an extraordinary capacity for growth. One can develop one's appreciation for friendship for many years and still not reach the stage at which further significant growth is impossible. Friendship continues to reveal new varieties and depths to be appreciated.[1]

The matter can be summarized briefly. The liking for ice cream shows little potential for growth. The liking for friendship shows a great potential for growth.

Is it better to develop one's likings or not to develop them? In ancient Greece the stoic school of philosophy taught that it is better to limit one's likings and not to let them develop. They thought that having many and great likings makes a person unhappy because it agitates him unpleasantly and frustrates him when he cannot get what he wants. They used to point out that no sooner has a person satisfied one desire than he is agitated by another, so no satisfaction is possible if one allows one's desires to grow.

This stoic position makes sense only on the supposition that the likings once developed will not be satisfied. This supposition is true in some cases. Often the means are not available to provide satisfaction. One must admit too that, in some cases, no sooner is one appetite satisfied than another arises, so that no state of satisfaction can be reached. The apparently insatiable appetites of certain people for money or power give rise to such cases. However, the supposition that likings once developed will not be satisfied is not true for all cases. Therefore the stoic position does not constitute an adequate solution to the problem.

Another aspect is shown if we reformulate the question. Which is the best situation for a person: to have no likings and therefore to have no need of satisfaction, or to have small likings and to be able to satisfy them, or to have great likings and to be able to satisfy them?

Given our previous definitions of "good" and "better" (greater good) the answer is evident. In the first situation, with no liking, no good is achieved. In the second situation, with small likings, a small good is achieved. In the third situation, with great likings, a great good is achieved. The third situation is by definition the best situation.

This answer corresponds rather exactly with common opinion. To have great desires and to achieve that which you desire is what people generally would agree is great happiness. Other things being equal, people would prefer to have great desires and to satisfy them rather than to have only small desires or no desires at all.

This answer, that it is good to develop likings, holds insofar as they can be satisfied. If a liking has no chance of being satisfied then it is better not to develop it.

Returning to the case of Charlie, we can say with some assurance that it is an important good for him to develop his liking for friendship. This appetite has great potential for growth and he is likely to be able to satisfy it to a considerable degree throughout his life. There is good reason to believe that if he is allowed to act selfishly his development of a liking for friendship will be hindered. On the other hand, if he is encouraged to act generously he is likely to develop a considerable appreciation for friendship. Therefore, in guiding Charlie, his mother is not simply imposing on him her own likes and dislikes. She is doing what is best for her son from the point of view of his own appetitive potential. She is guarding against the possibility that he might reach the age of twenty with his taste for ice cream intact but unable to share properly in adult human relationships.

Notice that what is good for Charlie is to develop his potential liking for friendship. Sharing the ice cream is good for him as a means to this development. We have not proved that sharing the ice cream is good for Charlie in itself, apart from being a means. For Charlie to share the ice cream is in accord with the desires of Charlie's young friend and the desires of Charlie's mother, so it is a good for them. For Charlie himself at this stage, however, it is a good only as a means to development.

We can sum up our conclusion of this part of the chapter in a fourth subsidiary rule: In order to maximize the achievement of the good (or of what one likes) one should develop those likings which can be satisfied. We will call this the rule of the development of likings.

We have stated the rule in a very general way, abstracting from the complications which arise in the real world. In real life because of limitations of time, energy, and attention one cannot develop all of one's likings. The best one can do is to develop some to a considerable degree and to put less emphasis on others. Furthermore, the development of a certain liking may well be detrimental to the development of another. For example, to develop one's appetite for revenge is certainly detrimental to developing love of enemies. The best we can hope to do, accordingly, is to develop that set of likings which will yield the greatest total good.

Thus far this chapter has established the meaning and validity of the rule of the development of likings. Next we will look at some of its implications for the intelligent direction of human activity.

B. Potential Appetites as Criteria for What Is the Greater Good

The appetites of one person may be very different from those of another. This person's appetites at this time may be very different from his appetites at another time. The actual appetites of a person at any one time may be difficult to analyze or even to determine. Such complexity and obscurity make it difficult to determine the relative strengths of actual appetites. Is it not a hopeless task to determine the relative strengths of potential appetites?

We will not presume that the task is impossible, however, until we have looked at it more closely. Immediately we are confronted by a fact which is hardly encouraging. We have no direct knowledge of potential appetites. We discover them only by deducing their existence from actual appetites.

An individual learns eventually to appreciate the plays of Shakespeare. This actual appreciation allows us to assert that before he actually liked these plays he had a potentiality to like them. Having discovered actual likings in some individuals, we can often conclude with some assurance that the potential for such likings exists in other individuals. Most adults exhibit some appreciation for friendship. There is reason to believe that those adults who have little or no appreciation for friendship have simply not developed their potential. We can conclude with some assurance that this newly born infant can, with the proper development, come to appreciate friendship. Though we cannot observe appetitive potential directly, we gain considerable knowledge of it from observation of actual appetite.

Next, an important distinction can be discerned between two types of likings. The first type includes physical desires, desires for food, drink and physical sexual pleasure, desire for sense pleasures generally. These likings exhibit the characteristics already noted concerning Charlie's love of ice cream. Normally one becomes capable of them more or less spontaneously in the course of physical maturation, with little need for learning or training. These likings may be experienced as powerful early in life. However, they show little potential for growth beyond the level made possible by physical maturation.

The second type of liking includes appreciation for friendship, appreciation for the intellectual discovery and contemplation of truth, and appreciation of what is beautiful. Usually these likings grow by means of training and learning. They have great potential for growth. Of course one may reach a stage of incapacity for growth even in this second type of liking. This would be the case for those near death or for those losing certain of their faculties. Normally, however, no matter how much one has developed in appreciating friendship, truth or beauty, one can still develop much more.

This distinction between the two types of liking gives a basis for further guidance for human activity. If one makes no effort to develop likings one will be dominated by the first type of likings, those which require little or no learning or training. Such a course of action goes against the rule that it is good to develop those likings which can be satisfied. One will be richer in satisfaction if one develops the second type of liking.

This matter can be illustrated by the example of an erotic relationship between a man and a woman. The appetite which arises spontaneously is the desire for the sensual sexual pleasure. This pleasure shows little potential for growth. In fact, frequent repetition will cause it to lose some of its intensity. If no effort is made to develop other aspects of the relationship it is likely to remain on this physical level. If other, more personal, aspects are developed the relationship will yield much deeper and more varied satisfactions for both partners.

We can now formulate another rule for human activity. Rather than live only by those likings which arise more or less spontaneously, we should, by training and learning, develop other likings which have great potential for growth.

It is important, then, to ascertain the relative potential strengths of different likings. In this task we can be more certain of our conclusions in some cases than in others. An adult who appreciates friendship can be quite certain that the liking for friendship is potentially greater than the liking for ice cream. One need not be seriously troubled by the possibility that Charlie has stumbled upon some depth of appreciation for ice cream that is hidden from the rest of us. At the other extreme, in some cases we do not even try to determine which of two likings has the greatest potential. Jane delights in the study of philosophy. Mary greatly enjoys the music of Beethoven, Mozart and Bach. Most of us would not even try to argue that the potential for liking philosophy is greater, or less, than the potential for liking music. We agree that the development of either of these great potentials is well worth the effort.

In other cases we have probable but not certain opinions about the relative greatness of potential appetites. This occasions controversy about what is good. When such matters are disputed we may be tempted to abandon the efforts to reach any solid conclusion. This would be a mistake. There are means we can use to reach a higher degree of probability. We can listen to proponents of each side argue their cases. We can compare our experience with the great people of other ages to see if there may be something we are missing. We can widen our appreciation of goods by trying to appreciate the values of those in cultures different from our own. If after considerable effort we have not yet reached certainty, we may have reached a degree of probability, a degree of wisdom, which is immeasurably better than pure ignorance. In Book One of the *Nicomachean Ethics* Aristotle warns that we should seek in ethics only that degree of certitude which the subject matter allows.[2]

C. Potential Dislikes and Evil

It is good to develop those likings we can satisfy. Is there any corresponding rule concerning dislikes? Is it good or bad to develop one's potential dislikes? Other things being equal, it is bad to develop one's potential dislikes. To have great dislikes whose objects are likely at times to be unavoidable means that one will suffer more evil than if one lacked such dislikes. Sometimes, however, a dislike is good as a means to an end. For example, it is good to develop a dislike of one's own boorish behavior if that behavior is preventing one from achieving some considerable good. Many dislikes which arise spontaneously (e.g., pain from lesions) are useful as means to prevent further harm.

D. Potential Likings and the Universality of Goods

If all people have a potential for a certain liking, then developing that liking is a good for all people. If everyone has a potential for liking friendship, then it is a good for everyone to develop a liking for friendship. It may be, however, that certain potential likings are shared only by some but not by all people. For example, it may be that only a few people have the potential to enjoy a certain state of consciousness achieved by a special kind of mental discipline. To develop this potential would be a good only for those who possess the potential.

We will not go into the question of which goods are universal and which are goods only for some people. That is a question of content rather than of method. A related point should be noted, however. If we describe a good in very general terms it is more likely to be a good for people generally. If we describe a good in more particular terms it is more likely to be a good only for a restricted group of people. For example, probably nearly all people have a considerable potential for liking the discovery and contemplation of truth. To develop that potential is a considerable good then for nearly everyone. Only a more restricted number of people, on the other hand, have the potential to enjoy the discovery and contemplation of the truth in the *Metaphysics* of Aristotle.

E. The Social Context for Learning about What Is Good

A person left alone to discover what is good will tend to follow those likings which arise spontaneously. The young, especially, if left to themselves will know little or nothing about those goods which can be appreciated only after learning and training. To facilitate appreciation of this latter type of good, the young and the undeveloped generally in a society are directed by those members who have learned to appreciate these goods. This direction may take the form of parents encouraging their children to share with their friends, or teachers encouraging students to study poetry which they do not yet appreciate. It may take the form of some people, whose appreciation of certain goods is highly developed, producing works of art which can help others to come to a similar appreciation.

In spite of encouragement and urging by parents, teachers, artists and others, people tend to remain attached to the goods they already appreciate, to remain with the familiar. Growth in appreciation for what is good requires a willingness to change, to leave what is good in order to discover something better. If one centers one's attention only on the desires of the present one will not experience any need to develop further desires. If one becomes aware of one's life as a whole, one realizes the possibility of greater desires being satisfied, the possibility of greater happiness. This awareness provides the motive for development (for "conversion," to use the term which often occurs in religious contexts).

Chapter Five

DIMENSIONS
OF THE GOOD

Particular events take on additional significance from their contexts. For example, a melody played on a piano is a sequence of individual notes. A note played by itself has a particular sound. The same note with the same sound heard as part of a melody has an additional significance. It is heard not in isolation but in relation to the notes which come before and those which come after. To hear each note in isolation is not to hear the melody.

In a similar way many human actions gain an additional significance from their context. The act of shaking hands has one significance when old friends meet, another significance when strangers are introduced, and still another significance when two people who have quarreled are reconciled. To point out another's mistake has one sort of significance when it is done to tease a friend, a different significance when a devoted teacher helps a student, and a third kind of significance when it is done out of spite. Clearly, one cannot judge whether an act is good, nor the extent to which it is good, if one does not grasp the contexts which give additional meaning to the act.

One important context arises from the fact that doing things of a particular kind makes one to be a person of a particular kind. If I frequently tell lies I constitute myself as a dishonest person. Once I realize that this is so there is a new dimension added to my choice about whether or not I tell the truth. I become responsible not only for the particular good or bad things I cause outside of myself by my choice. I become responsible for the kind of person I am and will become. At this point I can put more of myself into a choice. I choose one or other alternative not only because of its quality in itself but also because I choose to be a particular kind of person. In this way, one may choose to be loyal to a friend not only because of what it does for one's friend but also because one wills to be the kind of person who is loyal to friends.

Another dimension in the seeking of good enters when one becomes aware of a choice in the context of the whole of one's life or at least of a major part of that life. A man who habitually consumes too much alcohol at first views each choice to drink without considering this fuller context. At a particular moment, however, he may realize how his habit is affecting his whole life. If he continues in this habit he will end up his life miserably, his talents unused, his time wasted. At this point the choice before he takes his next drink is not concerned merely with the immediate goods and evils of the situation.

Frequently the realization of several dimensions may be combined. When the habitual drinker realizes that his choice involves the whole of his remaining life, he may also realize vividly the dimension of responsibility for the kind of person he is. He realizes what kind of person he has made himself to be. Insofar as others are affected by his actions, still another dimension may enter his mind. He may realize, for example, what he is doing to his family. His choice of good or bad then involves dimensions far beyond the immediate situation. To face this full responsibility is not easy, so there is a temptation at times to put the fuller dimensions of one's choice out of one's consciousness.

Finally, good and evil can be seen within a religious dimension. Scholars disagree even concerning the meaning of religion itself. It would be presumptuous to try to settle such controveries here. We will look at one aspect of human experience, an aspect which we will call religious, an aspect which adds a new dimension to the seeking of good.

An individual with a particular liking perceives the object of that liking to be good. A gourmet appreciates the fine food and so perceives it as a good. Were the appreciation for food the whole of the gourmet's appetitive life then a life of eating delicious food would appear to him to be the perfect life. Our particular gourmet, however, has other likings. He enjoys the company of friends. He likes German classical music and Russian novels. For him a life of eating delicious food is not sufficient. Suppose, however, that all of his actual likings are satisfied. Will he be completely satisfied? He can still conceive of the possibility of having other and greater likings and of satisfying them. That is, he can conceive of being happier. No matter how great a finite liking may be, one can think of a greater one. Correspondingly, no matter how great a finite good may be, one can think of a greater one. The notions of liking and of good have no intrinsic limits.

To sum up: that which satisfies a particular limited liking is a particular limited good; such a good is always incomplete for a human being who can conceive of something better. The only good which would not be incomplete for a human being would be a good which satisfies an unlimited liking. To possess such a good would preclude any possibility that a greater good could be achieved.

If one considers oneself to be in relationship to such a good, then a new dimension is given to moral life. Everything is at stake in one's choice for or against such a good. One's choice even of particular goods may be seen as implying a particular stance in relation to the unlimited and absolute good. The Judaeo-Christian tradition teaches that one's relation to the supreme good, God, is affected by one's choice or refusal of certain created goods.

Chapter Six

MORAL GOOD
AND MORAL EVIL

Before proceeding it will be useful to summarize several points discussed earlier.

Chapter One distinguished three factors in the moral act. One factor is the judgment of conscience that a particular course of action is morally good or morally bad. A second factor is the choice to act either in accordance with or against the judgment of conscience. The third factor involves the objective elements of the moral act. The objective elements include the act or course of action itself, and those realities affected by the action and which should be considered in deciding whether the action is morally good or bad.

"Morally good" can have either of two different meanings. An action is morally good in a subjective sense when the person's choice is in accord with his or her judgment of conscience—that is, when the person does what he or she judges is good. Objective moral goodness, on the other hand, belongs to an act apart from the actual subjective dispositions of the one who acts. When I say that to feed this hungry man at this time is objectively morally good I mean that the act itself is good and its effects are good quite apart from whether the person who does it is operating in a subjectively good way.

Probably when people think of moral goodness they usually are thinking of the subjective disposition of the person. This may make it confusing to speak of moral goodness in this objective sense as something ascribed to the action itself and its effects apart from the subjective disposition of the one who acts. However, it is important to emphasize this objective element of goodness which is involved in morality. In a sense the objective goodness is what is primary in morality. It is because an action and its effects are objectively good that one can rightly make the judgment that it is an action which is good to do. It is because he or she judges that it is an objectively good action that the morally good person chooses to do it.

In seeking criteria for moral judgments we have been seeking criteria for judging the objective goodness, not the subjective goodness, of a moral action and its effects.

At the beginning of Chapter Three we temporarily set aside the term "moral." That is, rather than looking immediately at objective moral goodness we reflected on objective goodness in a more general way. In the course of that reflection we have defined "good" and "evil" and have presented some criteria for deciding not only what is good or evil but also what is a greater good or a greater evil. It is time now to return to the consideration of that objective good and evil which are designated as moral.

A. Definition of Moral Good and Moral Evil

The moral good for an individual in a particular situation: (i) is a good as defined in Chapters Three to Five and as determined according to the criteria set down in those chapters, (ii) is a good which falls within the free choice of the individual in that situation, and (iii) is a good reckoned with a view to the whole of what is good for the individual.

The first part of this definition gives the general class to which the moral good belongs. Moral goods belong to the wider class of goods in general as these goods have been explained in the preceding chapters.

The second part of the definition states that moral goods constitute one particular group within the wider class of goods in general. Moral goods are those which are within the free choice of the individual. If I inadvertently cause some good to happen to someone this is not a moral good, because it was not the object of free choice. If I freely choose to cause it, this same good would be considered a moral good, insofar as it is the object of my free choice.[1] As moral acts are free acts, so a moral good must be some good which falls within the free choice of the individual. Since free choice is not the subject of this book we will not explore further this part of the definition.

The third part of the definition indicates what is specific about moral goods. Not all the goods which fall within the free choice of an individual are moral goods for that individual. Only those are moral goods which are good as reckoned with a view to the whole of what is good for the individual. At a particular moment there may be a great number of goods which fall within the free choice of an individual. Each is good in a particular respect. That is, each is good insofar as it is the object of some liking of the individual. Not all of them may be good in view of the whole of what is good for the individual. By pursuing one particular good an individual may cause himself harm, either by destroying some greater good or by causing some greater evil. Clearly such a particular good is not a moral good for this individual in this situation.[2]

The moral good need not be the greatest possible good in a situation. The moral good is any good which, in view of the whole of what is good for the individual, gives a preponderance of good over evil. In a particular situation there may be several morally good alternatives, some of which are morally better than others.

Our definition of moral evil will be parallel to that of moral good. Moral evil for an individual in a particular situation: (i) is an evil as defined in Chapters Three to Five and as determined according to the criteria set down in those chapters, (ii) is an evil which falls within the free choice of the individual in that situation, and (iii) is an evil reckoned with a view to the whole of what is good or evil for the individual.

When a lesser moral good is an alternative to a greater moral good, the lesser moral good is morally good simply, but morally evil in a relative sense. Suppose that in a particular situation X is a greater moral good and Y is a lesser moral good. Y is a moral good simply speaking, fulfilling the terms of our definition. There is another aspect to Y in this situation, however. It is an alternative to X. A choice of Y involves the rejection of X. The rejection of a greater good in favor of a lesser good has about it something bad. We express this aspect by saying that Y in this situation is morally bad in a relative sense.[3]

In a parallel way, something which is a moral evil simply is also a moral good in a relative sense when it is an alternative to a greater moral evil.

In certain situations all of the alternatives open to free choice may be evil according to the criteria we have established. In such cases none of the alternatives is objectively morally good simply speaking. (There will always be the subjectively morally good alternative—a choice of what one judges to be the best of the alternatives.) In such a case the alternative which is objectively morally best in a relative sense will be that alternative which provides for the least preponderance of evil over good.

B. Defense of These Definitions

Three main objections to our definition of moral good can be foreseen. Some opponents of situation ethics would object that our definition leaves the way open for situation ethics. We will defer to Part Three the examination of the case for or against situation ethics and the explanation of the extent to which this definition of the moral good does or does not lead to that ethical system. The problem of the definition of moral good is logically prior to the problem of situation ethics, so we will deal first with the former problem in this chapter before moving on to the latter problem in Part Three.

A second objection may be directed against defining the moral good as the object of liking. We have defined the good in general as the object of liking. The moral good is one type of good. Therefore part of its definition is that it is the object of liking. Some people may object to this.

The most obvious reason for such an objection is that very often that which is pointed out as the moral good is not liked. To give generously when one would like to spend the money on oneself, to abstain from certain sexual activities, to forgive one's enemies, to tell the truth even when it is embarrassing—these are generally considered to be morally good things, but they do not always appear to be particularly likable.

It is commonly thought, in fact, that the element of liking may detract from the moral quality of an action. If I help my neighbor by persevering through a task that I detest, that, by many people, would be considered an act morally superior to helping my neighbor by doing work which I thoroughly enjoy. Willingness to do the right thing in the face of dislike is commonly seen as a mark of moral virtue.

In responding to this objection it should be noted, first of all, that the same thing may be at one and the same time liked and disliked by the same person. Sitting up all night with a sick child may be an object of liking for the mother insofar as she loves the child and wishes to do what is best for it. It may, at the same time, be disliked by the mother because it goes against her desire for sleep. It is possible therefore, for one and the same thing to be morally good and the object of liking while also from another point of view being disliked.

Secondly, defining the moral good as the object of liking does not mean that the greatest moral good for an individual is that which he or she likes best at a particular moment. We have defined the moral good as the object of liking with the qualifications given in Chapters Three to Five. According to these qualifications the good is not determined only by one's actual liking at a particular moment. Accordingly it is consistent with our definition that the moral good be not liked but disliked by a person at a particular moment.

Rather than continue our argument in terms of the objection we will argue directly that part of the definition of moral good should be that it is the object of liking. Our argument will have two steps. First, we will argue that if the moral good is not the object of liking there is no reason to pursue the moral good. Second, we will argue that any moral good which there is no reason to pursue is not the moral good as commonly conceived.

We can begin the elaboration of the first step by recalling that a good may be an object of liking in either of two senses. In the first, and principal, sense, a good may be liked because it is itself positively attractive either as an end or as a means to an attractive end. In a second sense, a good may be itself an evil, an object of dislike, but a lesser evil, and be an object of liking because it is an alternative to a greater evil. The source of the liking in this second sense is not the attractive quality of the object itself but the dislike of the alternatives.

Next, what do we mean by "reason to pursue the moral good"? There are two kinds of reasons for acting or not acting. We can call them subjective and objective reasons. A subjective reason[4] is an appetite, such as hunger or fear. As has been explained in Chapter Three, the basic element in any appetite is either liking or dislike. An objective reason is some reality which can be the object of appetite. Food as the object of hunger is an objective reason for acting.

An objective reason becomes an effective reason for acting or not acting only when it is joined to a subjective reason. Food, for example, becomes an effective reason for acting only if there is a desire for food.

If the moral good is not the object of liking there is no subjective reason to pursue the moral good. This is a consequence of the meaning of the terms. All subjective reasons (appetites) moving on toward an object have as their basic ingredient an element of liking. Any effective reason for doing the moral good must, therefore, involve an element of liking.

The second step of our argument is that any moral good which there is no reason to pursue is not the moral good as commonly conceived. It is commonly supposed that the moral good is something which there are strong reasons to pursue. It is seen commonly as something of great practical importance, as an important goal in life, as in a sense *the* goal in life. A moral good which there is no reason to pursue would be none of those things. It would be something of academic interest, perhaps, but a thing one could disregard with impunity.

To sum up, it is essential to the moral good as commonly conceived that there be reasons for pursuing it. These reasons must contain, as their basic element, a liking for the moral good. It is then essential to the moral good that it be the object of liking. A definition should express what is essential to the reality which is defined. Therefore the definition of the moral good should include that it is the object of liking.

One might, of course, decide to define the moral good in a way which does not agree with the common conception of it. When one departs too much from common usage, however, one ceases to make sense except insofar as one might be supposed to have invented a private language. This would seem to be the case if one were to define the moral good in such a way that there need be no reason for pursuing it.

In view of our argument let us examine a couple of views of moral good which do not define it as the object of liking.

Some may define the moral good as that which God wills human beings to choose freely. We may ask what reason this gives for pursuing the moral good. More than one answer is possible.

The authors of this definition might even answer that there need be no particular reason to pursue the moral good, that such is not the point of moral goodness. We should answer that such a moral good may be an interesting subject for speculation, but it is not the goal of human activity which dominates our practical science of ethics, nor is it what people commonly mean by "moral good." We will have to look elsewhere for a definition of that reality which we were seeking under the title "moral good."

When asked what reason there is to pursue the moral good, the proponents of the above definition are more likely to say that of course there is a reason to pursue the moral good. We should pursue it because it is the will of God. We can then ask why one should do the will of God. Several answers are possible.

They may answer that we should do the will of God because if we do so God will reward us. What reason do we have to seek the reward? We like it. Our reason to pursue the moral good, in this case, is that it is liked as a means to an end which we like.

Alternatively, they may answer that the reason to do the will of God is that otherwise God will punish us. What is our reason for avoiding punishment? We dislike it. The reason to pursue the moral good in this case is that it is liked as an alternative to something we dislike.

They may answer that the reason to do the will of God is simply that it is the will of God. This does not help to further our analysis. The will of God becomes something I have a reason to do only if it is in some way an object of my liking. Perhaps my love of God generates a liking for doing his will. Perhaps my awe of God generates a liking for doing his will. If there is no liking, however, then the will of God remains for me a matter of theoretical interest only.

Of course it may be true that the moral good is the will of God; but to qualify as the moral good, the will of God must be something one has a reason to do, and this reason, ultimately, involves liking. It is essential to the moral good that it be the object of liking, and this should be included in its definition.

Another definition of the moral good is that it is what one is directed to do by a certain kind of moral experience. In this experience one becomes immediately aware that one should do or should not do some particular thing. The reason to do the moral good is given in the moral experience itself. It makes no sense to ask for other reasons for acting. The reason to act or not act is the experience itself, an experience of "oughtness" as some have designated it. The experience that a particular thing ought to be done is at the same time an experience that this thing is a moral good and the reason for doing it.

To relate this theory of the moral good to our own definition we must inquire about the nature of this moral experience. Is it a form of liking for the moral good, or at least does it contain such a liking? If it is, or does, this would explain how it is a reason for doing the good. This theory could then be quite compatible with our definition of the moral good as the object of liking. Perhaps, alternatively, the moral experience is a form of dislike for acting contrary to the moral good. By implication the moral good would be liked as an alternative to something that is disliked. This again would explain how the moral experience is a reason for doing the moral good, and again this theory could be compatible with our definition of the moral good. (It would, however, be a curiously negative explanation as to why one should pursue the moral good.) If, on the other hand, the moral experience involves neither liking nor dislike, then it gives no reason to do the moral good, and we have strong reasons for ignoring the moral good in favor of something that we like. To put the matter in slightly different terms, if the moral experience is a subjective experience moving us toward the moral good, then it falls into the category of things which we have defined as liking.

The same sort of argument which shows that moral good should be defined as the object of liking will show that moral evil should be defined as the object of dislike. If moral evil is not in some sense the object of dislike, no convincing reason can be given for avoiding moral evil.

A third possible objection against our definitions of moral good and evil is that they are not sufficiently specific. The objection would be that our definitions do not show adequately how the moral good and evil are different from other goods and evils which fall within the free choice of an individual in a particular situation.

There may be many goods among which one can choose in a particular situation. There are various physical goods such as food, drink and good health. There are different types of goods which supply intellectual satisfaction or aesthetic enjoyment. There are different sorts of fame, of wealth, and of friendship. Not every good which can be chosen in a particular situation is a moral good. How does our definition distinguish the moral good from other goods which might be chosen? It states that the moral goods are those which are good when account is taken of the total good of the individual. If, having considered the total good of the person, a particular pleasure can be seen to contribute to the greater good of the individual, then that physical pleasure is a moral good in that particular situation. On the other hand, the choice of this physical pleasure may rule out some greater good or produce some greater evil, thus detracting from the total good of the individual rather than adding to it. In such a situation the physical pleasure is not a moral good, though it is a good in a more general sense, being the object of a desire.

In our definition it is in the *particular situation* that a particular good is determined to be a moral good or not. We do not first list some general classes of goods as moral and certain other classes of goods as non-moral. Any good can become a moral good if in a particular situation it contributes to the total good of the person and falls within the free choice of the individual in that situation. Likewise, it is in a particular situation, according to our definition, that a particular evil is determined as a moral evil. Any evil may be a moral evil if in a particular situation it detracts from the total good or contributes to the total evil for the person and also falls within the free choice of the individual.

It is against precisely this aspect of our definition that the third objection would be directed. Many people would, implicitly or explicitly, categorize certain general classes of goods and evils as moral and other classes of goods and evils as non-moral. Among moral goods they might list such things as telling the truth, being faithful to one's spouse, or feeding the hungry. Such goods as the contemplation of truth, listening to a symphony or eating a delicious meal are commonly considered to be non-moral goods. Among moral evils many would list such things as theft, adultery or telling lies. Evils such as unpleasant sounds, hunger, boredom and physical discomfort might more frequently be classed as non-moral. In this view, a good is constituted as a moral good by some element or characteristic which belongs to a whole class of goods apart from a particular situation. Similarly according to this view an evil is constituted as a moral evil by some element or characteristic which belongs to a whole class of evils apart from a particular situation. According to this view our definitions of moral good and evil have missed these elements or characteristics and so our definitions do not adequately distinguish moral goods and evils from other goods and evils.

Is this a valid objection against our definitions? To test its validity, let us suppose that in a particular situation it is found that, using the theory of the objectors, the moral good is X. In the same situation the moral good according to our definition is Y. Is there any convincing reason for choosing X rather than Y? As indicated earlier, a convincing reason to choose anything must involve liking. A convincing reason to prefer one good to another must involve a greater liking. If one uses greater liking as a criterion, along with the qualifications that rational behavior demands, one is in fact using the method set forth in our definition of the moral good. In other words, only our definition of the moral good shows convincing reasons for choosing the moral good. We have shown earlier that a definition of the moral good is not satisfactory if it does not indicate convincing reasons for choosing the moral good.

Convincing reasons for avoiding anything must involve dislike. A definition of moral evil which shows convincing reasons for avoiding moral evil must, therefore, involve the element of dislike. Our definition does this, including also the qualifications that rational behavior demands. Any other definitions of moral evil are unsatisfactory because they do not show convincing reasons for avoiding moral evil.

This section may leave the reader with the impression that the moral theory here elaborated leads necessarily to situation ethics. That would be a false impression, as Part Three of this book will show. To take Part One apart from Part Three is to risk a serious misunderstanding of the meaning of the moral theory of this book.

C. Response to Ethical Relativism

From the point of view of the ethical theory we have presented, what response is to be made to ethical relativism?

Individual ethical relativism as described at the end of Chapter Two holds that the rule to be followed is to follow one's own desires in any situation. Chapters Three, Four and Five have made clear that even if one makes one's likes and dislikes the criteria for determining what is good, it is still not reasonable simply to follow the likes and dislikes one happens to experience at a particular moment. These chapters constitute an argument against individual ethical relativism.

The position of cultural ethical relativism was summarized in Chapter Two in three propositions. First, all moral norms are products of particular cultures. Second, no moral norms are accepted by all cultures. Third, no moral norm can be proven to be correct absolutely. That is, in arguing in support of any moral judgment one arrives ultimately at the fact that the basic norms on which any argument depends are accepted by some cultures and not by others. According to the cultural ethical relativist one cannot prove that any culture is right or wrong in accepting or rejecting any such basic moral norm. From the point of view of our ethical theory, what response is to be made to this cultural ethical relativism?

There is one point on which our theory agrees to some extent with cultural ethical relativism. In our theory the criteria for moral judgment include the appetitive potential of human beings. We do not have direct knowledge of these appetitive potentials. We become aware of them only when they are actualized. They are actualized differently in different cultures. The experience of people in one culture may give a different idea of appetitive potential than does the experience of people in another culture. Accordingly the criteria for moral judgment one discovers from one culture may be different from the criteria discovered from another culture.

This point being granted, it remains that our ethical theory is radically different from cultural ethical relativism.

The basic difference concerns absolute truth in moral matters. As was explained in Chapter Two, "absolute truth" here does not refer to a degree of certainty one may have concerning some proposition. It refers rather to the existence of a reality in relation to which a proposition is true or false. This point can be clarified by an illustration. People were deliberately kept ignorant of the identity of the body buried in the tomb of the unknown soldier in Paris. No one knows the identity of the body buried there. It was, however, the body of a particular soldier. There is a reality in relation to which a statement about the identity of the body is true or false. Even in this case then, in which all are ignorant, it is meaningful to speak of absolute truth because there is a reality in relation to which a proposition is true or false.

For cultural ethical relativism it is meaningless to speak about absolute truth in relation to moral norms. According to that theory, when culture A differs from culture B concerning some moral norm there is no reality in relation to which the position of either culture is true or false. In our ethical theory in every instance it is meaningful to speak about absolute truth in relation to moral norms. The correct moral norm is that which accords with the likes and dislikes of the person, with all of the qualifications noted in these chapters. These criteria exist in relation to which a moral proposition is true or false. These criteria exist whether or not we know them.

Our ability to discover the correct moral norms varies from one area to another. In some cases when two cultures have different moral norms it is difficult to know which one is more nearly right. In other cases one can find convincing evidence that the norms of one culture are more correct than are the norms of another. Just as there are cases in which we can judge that one individual has developed his or her appetitive potential more fully than has another, so in some cases a similar judgment can be made concerning two cultures.

It is not our purpose here to get into questions of content, questions of what norms we can accept as valid. However an illustration, necessarily oversimplified, may help to clarify the point at issue. In culture A we discover that people place a great deal of emphasis on external activity with little or no importance attached to contemplation. In this culture a person who refuses to engage in energetic external activity is liable to be blamed for being lazy. In culture B more emphasis is placed on contemplation, even to the extent that a contemplative life is seen to be superior to a life of external activity. Examining the people in culture A we discover that they have little or no appreciation for contemplation. Their preference for external activity is most plausibly explained as the result of a failure to appreciate any alternatives rather than as a result of any high development of their appreciation for external activity. In culture B the people seem to appreciate both contemplation and the values sought in external activity. It is reasonable to conclude from this that culture B has better criteria than culture A for making moral judgments which involve the relative merits of these two ways of life.

Of course in some cases we can be more certain than in others in judging between the moral norms of different cultures. One should be open to the possibility of learning from other cultures and one should guard against the tendency to prefer one's own cultural values only because they are familiar. Such an attitude of openness does not mean, however, that we suspend all moral judgments until we reach complete certainty on an issue.

While ruling out the two forms of ethical relativism, our ethical theory elaborated in these chapters allows for a considerable variation in moral judgments. Of course imperfection or outright error in ethical views accounts for some cases in which the moral judgment of one person differs from that of another. Another source of variation in moral judgment, differences between one situation and another, will be discussed in Part Three.

Our theory suggests still another source of such variation. Because of difference in appetitive potential something which is truly a great good for one person may be truly only a lesser good or no good at all for another. To achieve a certain kind of state of consciousness may be a great good for someone who can learn to appreciate; it cannot be said to be a great value for someone who does not have the ability to learn to appreciate it.[5]

Chapter Seven

TOWARD ADULT MORALITY

Obviously the moral life we have been discussing does not take place in a new-born infant. In fact it takes from fifteen to twenty years for a person to reach a stage which would be generally recongized as adult morality. The stages of this development present a rich field for study and also for speculation. Many different aspects of this development can be examined: the emotional development and the appetitive development generally, the growth of freedom and responsibility, cognitive development. This chapter will discuss several points about this development centered on this question: What are the principal factors involved in a human being's control of his or her actions? This brief study will, of course, not provide a comprehensive view of moral development. It will show, however, that the very meaning of "moral" changes as the person develops toward adulthood.

An infant does not act morally. An infant acts according to instinctual urges, according to built-in mechanisms, without taking account of reality. When a month-old boy gets hungry or begins to feel soggy, he doesn't look at his mother and think: "Poor old Mom. I've kept her pretty busy today. I'd better not disturb her." No, our baby is bothered by no such scruples. He doesn't bother to reflect on the matter at all. He feels hungry or wet, so he starts to howl. Nobody had to teach him how to howl or when to howl. It was probably his first reaction when he emerged from his mother's womb. His howling mechanism, like his digestive system, was in place and ready to operate at birth. It was a matter of instinctual behavior.

As the child matures he will begin to act in ways other than by instinct; but as long as he lives, instinct will remain a basic factor influencing behavior. Instinctual needs for food, drink and safety, instinctual fears and dislikes, will continue to be strong motives for his behavior.

As the child develops his instinctual reactions will begin to be modified by learning. At first this learning will not involve any intelligence or reflection. You can train a dog to obey by rewarding it when it obeys and punishing it when it disobeys. This kind of learning occurs in human beings. Our baby boy, for example, may be picked up and fed or changed every time he whimpers. When he howls, however, his mother is stern and not at all playful, and though he may eventually get fed or changed it is not nearly so pleasant an experience as the cuddling and comforting that goes on when he restricts himself to a whimper. In such a case whimpering is reinforced and howling is discouraged. He learns not to howl except in those cases when something serious triggers his howling reaction and causes it to override his newly learned response. This learning takes place even though the infant cannot yet understand or reflect upon what is happening.

When he is still quite young, well before he has to go to school, our young boy begins a new kind of learning—reflective and intelligent learning. He begins to adopt a certain type of behavior because he understands that it has satisfactory results. He begins to avoid certain other types of behavior because he understands that it can have painful consequences. When our young hero comes in from the back yard and tracks mud across the newly-cleaned kitchen floor certain unpleasant, perhaps even painful, results usually follow. When he takes off his shoes at the door and runs over to give his mother a big hug it is often good for a reward the next time the ice-cream boy passes by. Our lad has now entered the properly human world of calculating the effects of actions and behaving accordingly.

It is not only his parents who teach him. He learns from experience. He learns, for example, that boiling kettles are best left alone and that strange dogs and strange children should be approached with caution.

Once the child begins to use intelligence in directing his own actions, then he begins to apply, in a rudimentary way at least, those subordinate rules discussed in Chapter Three. He applies these rules even though he does not formulate them abstractly. He discovers that certain means cause certain ends, that certain causes produce certain undesired effects, and he begins to act accordingly. He learns to choose in accord not with the likes and dislikes of which he happens to be aware but with his whole range of likes and dislikes. He learns to choose in accord not with the likes and dislikes of which he is capable at the time of choice but with his likes and dislikes during the whole time affected by the choice. Beginning with a very limited application of these rules, the child will learn gradually to apply them in a more informed and intelligent way.

The child will be slower to apply the principles discussed in Chapters Four and Five. To the four-year-old boy it makes little sense to go against present inclinations in order to develop new and different inclinations. The child of that age will also be quite unable to grasp the larger contexts which give a fuller significance to individual actions.

Those caring for the child (normally the parents, and later others such as teachers) are not satisfied to let the child develop according to a random occurrence of likes and dislikes and insight. They hurry him along a certain path by urging on him certain types of behavior which he does not yet appreciate. The four-year-old is urged to share his toys. He is scolded for overly frank public discussion of family secrets or intimacies. Later he will be urged to study poetry and do all sorts of things which, he is assured, are good for him, but he does not appreciate their goodness.

There results a conflict between the child's own inclinations and what is urged on him by others. Even when demands by others are in accord with what is best for the child often they will conflict with the child's own inclinations at the moment. Because it is usually the parents who play the principal role in making these demands we will describe the resulting development as an interplay between child and parents. It is understood that other people besides the parents may play important roles in this development of the child.

The child accepts the parents' judgment about the goodness or badness of his actions and of himself. That is, for the young child ''good'' comes to mean those things which please the parents and ''bad'' comes to mean those things which displease the parents. At times the child may rebel against the real or perceived injustice of some parental demand or punishment, but he cannot sustain for long any independent evaluation of himself and of his actions. Even an adult gets much of his or her sense of the worth of self and of his or her actions from the evaluation by others. Much more is this the case for the child who has nothing which he recognizes as a basis for a counter-argument. When the four-year-old is told that tracking mud on the kitchen floor is bad he is usually not disposed to argue. He does not call his parents into conference and explain: ''You may think that tracking mud on kitchen floors is a bad thing. However, some authorities, with whom I happen to agree, regard it as a legitimate mode of self-expression.''

The demands of parents are strengthened because the parents are quasiomnipotent for the young child. They reward and punish him, and against their decisions he has no appeal. More important, parents supply the necessities of life, physical necessities such as food and shelter, psychological necessities such as security, acceptance and affection. Parental disapproval is a terrifying thing if it carries the implicit threat of rejection of the child. Parental approval, on the other hand, brings with it the promise of security, affection and general well-being.

Small wonder, then, that the small child accepts that he is good when his parents say that he is good, and that he is bad when his parents say that he is bad. This doesn't mean, of course, that our four-year-old boy always does what his parents want. Quite often he may find it a good deal more satisfying to be naughty, to swipe a few cookies or to punch his sister when she makes a nuisance of herself. When he does this, however, he recognizes that he is being bad.

At this stage the child experiences blame, shame, and guilt. He does something wrong and his parents find out and they blame him. This blame is really an attack on the child's sense of self. He gets much of his sense of self-worth from his experience that his parents treat him as someone special. When they blame him he sees himself lowered in the eyes of these omnipotent ones. Since he is disposed to accept their judgment, he becomes unworthy in his own eyes. He feels ashamed and guilty. The child experiences the parental judgment not merely as an external factor to be reckoned with in calculating rewards and punishments, but as something profoundly affecting his own sense of self and of self-worth.

At first the child feels shame or guilt only when the parent is actually present and blames him. He feels approval only when the parent is present and approves. Eventually he interiorizes the parental commands. When he does things which go against parental commands he blames himself and feels shame and guilt even if parents are absent and ignorant of what he has done. When he does things of which his parents approve he feels self-approval even if his parents are absent and unaware of his behavior. After a time he may forget all connection between his interior feelings and the parents who first caused them. He simply experiences an "inner voice," a spontaneous feeling of guilt or self-approval.

Probably there are several psychological processes by which this process of interiorization takes place. Simple conditioning may be a factor. If our four-year-old is scolded every time he is caught stealing cookies he may be conditioned to feel that way even when he performs the act without getting caught. The development may well involve some of the processes of identification and of repression which Sigmund Freud associated with the formation of the super-ego.[1] A good deal of the process of interiorization can be explained by the nature of the child's spontaneous response to a parent's praise or blame. The child does not only see this praise and blame as the expression of a parent's attitude. He accepts it as a correct evaluation of himself and of his actions. When his mother scolds him he not only becomes aware of his mother's attitude but he also feels that he is a bad boy.

This whole process takes place on the level not of abstract formulations but of concrete feelings. The child at this stage does not formulate a set of rules or standards of behavior. He has a fairly concrete notion of what a good boy is supposed to be like. Nor need the child consciously decide to strive for this ideal. The ideal arises spontaneously within him. His urge to be accepted, to be someone of value, spontaneously takes the form of an urge to conform to this ideal. Henceforth the conflict is no longer simply between his own inclinations and the demands of society. The conflict is between the inner demands of this ideal and certain other of his inner inclinations.

Many people, implicitly at least, identify these learned responses of guilt and self-approval[2] with conscience and make them the basic criteria for moral judgment. If someone says that his conscience is bothering him he may well mean simply that he has this feeling of guilt. When people cease to feel this sort of guilt about a certain type of behavior they may take that as a new perception that such behavior is not immoral. These learned feelings may even play a prominent part in some ethical theories, especially in some of the theories which appeal to a moral sense.

However, there are several undesirable results if these learned responses of guilt and self-approval are identified with conscience and made the principal criteria for moral judgment. One such undesirable result is that these responses are not always reliable guides to moral life.

They are not intelligent judgments based on a realistic appraisal of the actual situation. They are more or less automatic responses triggered by factors which may or may not be morally significant in the situation. They go back to the simplistic and unsophisticated responses learned in childhood. As a result sometimes we feel guilty about things which are not really immoral. Our inner feelings of guilt may make such excessive demands that they severely restrict behavior and destroy most of the enjoyment of life. On the other hand, we may fail to feel guilty about certain other things which cause real harm or destroy important goods. People may feel a great sense of relief when they stop feeling guilty about something. This may be a gain or it may be a loss. It depends on whether that something is really bad or not.

A second drawback about a morality based on these feelings of guilt and approval is that they are not the voice of the authentic self. They are the interiorized voices of someone else. They may represent demands fixated at an immature level when the child first had to cope with parental demands. They don't represent a personal appreciation of the goodness of what is good or the evil of what is evil. A person whose actions are controlled by these feelings has not yet assumed full responsibility for his or her life.

A third drawback of a morality based on these feelings of guilt or self-approval is that an emphasis on guilt can destroy one's sense of self-worth. The novel *Hawaii* developed the idea that Christian missionaries harmed the natives by stressing guilt. One can feel guilty for thoughts and desires which arise in ourselves quite spontaneously and against our wills. One can feel worthless and despicable quite apart from anything one can do about it. Such morality centers attention not on good but on evil.

Finally, a morality which stresses this feeling of guilt emphasizes repression, at least in the view of many psychologists. A strong sense of guilt may cause the conscious self to refuse to recognize some undesirable thoughts or feelings. These thoughts and feelings are repressed, put beyond consciousness. Repression, however, does not so much resolve a problem as hide it. The repressed material does not go away. It remains in the unconscious and from there it can cause undesirable effects. Strong repressed drives may break through into consciousness in disguised forms such as neuroses, irrational fears or compulsions. Even if there is no neurosis, at best the repressed material remains unintegrated into the total personality. It remains a part of the personality which does not develop by contact with reality and by intelligent insight. It remains in the primitive state it was in at the time of repression.

The fact that a morality based on these feelings of guilt and self-approval can have undesirable results does not mean that developing these feelings of guilt and of self-approval is a bad thing. It is probably a necessary stage in growing up. Before the child has developed all the requisites for a mature morality he or she is at least socialized. That is, the child interiorizes those attitudes which are necessary or useful for living in a particular human milieu. What is harmful to full human growth is to stop development at this point and to let one's whole system of values be nothing but a childish interiorization of parental attitudes. Even after one achieves a more mature stage of moral development, a well-formed habit of feeling guilt or self-approval in the proper situations can be a considerable aid to life.[3]

What will be involved in a more mature stage? One can interpret the topic so widely that a description of moral maturity will include all of the qualities of the morally good person. Our narrower description will focus on several elements in moral judgment discussed in previous chapters.

Morally mature persons will not be dominated by feelings of guilt and self-approval instilled in them by others. They will use their intelligences to make moral judgments according to the proper criteria. A child after he or she begins to direct his or her own actions by intelligence begins to apply in a rudimentary way the subsidiary rules discussed in Chapter Three. As persons grow toward moral maturity they gain the experience and insight necessary to apply these rules in an effective way. Furthermore, mature persons have developed their likings for a wide variety of goods, so their appreciation of goods is more reliable than is that of a child. On the other hand, mature persons recognize that they have not learned to appreciate all goods. They are able, then, to learn from others, to admit their own limitations, and to see that it is reasonable at times to go against present inclinations in order to develop their appreciation for other goods. The mature person is able to grasp the larger contexts which give fuller significance to particular actions. Finally, the mature person can follow the judgment of reason even when it goes against his or her present inclinations.

PART TWO

The Criteria for Moral Judgment: Sacred Scripture

In Part Two we will examine what valid criteria for moral judgment can be discovered with the help of Sacred Scripture.[1] *The focus will be mainly on the New Testament. To provide a background, however, the first three chapters of this part will examine several Old Testament concepts and themes.*

Chapter Eight

LAW AND COVENANT
IN THE OLD TESTAMENT[1]

It has been common, especially in certain ages, for Christians to contrast the Old Testament emphasis on law with the New Testament emphasis on love. To leave the contrast in this simplified form is to distort the Old Testament understanding of law and morality. It is, for example, to ignore the role of love in Old Testament morality. Moreover, according to the accounts of the Gospels, the polemic of Jesus against Jewish legalism is directed not against the Mosaic law but against the way some Jews of his time used the law. A more reliable view of Old Testament morality must view the Mosaic law in relation to covenant.

A. Law

When the New Testament speaks of the law, in some cases it refers not to any particular laws or code of laws but to the Pentateuch, the first five books of the Old Testament. In accordance with this usage the Old Testament can be designated "the law and the prophets." (See, for example, Mt 5, 17; Lk 16, 16; Jn 1, 45). In this book, however, by "law" we refer not to the whole Pentateuch but to the laws or codes of laws contained in it.

The Pentateuch contains several law codes dating from different centuries. The code of the covenant, Exodus 20—23, may date back to the first centuries after the Israelite conquest of Palestine. The Deuteronomic Code (Deuteronomy 12—26) played a part in the religious reform in Judah in the second half of the seventh century B.C. and dates from that time or from several decades earlier. Scholars are less unanimous on the dating of the Holiness Code (Leviticus 17—26) which is part of a larger collection of laws, the Priestly Code, which includes not only the laws in Leviticus but also others scattered throughout Exodus and Numbers. The decalogue (the ten commandments) presented in two similar but not identical forms (Ex 20, 1–17, Dt 5, 6–21) probably antedates all or nearly all other legal material in the Old Testament.

It is clear, therefore, that the laws in the Pentateuch did not originate as one code imposed upon Israel all at once. When a later code came into force it might have been because an earlier code had been lost or fallen into disuse or judged inadequate to a new set of conditions.

These codes contain diverse type of laws. Some laws govern ritual and worship. Other laws, such as most of the ten commandments, we would call moral laws; still others come closer to what we would consider civil laws. This threefold division into ritual, moral and civil law is not made by the Israelites themselves, however. For them, the laws taken together constituted God's directives about how they were to live, and they accepted them as such without clearly distinguishing ritual law from moral law or civil law.

Pentateuch laws assume several different forms. The casuistic form seems suitable for judgment of cases by a tribunal. These laws state a condition and what is to be done in that condition. Exodus 22, 5 is an example. "When a man causes a field or vineyard to be grazed over, or lets his beast loose and it feeds on another man's field, he shall make restitution from the best in his own field and in his own vineyard." These casuistic laws generally reflect the type of law common in the Near East at the time the Hebrew codes were formed. This gives grounds for the opinion that often these laws are not original with the Hebrews but were taken over from other peoples.

Certain laws are apodictic in form. They simply command. "Thou shalt not kill" (Ex 20, 13). These laws are more characteristically Hebrew, finding fewer parallels in non-Hebrew sources. They may have originated in the context of Israelite religious ceremonies.

A third type of law seems to be between the casuistic and the apodictic. A participle clause states a condition and the main clause states what is to be done. Like the casuistic law, they state a condition and what is to be done if that condition arises. Like the apodictic type, they are concise and imperative in style and are not particularly suitable for settling cases before a tribunal.

B. Covenant

The notion of covenant did not originate with the Hebrews. Of the forms of covenant in use in the ancient Near East, the Hittite form was especially close to the form of some of the principal covenants in the Old Testament. A covenant, like a modern contract, estblished certain rights and duties; but it went beyond this to establish a more comprehensive relationship between the covenant partners, a relationship which could not be adequately spelled out in the legal terms of a contract. From being enemies or strangers, the parties in the covenant might become allies, or friends, or even in some sense brothers bound by quasi-familial ties.

Secular covenants could be between equals or between a superior and an inferior party, between a king and a vassal, for example. In the latter case the superior normally would dictate the terms of the covenant. In the covenants between God and Israel, God dictates the terms.

Hittite covenants often had four main elements. First, when it was a covenant between a superior and an inferior party, the superior in a prologue would give a record of events. This might be a record of his own actions presented as benefactions to the inferior party. The prologue usually shows why the superior has acquired rights over the inferior. Second, certain stipulations were stated, obligations which one or both partners were to fulfill. A third part consisted of sanctions, punishments for the partner who failed to fulfill the stipulations, and perhaps rewards for dutiful observance. The sanctions might be reinforced by appeals to gods and by calling down blessings or curses. Finally, there was a ritual by which the covenant was sealed. This might involve a sacrifice, or writing out the agreement, or the erection of a monument as a sort of witness to the covenant, or eating a meal together.

The Old Testament speaks of secular covenants, such as that between Abraham and Abimelech (Gen 21). Much more important are the religious covenants. In many passages the relationship of God with men is expressed in the form of a covenant. God makes a covenant with Noah (Gen 9, 8–17) and with Abraham (Gen 15, 1–20). The great covenant which establishes Israel as God's people is the one God made with Israel during the exodus at Mount Sinai (Ex 19–24; Dt 1–30). Joshua 24 describes a renewal of this covenant. A covenant is made or renewed again at other important points in Hebrew history (see 2 Kgs 11, 17; 23, 1–3; Ezr 10, 3; Neh 9–10).

The Sinai covenant as described in Exodus and in Deuteronomy contains the four elements common in the Hittite treaties. In the prologue God recites the deeds he has done for Israel, especially his delivering her from slavery in Egypt (Ex 19, 4; Dt 4, 32–39). The stipulations include not only the ten commandments but also the code of the covenant in Exodus and the Deuteronomic Code in Deuteronomy. The sanctions in the immediate context of the covenant consist principally of rewards (see Ex 19, 5–6; 23, 22–31; Dt 6, 10–25; 8, 7–20). However, it is clear that though the Lord is slow to anger, abounding in love, yet there are punishments for the guilty (Ex 34, 6–7; Dt 7, 10). The ceremonies include sprinkling both the people and the altar with blood, a sacrifice, and a common meal. The people themselves accept the covenant and Moses writes down the agreement (Ex 24). Accompanying the covenant is God's manifestation of his power, glory, and holiness (Ex 19 and 24). A vivid awareness of God is at the core of the covenant.

By the covenant a special relationship comes into being between God and Israel, and will remain as long as Israel is faithful. God will become Israel's ally, fighting on her side (Ex 23, 22–27). God will guide his people. They become a kingdom of priests, a holy nation, God's special possession (Ex 19, 5–6). It is the re-establishment of this relationship that later prophets will have in mind in the repeated refrain they attribute to God: "I will be your God, and you will be my people."

The notion of covenant is flexible and was able to expand to include deeper insights and to apply to new situations. For example, the notion of covenant suggests the notion of election, the notion that God by his sovereign will had chosen Israel. Reflection on election yielded the insight that God acted out of love (see Dt 7, 6–7). Many of the prophets continue to express their religious message in terms of the covenant (see, for example, Is 54, 10; Jer 14, 21; Ez 16, 59–63; Dan 9, 4).

C. The Relation of Law and Covenant

Exodus and Deuteronomy present the law as part of the covenant, as the stipulations to be observed by Israel as their living by the covenant.

This context gives a special meaning to the Mosaic law. Since the moral law of the Jews is contained in the Mosaic law, this relationship to the covenant gives a special meaning to Israelite moral law.

One part of this special meaning is that all true Israelite morality is religious. For the faithful Israelite, there is no true morality which is autonomous from religion.

In the covenant, the Mosaic law was seen as the will of God. The moral law, as part of the Mosaic law, was thereby seen as the will of God. For the faithful Israelite, doing good had no other meaning than doing the will of God. This is the first way in which the covenant made all true Israelite morality to be religious.

God called upon the Israelites to respond to him in the covenant. This response was expressed in observance of the Mosaic law, including its moral elements. Israel's response to God is her motive for observing the moral law. This is a second way in which the covenant made all true Israelite morality to be religious.

We should examine further this response to God in the covenant. The response is, first of all, fear of the Lord. God reveals himself in the covenant as powerful, as almighty. He inspires fear. This fear, however, should not be merely the fear of power in the hand of a potentially or actually hostile person. True fear of God is religious awe based on a realization of who God is. He is the all-holy one who is beyond all that human beings can experience or conceive, yet he has broken into Israel's life and he is close to her. This awe fills Israel with the desire to do God's will, not simply out of fear of punishment or desire for reward, but because the realization of who God is robs one of any valid basis for pitting oneself against him.

Israel is also called to respond to God in gratitude. In the prologue to the ten commandments God states: "I am the Lord your God, who brought you out of the land of Egypt, out of the house of bondage" (Ex 20, 2). Israel is to show gratitude for this action by observing the commandments which follow. The remembrance of this intervention by God, recalled liturgically, is to serve as a continuing motive for Israel's faithfulness (see Dt 6, 20–25).

By the time of the writing of the Book of Deuteronomy it was realized that God made the covenant because he loved Israel (see Dt 7, 6–7). God does not reveal his love for Israel simply as a matter of information to satisfy someone's curiosity. He seeks a response of wholehearted love (Dt 6, 5) and this love, like the fear of the Lord and gratitude, constitutes a motive for doing God's will (Dt 10, 12–13).

One could think of the covenant law as something God arbitrarily imposed on Israel. Even in that case, presumably Israel's awe, gratitude, and love toward God could provide a motive for observing the law. However, the law is not something arbitrarily imposed but something which flows naturally from the covenant. Accordingly the covenant not only provides motivation for observing the law but also in a way justifies and makes sense of the law's content.

For the regulations governing Israel's explicitly religious acts, this is quite clear. In the covenant God gives Israel a realization of who he is. From this realization it follows naturally that one should have no other gods before him (Ex 20, 3) and that one should not serve idols (Ex 20, 5). A realization of who God is gives rise spontaneously to a desire to praise and worship him, and this desire underlies the Mosaic cultic ordinances.

Nor are the laws concerning self and neighbor mere arbitrary rules. They too flow naturally from the covenant. Especially according to Deuteronomy, in the covenant God reveals his love for Israel and his desire to grant blessings to her. Accordingly the laws of the covenant are seen as directed toward Israel's benefit. Already in Exodus we find expressions of this concern.

> If you ever take your neighbor's garment in pledge, you shall restore it to him before the sun goes down; for that is his only covering, it is his mantle for his body; in what else shall he sleep? And if he cries to me, I will hear, for I am compassionate (Ex 22, 26–27).[2]

In following the law, Israel was really exercising the compassion and love of God toward the neighbor. At the same time, Israel becomes aware of God's sublime wisdom. To have the law is to share in that wisdom (see Dt 4, 6–8). No one else could know as well as God how Israel can act wisely to attain her true happiness.

In a primitive understanding of the covenant, the rewards and punishments appear as ways to force or buy Israel's conformity to the law. In reality, however, the "punishments" are the inevitable and natural results of rejecting wisdom. When one neglects the correct ways of attaining the good, one ends up with something not so good. The rewards are not extrinsic to the law. They are the natural results of acting wisely. God loves Israel and desires her happiness. His laws show the way to enter that happiness. The rewards and punishments help insert the covenant into salvation history. The prologue indicates that history in the past, how God has put Israel on the way of salvation. The rewards indicate the goal, the salvation which results if Israel remains on the way. The punishments indicate the natural results of Israel abandoning that way.

Just as true Israelite morality is religious, a response to God in the covenant, so true Israelite religion is moral. True Israelite religion does not consist only in explicit act of worship. It involves the whole of life. The prophet Amos especially developed this point. God is not some little tribal deity interested only in some burnt offerings or some court rituals in his honor. God is the Lord, the Lord of every being. He is to be served in all of life—in helping the poor and the weak, in being fair to one's workers, in caring for the sick. This point, taken up by later prophets, is at the core of the moral teaching of Jesus, for whom the second great commandment is to love one's neighbor as oneself. James says "Religion that is pure and undefiled before God and the Father is this: to visit orphans and widows in their affliction . . ." (Jas 1, 27).

The true Israelite sense of the law came from the profound religious experience involved in the covenant. In order to preserve this experience it had to be somehow captured in words and images in order to pass it on to later generations. Each succeeding generation would be called to relive that profound religious experience. It seems almost inevitable, however, that at times people will not relive the experience, that they will have only the words. At such times for the Jews, the law loses its spirit, becomes a thing in itself and not the response to God and his plan of salvation. The law becomes absolutized and legalism takes over.

While the Jews remained conscious of the covenant they were reminded that God had first gratuitously chosen Israel and promised her salvation. In this context it is clear that observance of the law, while it is required of the Jews, is not the original cause of their salvation. That original cause is God's sovereign choice. Once the law is dissociated from the religious experience of the covenant, it can easily appear that it is observance of the law which first earns salvation and God's love. Having lost sight of the covenant, some Jews lost sight of the purpose and meaning of the law. The focus shifted to the self and to actual observance. One centers attention on the fact that one observes the law, and so one is in the right. One loses any perspective by which one can choose between conflicting laws. If one is interested simply in one's own subjective being in the right, transgression of some minor ritual regulation can seem as important as neglect of some basic value. Either transgression puts you in the wrong. Finally, having lost sight of the covenant one loses sight of the positive motives for observing laws, love of God, faithfulness and gratitude to him. One focuses only on one's dread of being wrong.

Chapter Nine

OLD TESTAMENT NOTIONS
OF FLESH AND SPIRIT

Although the terms "flesh" (Hebrew—*basar*) and spirit (Hebrew—*ruah*) may be used in slightly different ways in different books, there are certain meanings attached to these words rather generally in the Old Testament. A knowledge of these meanings helps in understanding the key New Testament terms "flesh" (Greek—*sarx*) and "spirit" (Greek—*pneuma*).

A. Flesh[1]

"Flesh" in the Old Testament can have any of several non-religious meanings. Job says to God: "Thou didst clothe me with skin and flesh, and knit me together with bones and sinews" (Job 10, 11). The context here is religious but "flesh" refers only to the meaty or muscular parts of the body. These, together with skin, bone and sinew, are seen to make up the whole body.[2] "Flesh" may refer to the body generally, not merely to the fleshy parts. When Ahab hears the words of Elijah he tears his garments and puts sackcloth upon his flesh (1 Kgs 21, 27). "Flesh" may indicate the whole person, without singling out the bodily aspect. The psalmist speaks of his flesh yearning for God (Ps 63, 1). Flesh can refer to kinfolk, as when Abimelech reminds his kinsmen that he is their bone and their flesh (Jgs 9, 2). "All flesh" can indicate animal life generally (Gen 6, 17) or all mankind (Gen 6, 12ff).

In many passages of the Old Testament "flesh" takes on connotations which enable it to express certain Hebrew insights into human existence. These connotations are important for understanding Hebrew religious attitudes.

First, when the Old Testament refers to human beings as flesh this can indicate that they are weak and fragile. Behind this connotation is the creation story in Genesis. The Lord God molds man out of dust and breathes into his nostrils the breath of life, and man becomes a living being (Gen 2, 7). Why dust? When a human being dies, when the breath of life leaves him, he decomposes and becomes dust. A man is a bit of dust which for a time is made to live by the mysterious breath of life which he cannot give to himself. The Lord says: "My spirit shall not abide in man forever, for he is flesh" (Gen 6, 3). Job sees in this image an expression of man's radical dependence on God. "If he (God) should take back his spirit to himself, and gather to himself his breath, all flesh would perish together, and man would return to the dust" (Job 34, 14–15). A human being has, as it were, borrowed breath from God for a few years. Then all flesh withers, like the grass (Is 40, 5–8).

The weakness of the flesh is contrasted with the power of God. The Egyptians are not omnipotent, Isaiah reminds his countrymen. They are men and not God, and their horses are flesh and not spirit (Is 31, 3). Hezekiah rallies his people against Sennacherib: "Be strong and of good courage. Do not be afraid or dismayed before the king of Assyria and all the horde that is with him; for there is one greater with us than with him. With him is an arm of flesh; but with us is the Lord our God, to help us and to fight our battles" (2 Chr 32, 7–8). Accordingly, it is a grievous mistake to trust in flesh rather than in the Lord (see Jer 17, 5–7).

In depicting flesh as weak, Old Testament writers do not necessarily mean that it is evil in itself. The human creature of flesh is created by God (Job 10, 11). The flesh is pictured as yearning for God (Ps 63, 1) and as singing for joy to the living God (Ps 84, 2). The great change foreseen by Ezekiel consists of God replacing man's heart of stone with a heart of flesh (Ez 36, 26).

The flesh, the human being both physical and personal, is a good creation of God. This does not mean that it should be the basis for one's trust. The flesh is fragile. What strength it has it receives from God. Even abstracting from the sinful tendencies shown by the flesh in its actual condition, one should still trust not the flesh but God who is the source of all strength.

B. Spirit[3]

The Hebrew word *ruah* has several meanings. One basic meaning is breath. Job complains: "He will not let me get my breath (*ruah*)" (Job 9, 18). *Ruah* as breath is easily associated with life. Animal life is referred to as "all flesh in which is the breath (*ruah*) of life" (Gen 6, 17; see also Gen 7, 15; 7, 22). The psalmist points to the lack of life in idols by noting: "Nor is there any *ruah* in their mouths" (Ps 135, 17). So close is the association of life and breath that in some passages it is difficult to know which concept is intended by *ruah* (see, for example, Jer 10, 14; 51, 17). In some cases the Hebrew authors may have both concepts in mind without intending to make any distinction.

Ruah can refer to the inner self of a person. The psalmist prays: "Into thy hand I commit my spirit (*ruah*)" (Ps 31, 5). Good news causes the *ruah* of Jacob to revive (Gen 45, 27). Job's *ruah* is broken (Job 17, 1). It seems that breath becomes associated with life, and life becomes associated with the one who lives, the one who thinks, feels and acts. The term *ruah* can then refer to breath, or to life, or to the one who lives.

God is presented as possessing *ruah*. Often the *ruah* of God seems to refer to the self or the mind of God. The prophet Micah asks: "Is the spirit (*ruah*) of the Lord impatient?" (Mi 2, 7). The psalmist asks: "Whither shall I go from thy spirit (*ruah*)?" (Ps 139, 7).

Another basic meaning of *ruah* is wind. Eliphaz, Job's friend, asserts: "He (the wicked man) will not escape from darkness; the flame will dry up his shoots, and his blossom will be swept away by the wind (*ruah*)" (Job 15, 30). The wind, like other things in nature, is created by God and is under his power (see Ps 135, 7; Am 4, 13). Some passages depict God as present in a special way in the wind. Adam and Eve sense God's presence in the garden in the wind (Gen 3, 8). For the psalmist, God comes swiftly upon the wings of the wind (Ps 18, 10). The wind is an apt expression for God's presence. It is present and powerful, yet it remains unseen and uncontrolled.[4]

In numerous passages *ruah* is seen as God's agent in historical events. In some of these passages *ruah* is clearly identified with wind. At the end of the flood, "God made the *ruah* blow over the earth and the waters subsided" (Gen 8, 1). An east wind brings the plague of locusts upon Egypt and a west wind drives them away (Ex 10, 13–19). The wind drives back the sea so that the fleeing Israelites can cross over (Ex 14,

21). The wind can be an instrument of God's wrath (see, for example, Ez 13, 13). In some passages the two basic meanings of *ruah* are combined and *ruah* is seen both as wind and as God's breath. After the wind parts the sea and Israel escapes, Moses and the people sing: "At the blast (*ruah*) of thy nostrils the waters piled up: the floods stood up in a heap; the deeps congealed in the heart of the sea" (Ex 15, 8; see also 2 Sam 22, 16; Is 11, 4).

The *ruah* of God, whether conceived as breath or as spirit or as wind, is present and active in creation. "The earth was without form and void, and darkness was upon the face of the deep; and the *ruah* of God was moving over the waters" (Gen 1, 2). Job recalls: "By his *ruah* the heavens were made fair" (Job 26, 13). For the psalmist it is: "By the word of the Lord the heavens were made, and all their host by the *ruah* of his mouth" (Ps 33, 6).

Ruah in human beings comes from God (see Is 42, 5; 57, 16). It is a temporary gift from God, for human beings have a fragile hold on life. "He (God) remembered that they (the Israelites) were but flesh, a wind (*ruah*) that passes and comes not again" (Ps 78, 39). It is as though God lent *ruah* only for a time. Then the Lord said, "My spirit (*ruah*) shall not abide in man forever, for he is flesh" (Gen 6, 3). This recalls the image of God breathing into the dust and making it into a living man (Gen 2, 7). The psalmist continues the same image: "When thou takest away their *ruah* they die and return to the dust. When thou sendest forth thy *ruah* they are created" (Ps 104, 29–30; see also Job 34, 14–15; Eccl 12, 7).

Ruah is involved in giving not only physical life but the whole fullness of what life is to be. Ezekiel pictures Israel in its sad state as dry bones strewn in a valley. God says to the bones: "Behold I will cause breath (*ruah*) to enter you, and you shall live" (Ez 37, 5). The *ruah* comes into the bones; they take flesh upon themselves and rise up as living human beings.

In some cases God gives *ruah* to people, either temporarily or permanently, to perform special works. The spirit comes upon King Saul and he prophesies (1 Sam 10, 6). The spirit speaks through David (2 Sam 23, 2). The spirit in Joseph enables him to judge and act wisely (Gen 41, 38). Some of the spirit which was in Moses is put into the seventy elders and they prophesy (Num 11, 25). Joshua receives the spirit to enable him to lead Israel (Dt 34, 9). Elisha receives a double share of the spirit of Elijah and is enabled to work wonders (2 Kgs 2, 9–15). The spirit is present in a special way to enable the prophets to fulfill their tasks (see, for example, Ez 2, 2; 11, 5; Zech 7, 12).

Psalm 51 presents *ruah* as the source of the revival of life in the repentant sinner.

> Create in me a clean heart, O God,
> and put a new and right spirit (*ruah*) within me.
> Cast me not away from thy presence,
> and take not thy holy spirit (*ruah*) from me.
> Restore to me the joy of thy salvation,
> and uphold me with a willing spirit (*ruah*) (Ps 51, 10–12).

It may be useful here to summarize. *Ruah* can mean breath. It can mean life and the inner self of a person. *Ruah* can also mean wind. Whether seen as breath, as spirit, or as wind, the *ruah* of God is presented as active in the world. Human beings possess life in a temporary and insecure way. God gives life, *ruah*, to human beings, both physical life and the fuller life of the faithful Israelite. God is pictured as breathing his *ruah* into human beings to enliven them.[5]

Chapter Ten

THE NEW TESTAMENT: FULFILLMENT OF PROMISE

Israel's religion directed the vision of its followers toward a future in which God's promises of a better life, of salvation, would be fulfilled. Hope is central to the Old Testament message. This hope rests on Israel's belief that her God is the Lord of history and that he has Israel's welfare at heart. Just as God has intervened in the past to bring Israel toward a better life, so will he act in the future. This better future need not follow automatically, however. Israel can jeopardize her future by sinning, by refusing to enter into God's plan. History is not a mechanical unfolding of developments predetermined by the potentialities of its participants. It is a drama of free persons.

God's promises of a better future are recorded in various books of the Old Testament. Some promises are very general.[1] Others are more specific. Some promises were seen by the Jews as having been fulfilled in events recorded in the Old Testament itself. The return of the Jews from exile in Babylon is an example of such a fulfillment. In other cases the promises can easily be interpreted as applying to a future beyond Old Testament times. For example, certain prophecies concern a messiah, an anointed one, who is to establish God's rule. Some Jews may have seen some of these prophecies as fulfilled in some Old Testament figure. However, many contemporaries of Jesus looked forward to a messiah still to come.

The New Testament writers explain Jesus and events in the early days of the Church as fulfillments of Old Testament promises. To a large extent it is these Old Testament promises which provide the conceptual tools by which the early Christians, including the New Testament authors, understand Jesus and events in the early Church.[2]

Some New Testament passages express only in a quite general way the conviction that Jesus is the fulfillment of Old Testament promises.[3] In other passages quite particular events in the life of Jesus are related to earlier prophecies.[4] It is especially the suffering, death and resurrection which are presented in this way. According to the New Testament, the first dawning of understanding of these events came to the disciples when they were able to relate them to Old Testament prophecies. It is thus that Jesus gave understanding to the disciples on the road to Emmaus (Lk 24, 25–27). Apparently he used the same procedure to bring understanding to the disciples in Jerusalem (Lk 24, 44–47). According to the Acts of the Apostles this same procedure is used by the disciples when it becomes their turn to give enlightenment to others.[5] The Gospels too present this same way of gaining understanding of the passion, death and resurrection of Jesus.[6]

There are several themes in Old Testament prophecy which are used by New Testament authors to explain the significance of Jesus. One such theme concerned a future king of the Davidic line.[7] When the New Testament authors identify Jesus as Son of David[8] they are using this Old Testament concept to show who Jesus is. Again, Jesus' answer to the messengers from John the Baptist (Mt 11, 4–6) seems to provide an understanding of himself in terms taken from Isaiah (see Is 29, 18–19; 35, 5–6).[9]

One important promise linking the Old and New Testaments concerns the new covenant. Old Testament prophets became aware that Israel by its sinfulness had broken the covenant between God and Israel. They hoped for a time when the fuller covenant relationship would be restored. For example, each time he presents God as saying: ''I will be your God, and you will be my people,'' the prophet is referring to a restoration of that fuller covenant relationship. Eventually, however, some of the prophets began to speak not in terms of a revival of the covenant but of the creation of a new covenant. Apparently they see the need of some radically new intervention by God to break the hold of sin upon Israel.

> Behold, the days are coming, says the Lord, when I will make
> a new covenant with the house of Israel and with the house of
> Judah, not like the covenant which I made with their fathers

when I took them by the hand to bring them out of the land of
Egypt, my covenant which they broke, though I was their husband, says the Lord. But this is the covenant which I will make
with the house of Israel after those days, says the Lord. I will
put my law within them, and I will write it upon their hearts;
and I will be their God, and they shall be my people (Jer 31,
31–33).[10]

This new covenant will be different from the old, according to Jeremiah, because God will put the law within the people, writing it upon
their hearts. The Mosaic covenant had a law written on stone tablets. Such
a law remains ineffective if it remains merely written on stone while people choose not to follow it. What is needed is an interior change in people
which will move them to follow God's law. With the people upholding
their part of the relationship the new covenant can endure.[11]

According to Matthew, Mark and Paul, Jesus at the Last Supper
presented his own sacrifice as enacting the new covenant.

Now as they were eating, Jesus took bread, and blessed, and
broke it, and gave it to the disciples and said, ''Take, eat; this
is my body.'' And he took a cup, and when he had given thanks
he gave it to them, saying ''Drink of it, all of you; for this is
my blood of the covenant, which is poured out for many for
the forgiveness of sins'' (Mt 26, 26–28; cf Mk 14, 22–24; 1
Cor 11, 25).

On the occasion of the Mosaic covenant the blood of sacrificed animals was sprinkled over altar and people to signify the living unity established between God and his people. In the new covenant the blood of
Jesus poured out in sacrifice establishes a new unity between God and
his people.[12]

Many prophetic texts in the Old Testament look forward to a special
pouring forth of the Holy Spirit. The Spirit will rest upon that descendant
of David upon whom many Israelites rested their hopes. This shoot from
the root of Jesse, aided by the Spirit, will bring a reign of wisdom, justice
and peace (see Is 11, 1–16). The Spirit will rest upon that suffering servant
foretold in Deutero-Isaiah (see Is 42, 1–6) with whom, according to the
Gospels, Jesus identified himself (see Lk 18, 31–33; Mt 20, 25–28). The

prophets foresee a time when God's spirit will be poured out upon the whole community, producing wonderful effects (see Is 4, 4–6; 32, 14–20; 44, 3–5). The Spirit will come upon even the common people (Jl 2, 29). The Spirit will cause an inner transformation.

> For I will take you from all the countries, and bring you into your own land. I will sprinkle clean water upon you, and you shall be clean from all your uncleannesses, and from all your idols I will cleanse you. A new heart I will give you, and a new spirit I will put within you; and I will take out of your flesh the heart of stone and give you a heart of flesh. And I will put my spirit within you, and cause you to walk in my statutes and be careful to observe my ordinances. You shall dwell in the land which I gave to your fathers; and you shall be my people, and I will be your God (Ez 36, 24–28).

Ezekiel here sees the Spirit accomplishing things similar to those which Jeremiah saw as accompanying the new covenant.

Some Jews may have seen some of these texts concerning the Spirit as fulfilled by events relatively close to the time the prophecies were made.[13] Nevertheless, the New Testament authors see these prophecies as fulfilled in Jesus and in the early Church. They relate that the Holy Spirit[14] was poured forth first upon Jesus himself. The Synoptic Gospels present Jesus as receiving the Holy Spirit at his baptism by John the Baptist (Mt 3, 16; Mk 1, 10; Lk 3, 22). Immediately the Spirit moves Jesus to go into the wilderness (Mk 1, 12). Jesus then embarks on his ministry full of the Holy Spirit and led by the Spirit (Lk 4, 1). By the Spirit Jesus expels demons (Mt 12, 28). In Acts 10, 38 Peter explains that God anointed Jesus with the Holy Spirit and with power. For Paul, the Spirit raised Jesus from the dead (Rom 8, 11).

Peter explains (Acts 2, 33) that Jesus, having received the promise of the Holy Spirit, pours it out upon others. As Paul puts it, Jesus became a life-giving Spirit (1 Cor 15, 45). The Spirit in Jesus passes on to others the life which is in Jesus. The Spirit is identified as the Spirit of Jesus (Phil 1, 19).

The baptism of Jesus, unlike that of John the Baptist, is a baptism not only with water, but with the Holy Spirit (see Mt 3, 11; Lk 3, 16; Jn 1, 33). This means that John's baptism preceded the pouring forth of the

Spirit, prepared the way for it, but was not the actual pouring forth. For the fourth Gospel, that which is wrought by water and the Spirit is a rebirth, a new life (Jn 3, 5). In the fourteenth chapter of this same Gospel Jesus promises to pray to the Father to send the Holy Spirit. In Chapter 7 Jesus talks to his audience about this life they will receive when they receive the Spirit. These promises that the Spirit will come are pictured as fulfilled in the early community of believers. They are fulfilled dramatically on Pentecost (Acts 2, 1–4), an event which Peter explains by reference to the prophecy of Joel (Acts 2, 16–21). Others who wish similarly to receive the Holy Spirit may do so on condition that they repent and are baptized (Acts 2, 38).

The Acts of the Apostles recounts several occasions when the Holy Spirit came into a group of believers. Not only did the Spirit come upon groups for a first time (Acts 8, 14–17; 19, 6); a group of friends of Peter and John, friends who presumably had received the Holy Spirit already, was seized in a special way by a further outpouring of the Spirit (Acts 4, 31). On at least some occasions the coming of the Holy Spirit was accompanied by external manifestations sufficiently obvious to assure witnesses that the Spirit had indeed been poured forth on that occasion (see, for example, Acts 10, 44–47).

There seems to have been a special gift of the Spirit to the men charged with spreading the faith. According to Acts 1, 5 and 8, Jesus promises the apostles not only that they will be baptized by the Holy Spirit but that on this occasion they will be given special power. The fourth Gospel presents Jesus as breathing upon the apostles on the occasion of sending them forth and saying: "Receive the Holy Spirit" (Jn 20, 21–23). In Matthew, Jesus urges his disciples in their future persecution not to be anxious about what they are to say before authorities, because the Spirit of their Father will be speaking through them (Mt 10, 20). The behavior of the apostles after Pentecost manifests a new power and sense of purpose. The Acts of the Apostles presents the Spirit as accompanying the apostles in their ministry. Peter is filled with the Spirit when he addresses the assembled rulers, elders and scribes (Acts 4, 8). The Spirit guides Peter (Acts 10, 19; 11, 12), sends forth Paul and Barnabas (Acts 13, 4) and warns Paul (Acts 20, 23). The decision of the apostles assembled in Jerusalem in presented as a decision by the Spirit (Acts 15, 28).[15]

Chapter Eleven

THE LIFE OF THE SPIRIT

In this chapter we will examine some aspects of the life given by the Spirit, beginning with the Pauline[1] writings and then reflecting systematically on the meaning of *agape,* which is Christian love.

A. The Effects of the Spirit

As in the Old, so in the New Testament, Spirit can best be understood in relation to flesh. We will look briefly then at the meaning of flesh[2] according to St. Paul.

"Flesh" can have any of several meanings in St. Paul. It can refer to the physical body. Paul speaks of an ailment of the flesh (Gal 4, 13).[3] The term may highlight the external, visible aspect of a human being. Paul states that the real Jew is not the one who is so outwardly, nor is true circumcision something external and "in the flesh" (Eph 2, 11; cf 1 Cor 5, 5; Gal 4, 23; 4, 29). "Flesh" can denote a bond of race (see Rom 9, 5; 11, 14). In other passages "flesh" refers to human beings in a more general way, not merely as physical. When Paul insists that he did not confer with flesh and blood (Gal 1, 16) he means that he did not confer only with human beings. He speaks of a mind of flesh (Rom 8, 7; Col 2, 18). "Works of the flesh" include such things as pride and idolatry (Gal 5, 20; 6, 12).

For Paul, as for the Old Testament authors, man, flesh, is weak. Paul does not dwell on the physical weakness and fragility of the flesh. It is the weakness of the whole person, especially in moral and religious aspects, that attracts his attention. Accordingly he adopts a particular way of speaking to the Romans accommodated to the weakness of their flesh (Rom 6, 19). Man is weak not only in comparison with God but also in comparison with other forces abroad in the world (see Eph 6, 11–13).

Does Paul see the flesh (i.e., the human reality as such) as sinful? Certain expressions could suggest that he does. "We know that the law is spiritual; but I am carnal (literally, fleshly), sold under sin" (Rom 7, 14). "Those who belong to Christ Jesus have crucified the flesh with its passions and desires" (Gal 5, 24; see also Rom 7, 5; 1 Cor 2, 14; Gal 3, 3; 5, 13).

Before concluding simply that for Paul the flesh is sinful, some distinctions should be made. First of all simply to be flesh, to be human, does not mean that one is necessarily sinful. Jesus was the Son become flesh. He was "manifested in the flesh" (1 Tim 3, 16).

What of other men in their actual state? What does Paul say about their sinfulness? Here it is useful to distinguish two meanings Paul gives to the expression "in the flesh." At times it refers simply to living in this world. For example, Paul debates whether it would be better to remain in the flesh or to depart and be with Christ (Phil 1, 22–24). In other passages to live "in the flesh" is to be in a state of life which the Christian has left behind. "But you are not in the flesh, you are in the spirit, if the Spirit of God really dwells in you" (Rom 8, 9). Life "in the flesh" in this second sense is life according to the human faculties of the human being, apart from any special intervention of God. Accordingly Paul can speak of Ishmael as born to Abraham and Hagar "according to the flesh" whereas Isaac was born to Abraham and Sarah through the promise (Gal 4, 23). Elsewhere Paul seems to speak of the life "in the flesh" in this second sense as living "according to the flesh," whereas life "in the flesh" in the first sense (life in this world) need not be life "according to the flesh." "For though we live in the flesh we are not carrying on a war according to the flesh" (2 Cor 10, 3).

To live in the flesh in the second sense, to live according to the flesh, is to be involved in sin, according to Paul. All men in fact have sinned. "All (Jews and Gentiles both) have sinned and fall short of the glory of God" (Rom 3, 23). The flesh, unaided human power, is inadequate to attain salvation. "I tell you this, brethren: flesh and blood cannot inherit the Kingdom of God, nor does the perishable inherit the imperishable" (1 Cor 15, 50; see Gal 6, 8).

To live "according to the flesh" means to live according to the sinful desires which arise in human beings as they actually are. "While we were living in the flesh our sinful passions, aroused by the law, were at work in our members" (Rom 7, 5). These desires of the flesh include more than physical passions. "Among these (worldly things) we all once lived in the passions of our flesh, following desires of body and mind, and so we were by nature children of wrath, like the rest of mankind" (Eph 2, 3). The desires of the flesh lead to such works of the flesh as immorality, impurity, licentiousness, idolatry and anger (see Gal 5, 16–20).

Flesh, unaided human nature, is inadequate not only because of its sinful passions but also because of its lack of wisdom. Human wisdom alone is unable to guide people to salvation.

> Let no one deceive himself. If any one among you thinks that he is wise in this age, let him become a fool that he may become wise. For the wisdom of this world is folly with God. For it is written, "He catches the wise in their craftiness," and again, "The Lord knows that the thoughts of the wise are futile" (1 Cor 3, 18–20; cf 1 Cor 1, 26–31; 2 Cor 1, 12; Col 2, 18–23).

Since the flesh is so inadequate for salvation, it cannot be the basis for true trust. "For we are the true circumcision who worship God in spirit and glory in Christ Jesus and put no confidence in the flesh" (Phil 3, 3; see also 2 Cor 1, 9; 3, 5).

Is the Christian also sinful, according to St. Paul? He makes clear that the Christian is to "put on the Lord Jesus Christ and make no provision for the flesh, to gratify its desires" (Rom 13, 14). The Christian lives by a new principle, and this is to live by faith (see Gal 2, 20). The Spirit coming upon the Christian is the source of good acts by the Christian. To this life of the Spirit we will now turn. We should first note, however, that Paul does not believe that the Christian suddenly becomes utterly sinless. His warnings against sinful behavior in the Christian community (e.g., Rom 16, 17–20) make that clear.[4]

The classical Greek term for spirit, *pneuma*,[5] like the Hebrew *ruah*, denotes a current of air, either wind or breath, and it comes to mean life, or a principle of life, or self. It can also denote an attitude of mind. In pagan Greek literature *pneuma* can have a religious significance, denoting the active presence of a divine being. A person can be in the possession of *pneuma*, as in the case of an inspired prophet, who acts not so much by his own powers as by the power of the *pneuma* which possesses him.[6] Thus the Greek term is well suited to express a notion in Paul which owes much to the Old Testament Hebrew term *ruah*.

Paul sometimes uses *pneuma* to indicate a reality other than the divine. In expressions such as: "The grace of our Lord Jesus Christ be with your spirit" (Gal 6, 18; Phil 4, 23; 2 Tim 4, 22; Phlm 25) "spirit" seems to indicate the inner self. In expressions such as "I serve God with my spirit" (Rom 1, 9) again "spirit" seems to denote the inner self (so too in 1 Cor 5, 3–5; 16, 18; 7, 34; 2 Cor 2, 13; 7, 1; 7, 13; Col 2, 5). "Spirit" may also indicate an attitude as in the reference to a spirit of gentleness (1 Cor 4, 21). Other expressions which at first reading might seem to refer merely to an attitude in fact may refer to the presence of the Spirit of God. This is true of 2 Timothy 1, 7: ". . . for God did not give us a spirit of timidity but a spirit of power and love and self-control" (see also 2 Cor 4, 13; Eph 1, 17).

Usually "spirit" in Paul refers to the Spirit of God. Paul, like the other New Testament writers, sees his time as the time of the fulfillment of the promises of the outpouring of the Spirit. God has sent his Spirit upon mankind (see 1 Thess 4, 8; 2 Cor 11, 4; Gal 3, 2). God's Spirit dwells in the Christian (see Rom 8, 11). Those in whom the Spirit dwells are called temples of God (1 Cor 3, 16) and temples of the Holy Spirit (1 Cor 6, 19). The Christian is to be filled with the Spirit (Eph 5, 18) and aglow with the Spirit (Rom 12, 11). The fact that in these last two texts the active presence of the Spirit is a matter for exhortation reminds us that the human person is called upon to play his or her part, choosing to let the Spirit be present and active. Paul sees himself as the minister of a new covenant which is "not in a written code but in the Spirit" (2 Cor 3, 6; see 2 Cor 3, 3–8; Rom 7, 6; Gal 3, 14). This seems to indicate that Paul interprets the events of the early Church as a fulfillment of Jeremiah 31, 31–33. He speaks of "desires of the Spirit" in people (Gal 5, 17). In the Mosaic covenant the law written on stone stated the correct way to act. In the new covenant the Spirit produces inner desires by which people are moved to act in the correct way.

The Spirit is seen as the source of a great variety of effects and works in the individual. The Spirit brings about a new birth (Gal 4, 29). The Spirit justifies (1 Cor 6, 11) and sanctifies (2 Thess 2, 13; 1 Cor 6, 11; Rom 15, 16) the Christian. The Spirit makes people to be in the likeness of God (2 Cor 3, 17–18). Because Christians are sons of God, God has sent the Spirit of his Son into their hearts crying: "Abba, Father" (Gal 4, 6). That is, since we live by the same Spirit as Jesus, we have the same attitude to the Father as he had. The Spirit gives strength (Eph 3, 16), freedom (2 Cor 3, 17–18), peace and joy (Rom 14, 17; 15, 13; 1 Thess 1, 6), and hope (Rom 15, 13; Gal 5, 5). The fruits of the Spirit include joy, patience, kindness, goodness, faithfulness, gentleness, self-control (Gal 5, 22–23). The Spirit brings eternal life (Gal 6, 8).

Some gifts of the Spirit, or "charisms," are given not so much for the benefit of their possessor as for the whole community of believers. Among these gifts are the power to heal or to work miracles, the gifts of prophecy, of tongues, and of interpretation of tongues (see 1 Cor 12, 7–11; 14, 1–5). The working together of these diverse gifts to build up the community is also the work of the Spirit, who is the principle of unity and peace (see 1 Cor 12, 1–30; Eph 4, 3–4).

Of special importance is the role of the Spirit in communicating the truth which is the basis for Christian life. The previous chapter has explained how the Gospels and Acts present the apostles' work of spreading the word as especially guided by the Holy Spirit. For Paul, it is the Spirit who first reveals the mystery of Christ to the apostles and prophets (Eph 3, 5). The Spirit entrusts the truth to bishops such as Timothy in order that they may pass it on (see 2 Tim 1, 14). On the side of those receiving the message, the Spirit gives faith (1 Cor 12, 9) and helps people discern the truth and understand what is happening in their lives as Christians (1 Cor 2, 12–16; 14, 37).

Paul speaks of his message being "in demonstration of the Spirit and power" (1 Cor 2, 4) and says that the Gospel he delivered came "not only in word but also in power and in the Holy Spirit" (1 Thess 1, 5). Here the Spirit is associated with power in the communication of the message, but it is difficult to know precisely how the Spirit intervenes in such cases. Perhaps the Spirit gave Paul the power to speak very effectively. Perhaps the Spirit worked inwardly on the listeners to enable them to receive the message and to be powerfully affected by it. Perhaps the Spirit worked external signs or wonders which attested to the truth of the message.

The Holy Spirit is presented as a seal or guarantee for the Christian (see 2 Cor 5, 5; Eph 1, 13–14; 4, 30). It is not easy to know precisely what action of the Spirit is involved here. In some cases at least it seems to be a matter of external manifestations of the Spirit showing that the

Spirit is present and active and so the message being delivered can be accepted as coming from God. We know from Acts that the coming of the Spirit on several occasions was an externally manifest event. Peter in Acts 2, 14–21 points to the gift of tongues as a sign that the Spirit has been poured forth in fulfillment of the promise. The external signs caused by the Spirit here serve as a guarantee that Peter's announcement of the fulfillment of the Old Testament promise is true. Paul may have some similar experiences in mind when he speaks of the Holy Spirit being a seal or guarantee. In 2 Corinthians Paul is trying in some sense to show to the Corinthians that his credentials are sound and so they should accept his message. In so doing he lists a number of good things he has done and hardships he has endured, and with these he lists the Holy Spirit. ". . . but as servants of God we through patient endurance . . . by purity, knowledge, forbearance, kindness, the Holy Spirit, genuine love, truthful speech . . ." (2 Cor 6, 4–7). Because the Holy Spirit is listed among externally manifest realities which commend Paul to the Corinthians, it seems likely that the Holy Spirit is here seen as commending Paul by being the source of external manifestations which have this effect. Elsewhere Paul states: "For I will not venture to speak of anything except what Christ has wrought through me to win obedience from the Gentiles, by word and deed, by the power of signs and wonders, by the power of the Holy Spirit . . ." (Rom 15, 18–19). The most obvious meaning of this text is that the Holy Spirit has worked signs and wonders (as well as being at the source of Paul's words and deeds) and that in this way the Holy Spirit has enabled Paul to win obedience from the Gentiles. (On the other hand, it is possible that Paul sees the intervention of the Holy Spirit in this case as an internal working in the Gentiles which complements the external words and signs.[7]) The whole new way of life in the Christian communities, including prophecy, peace, love, etc., could be compelling evidence that the promised outpouring of the Spirit had occurred and the message by which this community lives is to be taken seriously. The Corinthians themselves show Paul that they have received the Spirit and belong in the new covenant written on human hearts (2 Cor 3, 3). If such evidence could be found even in such a fractious community as that at Corinth, surely the intense Christian life in the more fervent communities could be convincing evidence of the truth of the Christian message.

Agape (love) is a gift or fruit of the Spirit (Gal 5, 22; Rom 5, 5; Col

1, 8). In fact it is the primary work of the Spirit (1 Cor 12, 31–13, 13). We must give special attention to this particular gift.

Agape in classical Greek denotes a kind of brotherly love. It is one of several words, and not the most common, used in classical Greek to signify love. It is adopted by the New Testament writers to denote both the love of the Father and of Jesus for human beings and the love which Christians, in imitation of God, are to have for other human beings.

To discover the nature of *agape* we must begin with God's love for human beings. This love is made visible especially in Jesus, so it is in Jesus that the nature of *agape* appears most clearly.

God's love for us in Jesus is gratuitous. That is, it is given generously quite apart from any merit on our part. "Why, one will hardly die for a righteous man—though perhaps for a good man one will dare even to die. But God shows his love for us in that while we were yet sinners Christ died for us" (Rom 5, 7–8; see Eph 5, 2; 5, 25–26). God's love revealed in Jesus is generous, self-giving. Jesus, though he was in the form of God, emptied himself for our sakes (Phil 2, 1–8). God's love is universal, for he desires all men to be saved (1 Tim 2, 4).

We Christians are to imitate God by loving others as God has loved us. "Therefore be imitators of God, as beloved children. And walk in love, as Christ loved us and gave himself up for us . . ." (Eph 5, 1–2). This love is to be like the love Jesus Christ has for us. Christ generously emptied himself, humbled himself and sacrificed himself for the sake of others, and Paul exhorts Christians to have that same mind (Phil 2, 5–8). The self-sacrificing love of Christ for the Church is the model for the Christian husband's love for his wife (Eph 5, 29–32). The Christian's love must be gratuitous, repaying evil with good, taking no vengeance, but helping enemies (Rom 12, 17–21); this is similar to the love of Jesus, who died for people while they were still sinners (Rom 5, 6–8). Christians should love all men (Gal 6, 10) just as God does (1 Tim 2, 4). They should love especially the lowly (Rom 12, 16) as Jesus did.[8]

Love is the fulfillment of the whole law. Owe no one anything, except to love one another; for he who loves his neighbor has fulfilled the law. The commandments, "You shall not commit adultery, You shall not kill, You shall not steal, You shall not covet," and any other commandment, are summed up in this

sentence: "You shall love your neighbor as yourself." Love
does no wrong to a neighbor; therefore love is the fulfilling of
the law (Rom 13, 8–10; cf Gal 5, 14).

Paul states that love is the fulfillment of the law, not its replacement. It
is not a matter of loving and then not caring about the relationship of
one's actions to any laws. The commandments are summed up in love of
neighbor. The point of the commandments which Paul has in mind is to
do good to one's neighbor. He who loves his neighbor truly is moved to
do good to him and so out of an inner urging the one who truly loves
accomplishes that which the commandments demand.

Because love expresses itself in action it is the basis for other virtues.
The beautiful description of *agape* in 1 Corinthians 13 gives examples of
the kinds of virtuous behavior which spring from love. One who loves is
patient, is kind, bears all things, believes all things, hopes all things,
endures all things. One who loves is not jealous, boastful, arrogant, rude,
irritable or resentful. Elsewhere Paul gives love as the motive for not
giving scandal (1 Cor 8, 9–13) and for working (Eph 4, 28).

B. Agape: Systematic Discussion

First we will try to relate the New Testament notion of *agape* to
concrete experience. Then we will look at the love of neighbor in relation
to the love of God.

When we try to relate Paul's notion of *agape* to our own experience,
a problem arises. Are we really capable of this kind of love? One may
answer that by mere human power this love is not possible, but that by
God's power it is not only possible but obligatory. If this is the case,
however, we should experience that we have this love, if we consider
ourselves more or less faithful Christians. But do we experience it? Do
we experience a love for people who do nothing to deserve it, who are
our enemies, who insult or offend or threaten or harm us? Toward such
people we habitually react with such impatience, outrage, distaste,
hatred, or some other negative emotion that real love of them seems to
be remote from our experience. Faced with such people it may seem that
the best we can do is to will good to them, do good to them if possible,
in spite of not loving them. At this point some might claim that to love

someone is to will good to them, so we really love these people. This, however, seems to be stretching rather far the meaning of love. If I will good to someone not for his own sake but for some other reason (e.g., to avoid eternal damnation, or in order that he be grateful to me or in order to appear magnanimous), this is not what most people consider as love. Nor does it seem to be the kind of love that Jesus had nor does it seem to be the love intended in that second great commandment which prescribes that we should love our neighbor as ourselves.

To identify more precisely the experience of *agape* it is useful to begin by distinguishing two different ways of being aware of other persons. In the first way we become aware of another person "from the outside" as it were. This awareness is closely tied to characteristics which are externally manifest—physical appearance, sound of voice, etc. This awareness of the other person is from the point of view of the observer, of the one who is aware of the other. For example, by this first kind of awareness I become aware of this person as he relates to my vision as being a certain color, size, shape. I become aware of him as obstructing my view of a window, as a threat to my comfort, as a possible ally in an argument. This kind of awareness is awareness of the other person as an *object*.

In a second kind of awareness of another person I am aware of the other "from the inside." I become aware that this person is another self, another center of consciousness and experience, someone who thinks, who feels, who can be sad, happy, disappointed or excited. I don't simply know that the other person thinks, feels, etc. In some sense I think or feel with the other person, from inside of the other person. When someone close to you suffers a bitter disappointment, for example, you don't merely judge that the person is experiencing certain feelings, but in a way you feel those feelings with the other person, from the point of view of the other person. This second kind of awareness is awareness of other persons as *subjects*.

Probably in most cases we are aware of other persons in both of these ways at the same time, but the proportions differ from case to case. On my way to work in the morning I habitually drive by an open newspaper kiosk attended by a shabbily dressed old man. On the normal day I am aware of this old man mainly in the first way. On a certain day, however, it is cold and blustery and the old man seems to be suffering from the severe weather. I wonder why he is out in such cold weather at his age, and then I reflect that probably he has no choice if he is to keep this job which gives him a meagre but necessary income. In the course of these reflections I become aware of the old man in the second way to a greater extent than I did formerly.

One can sometimes become intensely aware of a person in this second way, aware with such intensity that one becomes quite forgetful of one's own point of view and quite caught up with the point of view of another. A certain farmer has spent many years building a herd of fine beef cattle. He has worked hard, has enjoyed his work, and is quite proud of the reputation of his herd. Eventually, however, he grows too old to run the farm, so he sells the land, the equipment and the herd. His daughter, who understands him well, is keenly aware of her father's sense of loss and emptiness as he prepares to leave the place which has been his home for many years, to which he brought his bride, where they raised their children, suffered hardships together and achieved a modest success. His daughter is not experiencing the event from her own point of view but is very much caught up in the feeling and the meaning of the event for her father.

This second kind of awareness does not stop at mere cognitive awareness. It involves appetitive response. This appetitive response, like the awareness, is not from the point of view of the one who is aware, but from the point of view of the one of whom he or she is aware. In the example in the last paragraph, the daughter feels the sense of loss, the sense of sadness, of her father. That is, she is not responding for herself to something that is simply happening to her. What is happening affects her because it affects her father, and she feels the sense of loss, the sadness, not for herself but for her father.

The appetitive reactions which accompany the second kind of awareness of persons are usually, if not always, favorable to the persons. One is happy because the other is happy, sad because the other is sad. Besides happiness and sadness these appetitive reactions favorable to the other person include fear, excitement, hope, and many other emotions. Underlying them all is an attitude of willing good to the other person, and this attitude has several of the qualities which are essential to *agape*. First, it is a generous attitude. One desires good to the other person not for the sake of oneself but for the sake of the other person.

Second, this attitude of willing good to the other person is usually, if not always, gratuitous. When one is aware of the other person as another center of consciousness one can will good to the other quite apart from whether the other has earned this good by any actions. You can will good to the other even if the other has done something offensive or is threatening or harming you. Suppose, for example, that you have an enemy who in doing something to benefit himself has harmed you. Furthermore, he has been abusive to you on several occasions in which you have argued with him. You spontaneously have become angry with him. You dislike him and want to lash out at him, to punish him. These are dispositions quite the opposite of *agape*. Under the influence of these dispositions you are very little aware of the person as another center of consciousness. You view him almost entirely from your own point of view, how he has affected your plans, sensitivities, etc. Then one day you see him in a moment of disappointment and distress, and you have sympathy for him. You become more aware of him as a self, as one who feels pain, who has hopes and ambitions just as you do, and also weaknesses just as you do. You become aware of things from his point of view. You don't approve of his attitude, but you begin to wish he were happy. Your wish does not come about because he has earned it. You are simply aware of him as a person who is unhappy, and it is a shame that a person is not happy. You don't lose all of your old distaste for the individual but you become aware of something new in your attitude toward him.

This attitude of willing good to the other person because one is aware of him or her in the second way fulfills in a striking way the precept that one should love one's neighbor as oneself. In a real sense the other of whom I am aware in this way becomes incorporated into my self. This happens first in a cognitive way. I more or less lose awareness of myself in centering my attention on the other person and experiencing things from his point of view. This happens in an appetitive way because I begin to respond appetitively to things not for myself as a separate being but for the sake of the other. In this act of incorporating the other person my own self is enriched. I cease to exist merely as a separate center of consciousness with my limited point of view and my narrow appetitive horizons. Dying to a "selfish" narrow definition of myself, I rise to a new and richer self, without taking anything away from the other person whom I have incorporated.

Before concluding that we have adequately defined Christian *agape* we must take account of the twofold calling of the Christian to love God and to love neighbor.[9] Paul and other New Testament writers describe love of neighbor as being gratuitous. Is the Christian called to have this same kind of *agape* for God? Some would answer negatively, pointing out that our love for God is not gratuitous because God deserves our love. Our love is a response to the good things God has done. However, this answer seems to take account only of part of the matter. It is true, of course, that God deserves our love because of what he does, and we should love him for what he has done, and so we can have a love for him which is not gratuitous. Nevertheless, it seems that this need not prevent us from loving God in another way, the way that comes with the second kind of awareness of persons. If we can and should love our neighbors in this gratuitous way, even if they also deserve by their actions to be loved, it seems we can and should love God in this gratuitous way. Of course we cannot will to God some good which he lacks, but we can rejoice that God already possesses all the good which we could will for him.

There remains one major difference between our *agape* for God and our *agape* for neighbor. We should love God as our supreme good, and we should not love our neighbor as our supreme good. This statement requires some explanation.

By "supreme good" we mean that good or complex of goods which satisfies all the desires (likings) of the person. All people desire such a supreme good. That is, all people seek to satisfy not only one or other desire but all of their desires.

In a sense, all people desire God as their supreme good. No matter how many finite goods are attained, an intelligent being can always realize that it is conceivable that one might have even greater desires satisfied by even greater good. That is, an intelligent being can always conceive of a greater being which would make him or her happier. Since no finite good can give the full happiness which rules out any desire for more, so the person in seeking the satisfaction of all desires is in some way seeking the supreme good, God.

While in some way seeking God a person can at the same time have the contradictory attitude of seeking some finite good or complex of goods as though it were the supreme good. This person is caught up in the desire for certain finite goods, and does not focus on this other aspect of life which reveals the inadequacy of finite goods and the need for God. This lack of attention to the infinite good may be the consequence of denying that God exists; however, even those who acknowledge that God exists do not necessarily in fact explicitly choose him as their supreme good.

If what we said earlier about the propriety of a gratuitous love of God is true, then the love for God as our supreme good should not be a selfish love. That is, we should not first define our desires and needs selfishly and then introduce God as the one who satisfies these needs and desires. Rather, God is the one who satisfies our desires after those desires are stretched beyond selfish limits because we have become aware of persons not merely as objects but as subjects.

We have discussed Christian love for neighbor and Christian love for God. We will look now at the relationship between the two.

In the parable of the last judgment in the Gospel according to Matthew, the good that is done to a neighbor is seen as done to God. ''Truly, I say to you, as you did it to one of the least of these my brethren, you did it to me'' (Mt 25, 40). This suggests that love for neighbor is implicitly love for God. To understand how this is so it is helpful to describe four different states of human beings regarding *agape*.

The first state is complete selfishness. (Normal adults do not exist in this completely selfish way, but some sociopaths come close.) A person in this state is aware of other persons only as objects. He has none of the generous reactions to others which result from awareness of others as subjects. This person experiences certain desires—for good, for physical comfort, for fame, etc.—and seeks to satisfy them. When other people help him satisfy his desires they are seen as means to that end. When they prevent the satisfaction of his desires they are seen as enemies. When they do neither of these things they are seen as irrelevant.

The second state is selfish, but not complete selfishness. Along with his selfish desires, a person in this state occasionally becomes aware of people as subjects and wills good to them as a result of this awareness. However, for him this awareness of other persons and generosity toward them is only one awareness among many, one motive among many. He gives this awareness and this generosity no priority. The generous willing of good to others affects his decisions in some cases simply because that is how he feels at the time. He does not see this generous love as the way to a fuller life and he does not set about deliberately developing this potentiality of his nature.

The third state is a sort of truncated *agape*. A person in this third state recognizes this generous love as the way to a fuller life. He deliberately tries to develop this ability. He habitually and deliberately gives this love of others the dominant place in determining his decisions. However, he also sets limits to his love. He cultivates this love for a particular circle (family, or a close circle of friends, or members of a particular larger group) but he excludes others. The good of some people becomes his good, the object of his willing of good to them, but the good of other people is not his good. By drawing a limit in this way, he excludes God, for he has set as his supreme good something finite.

The fourth state is true *agape*. A person in this fourth state sets no limits to the number of people he loves with a generous love. It is true that only in a vague way can this person actually love all people, because only in a vague way can he become aware of them as subjects. Nevertheless, he has not set limits to his love, and undertakes to love in this generous way whomever he meets. His refusal to set limits to his love means that he has not taken any finite good as his supreme good. In this he goes along with, rather than contradicts, the orientation of his nature toward God as the supreme good. Thus this *agape* for other people is implicitly *agape* for God.[10]

Just as true *agape* for one's neighbor is implicitly *agape* for God, so true *agape* for God implies *agape* for neighbor. This is apparent in several ways. God is *agape*, as 1 John 4, 16 states. If I choose God as my supreme good, whom I value above all else, logically I will try to become as much as possible like God, and so to love as he loves. Furthermore, *agape* for God makes us will what God wills, just as we would in any other case want what our beloved wants. God wills the good of all people. Therefore our love for God makes us will good to all. Finally, persons are like God, made in his image. In spite of sin, people never completely lose their likeness to God. If we love God we will love others insofar as they are like God. This means that we will love them insofar as they are persons, apart from whether they have earned our love by their actions.

C. A Note on Altruism

By "altruism" here we mean desiring good for another person for the sake of that other and not because of benefit to oneself. Altruism both leads to doing good for others and causes rejoicing because of the good the other enjoys. Clearly, an ethics based on *agape* is an altruistic ethics.

It may seem that an altruistic ethics cannot be reconciled to the type of ethics explained in Part One. There we explained the objective moral good in terms of developing appetites and fulfilling them, and this state of fulfilled desires constitutes happiness. Altruistic ethics, on the other hand, seems not to aim at happiness—at least not at the happiness of oneself. Altruism, it seems, demands that one be ready when necessary to sacrifice one's own happiness for the good of another.

In dealing with this difficulty we should first consider how happiness is the goal of any ethics or of any human endeavor. When we fulfill a desire (a liking) we are happy; but we do not fulfill the desire in order to be happy, as though the happiness were some additional thing which comes along with the fulfillment of the desire. Rather, happiness is simply the state of fulfilled desire. We seek happiness, true, but that simply means that we seek to fulfill desires. What is primary here is the object of the desire, which when attained satisfies the desire. It is this object which is desired. Suppose that I am hungry, desire food, get some food, eat it, and this makes me happy. It is the eating of the food that I desire. I do not eat the food in order to make me happy, as though happiness were a goal and eating the food a means to that goal. Rather, the goal is the eating of the food. The happiness is simply the state of attaining the goal which is desired.

If happiness is the state of desire being satisfied, then with altruistic desires happiness results when one attains what one desires, the good of the other person. The reason why this truth is obscured in some cases is the relative weakness of altruistic desire in those cases. When my altruistic desire is relatively strong, then when the good of the other is attained I am more or less as happy as if I had attained an equivalent good for myself. When my altruistic desire is weak, my happiness at the good of the other is relatively small, and may be overshadowed by any discomforts that have come to me as a result of my generous giving to another. Here I have not developed my altruistic desire enough truly to appreciate the good which happens to the other. Yet I may dutifully pursue an altruistic course of action because I have been assured that in that direction lies the true good, though I am not yet able properly to appreciate it. My "altruism" is a sort of grim determination to do good to others even though I don't much like it.

Chapter Twelve

THE NEW TESTAMENT
AS GUIDE TO ACTION

Throughout this book the term "moral good" has a wide meaning, and includes explicitly religious goods which people should pursue. In discussing the New Testament we will use this term in this wide sense. The term is not used in the New Testament itself.[1]

In the New Testament morality is presented mainly in religious terms, in terms of attaining a right relationship with God. The New Testament makes clear, however, that in order to attain a right relationship with God one must strive for certain goods which are not explicitly religious.[2] Especially must one seek a right relationship with one's neighbor by *agape* and by seeking in various ways the goods of one's neighbor. In the New Testament the explicitly religious part of morality involves certain requirements in other parts of morality.

Characteristically the New Testament does not discuss the moral good in itself. It discusses it primarily in a religious context. What we might call the moral good is identified in the New Testament in religious terms—e.g., as the will of God, the service of God, or the works of the Spirit. Nor does the New Testament give a philosophical theory which sets forth criteria for discovering what actions are morally good. How does the New Testament help us to discover what is morally good? To answer this we must focus once again on the role of the Holy Spirit in Christian life.

A. The Spirit as Replacement for the Law

We have seen that Old Testament writers looked forward to a time when people would be more faithful to God than they had been in the past because they would have a law written on their hearts and not merely on stone tablets. The Spirit would be poured forth, bringing new life to people, transforming them inwardly. The New Testament authors consider that these promises have been fulfilled in their own day. For Paul, the Spirit has in a certain way replaced the Mosaic law. He speaks of himself and others being "ministers of a new covenant, not in a written code but in the Spirit; for the written code kills, but the Spirit gives life" (2 Cor 3, 6). Elsewhere he states: "But now we are discharged from the law, dead to that which kept us captive, so that we serve not under the written code but in the life of the Spirit" (Rom 7, 6). The Christian has been set free by Christ, and this includes being freed from the Mosaic law, as Paul argues in the Epistle to the Galatians. However, this does not mean that the Christian may ignore good actions. He is called to love, to walk by the Spirit and to produce various fruits of the Spirit (see Gal 5, 13–26).

At this point we will introduce material from Part One to understand and interpret what it means that the Spirit serves in some way to replace the Mosaic law.

The Holy Spirit gives new life, transforming people inwardly. One aspect of this work of the Spirit is, to use philosophical language, the production of new or intensified appetites in the person. A primary appetite produced by the Spirit is *agape*. There are further appetites produced by the Spirit, appetites to do the various works of the Spirit, the various good things which God wills the Christian to do.

It is possible to distinguish two ways in which, by producing appetites, the Holy Spirit replaces the Mosaic law. (By producing appetites the Spirit also to a certain extent replaces all written law.) First, the Holy Spirit motivates the person to do the good which God wills. He gives the person the desire to do what is good. The written law commands but does not give the inner desire to obey, so unfaithfulness follows. The written code then condemns, or, in Paul's phrase, it kills (2 Cor 3, 6). To the person who lacks the appetite to do good, the law is a burden. If he obeys, it is out of fear, as a slave might obey. The person who is given the proper appetites by the Spirit will do good not out of fear but out of desire for the good. A mother who loves her child cares for that child willingly, with no need of a written law to urge her. So the person moved by the Spirit has no need of urging by a written law. That urging is "written on the heart."

The Holy Spirit replaces the law also by being a guide informing the person concerning what is good. The New Testament speaks often of the Spirit guiding people. Probably such guidance takes place in many different ways. The way that interests us most here is that pervasive guidance which comes automatically every time that the Spirit produces an appetite in a person. As was explained in Part One, we recognize that something is good when we have an appetite for it, and we recognize that something is evil when we have an appetitive aversion to it. If I like a piece of music, or an apple, or a novel, by that very fact I recognize that the object of the liking is good. When a mother loves her child, she spontaneously recognizes that the preservation of the child's well-being is something good. If one has an aversion to a certain food, or to dishonest behavior, or to cruelty, one spontaneously perceives the object of that aversion to be evil. So if the Holy Spirit puts in me a desire to praise God, or a love of honesty, I explicitly recognize the object of the desire to be good. Without the desire to praise God I may believe that such praise is a good thing, because Scripture says so and my fellow Christians agree, but I do not experience for myself that such praise is good.

The New Testament says little about aversions produced by the Spirit, but there is no reason to believe that the Spirit who gives desires for what is truly good would not also give aversions to what is truly evil. In fact it seems like a psychological necessity that one who has been given a desire for a particular good would pick up an aversion to the evil which is the opposite of that good.

In summary, the Holy Spirit by giving people certain appetites replaces written law in two ways, by moving them to do good and avoid evil and by showing them what is good and what is evil.

How is this working of the Spirit related to moral judgment in particular cases? Such moral judgments require factual knowledge (knowledge of what is) and normative knowledge (knowledge of what ought to be or ought not to be). Suppose that a woman must decide whether she should undergo a painful and expensive operation. To make a correct judgment she must know certain facts: What is her own physical condition? What is the likelihood of her survival without the operation? With the operation? What side-effects might accompany the procedure? Does she have young children who depend upon her? Such factual knowledge, necessary as it is, does not by itself give a basis for judging what is to be done, because it does not, as factual, say what is good and what is evil. This knowledge of what is good and what is evil, the necessary second component for the judgment, is what we mean by "normative knowledge."

Suppose that a person were completely transformed by the Spirit so that the only appetites he has are appetites produced by the Spirit. Such a person would spontaneously have the correct normative knowledge for judging what is the morally good thing to be done in a particular case. He would still have to struggle with complex problems of fact, but concerning norms he could dispense with theories, authorities and moralists and depend on his own likes and dislikes.[3]

Unfortunately, we are not completely transformed by the Spirit. When your thoughtless neighbor has for the third straight morning blocked your driveway as you are trying to hurry off to work, among the warm sentiments which well up within you there may be one or two which you recognize as not coming from the Spirit. The Spirit and the flesh battle against each other, and until one can recognize which appetite comes from the Spirit one does not know which appetite to trust as a guide to what is good or evil.

How does one discern which appetites come from the Spirit? This is how the central problem of moral norms is posed for the Christian. The first basis for such discernment is the New Testament.

B. The New Testament as Basis for Discerning What Comes From the Spirit

Some passages in the New Testament refer explicitly to the Spirit and to the kinds of desires or behavior which proceed from the Spirit. Other passages indicate what is good, what is the will of God, but make no mention of the Spirit. These too can be a valid basis for deciding what is from the Spirit, because for the Christian to do good, to do the will of God, and to do the works of the Spirit are in reality the same thing.

It will be helpful to distinguish four different categories of New Testament indication of what comes from the Spirit.

1. Statements To Be Interpreted Literally

Some New Testament statements of what is morally good are meant to be understood literally. These can take any of several different forms. Some are in the form of commandments. Jesus tells the rich young man that he must obey the commandments in order to enter eternal life, and then he gives examples of the commandments, including: "Thou shalt not kill" (Mt 19, 16–19). There are less formal statements, such as Paul's expressed opinion that in view of the impending distress it is well for the unmarried to remain unmarried (1 Cor 7, 25–27). Elsewhere Paul speaks of the works of the flesh to be avoided and the fruit of the Spirit to be sought (Gal 5, 19–23). Jesus commands his disciples to preach and baptize (Mt 28, 19–20). Directives concerning good action take up a considerable portion of the New Testament, and many of them apparently are meant to be taken literally.

Several steps must be taken in order to use these statements as guides in particular situations. First it is necessary to determine as accurately as possible what type of behavior is being commanded or prohibited. In certain cases this presents little difficulty. The second chapter of the Epistle of James instructs its readers to show no partiality, and then it spells out examples of partiality. It is not difficult to know what general type of behavior is being condemned. Not all passages are so easy to understand. The First Epistle of John states that if anyone sees his brother sinning he is to pray for him, but then adds that this does not mean that one should pray for one who is committing a "sin unto death" (1 Jn 5, 16). It is not easy to know what constitutes a sin unto death in this context, so it is difficult to know precisely what the epistle is requiring in certain cases.

A second step necessary in using a New Testament statement as a guide in particular cases is to determine to whom the statement applies. It may apply only to one or to a few individuals, or it may apply only to individuals in a very special situation. To apply such statements more generally would be a mistake. After curing a leper Jesus tells him to say nothing to anyone (Mt 8, 4). This cannot be used as a basis for a rule against publicizing miraculous cures. Before sending his disciples out to preach Jesus gives them instructions (Mt 10, 5–42). It requires some care to determine which instructions apply principally to these disciples on this particular occasion and which instructions apply generally to preachers of the word.

Some New Testament moral teachings obviously are meant to apply generally. Even in such cases, however, one must still ask whether the norm applies universally or whether certain exceptions might be made. Scholars agree that Jesus' prohibition of divorce (Mt 19, 3–9); Mk 10, 2–9) applies generally. They do not agree as to whether it allows for some exceptions.[4]

A third step in using New Testament statements as guides is to discover what sort of behavior will fulfill the norm in this particular situation. In some cases a knowledge of the general type of behavior commanded or prohibited (step one) indicates clearly what kind of behavior is required in the particular situation. This is the case especially with prohibitions. Jesus' general prohibition of divorce, if it applies to a particular situation, also makes quite clear what type of behavior in the particular situation will fulfill the norm and what type will contradict the norm. In other cases the knowledge of the general type of behavior commanded or prohibited does not indicate clearly what kind of behavior will fulfill the norm. It is relatively easy to know the general meaning of the words of 1 John 3, 17–18: "But if any one has the world's good and sees his brother in need, yet closes his heart against him, how does God's love abide in him? Little children, let us not love in word or speech but in deed and in truth." It is not always clear what kind of behavior will best fulfill this norm in a particular situation. Should one impoverish oneself in order to help those in immediate need? Would it be better to keep some of one's goods in order to earn more income from which more help might be given to others later?[5]

Some of the problems raised by these three steps belong not to the discipline of Christian ethics but to the discipline of scriptural interpretation. These problems will not be dealt with extensively in this book. Some of the problems which belong to the discipline of Christian ethics will be discussed at some length in later chapters.[6]

2. Apparently Impractical Statements

Certain normative statements in the New Testament present not only the problems just discussed but also a further problem of interpretation.

For example, in Matthew's account of the Sermon on the Mount Jesus states: "If your right eye causes you to sin, pluck it out and throw it away; it is better that you lose one of your members than that your whole body be thrown into hell. And if your right hand causes you to sin, cut it off and throw it away: it is better that you lose one of your members than that your whole body go into hell" (Mt 5, 29–30). Have you ever met a one-eyed Christian who explained that some years ago he had plucked out his eye because it was causing him to sin? If such persons are rare, it seems to leave three alternatives. First, possibly Christians are finding that their eyes almost never cause them to sin. Second, possibly Christians find that their eyes do cause them to sin, but they almost always compound the sin by refusing the remedy prescribed by the Sermon on the Mount. Third (and this is much the most likely alternative), Christians generally do not accept this statement as applying to life in a practical way.

It is not a question of the impracticality of only one or two isolated statements. A considerable number of the sayings of Jesus present the same problem. The Sermon on the Mount, that central charter of Christian morality, contains several other problem statements. It states that one is not to swear to anything (Mt 5, 36), a saying which is apparently contradicted by the long tradition among Christians of taking oaths. If any one would sue you and take your coat, you are to let him have your cloak as well (Mt 5, 40). This is contradicted by the long-standing practice among Christians of defending oneself in court against lawsuits which appear to be unjust. Outside of the Sermon on the Mount Jesus is quoted as saying that one should hate his own father and mother, wife, children, brothers and sisters (Lk 14, 25–26). We are to call no man father or master, for God alone should have these titles (Mt 23, 9–10). We are not to seek what we are to eat or what we are to drink (Lk 12, 29). When we give a dinner or a banquet we are to invite not our friends or brothers but the poor, the maimed and the blind (Lk 14, 12–13).

These texts seem to leave us in a dilemma. On the one hand, there are strong reasons why Christians have not followed them in the past. The problem of interpretation is not that to follow them would be difficult. The Christian must be prepared to do difficult things. The problem is that, even if you allow for exceptions, these statements do not seem to be right as general rules, and yet they are stated as general rules. Is plucking out one's eye usually the best way to deal with a situation in which seeing has caused one to sin? Traditional Catholic moral theology would call plucking out an eye a mutilation, and would not allow it if other, less destructive, ways could be found to deal with the situation. Should one really not be concerned about what one will eat or drink tomorrow? Is the improvidence of irrational nature really a good model for human beings who can provide for their needs by the use of reason?

The alternative seems to be to decide that these rules are not practical as they stand, so they are not to be followed or at least they are to be followed only when they have been "interpreted" to say something quite different from their literal sense.

To attempt to decide which New Testament norms are practical and which are impractical presents its own pitfalls, however. Having kept that which one judges practical in the New Testament, and discarded or modified the rest, one ends up with a morality according to one's own mind, not according to the New Testament. One's sole concession is that where the New Testament happens to conform to one's own judgment one may keep the New Testament wording. We accommodate the Gospel to our views, rather than being judged by the Gospel. We cease to find in the New Testament the measure of our own sinfulness, our falling short, our need to appeal to God's mercy, our need for conversion. This is far from the mind of Jesus, who did not come to lull our consciences into a feeling of security. He came to root up, to cast fire on the earth. Having sifted out of the New Testament as impractical anything which does not fit our human perceptions, we may then make the discovery (and publish it in scholarly journals) that there is nothing specific about New Testament morality which would set it apart from other morality. By our picking and choosing we rob Christian life of what is special about it, its richness, its challenge, its evidence that a new life has been poured forth in the world.

We have described the results of a rather thoroughgoing process of rejecting or modifying those New Testament statements which strike one as impractical. Perhaps few Christians are selective in so complete a way. Even a lesser degree of this kind of selectivity, however, seems to move one in an illegitimate direction.

The selectivity we have described involves a person using his own criteria, whatever they may be, to make the selection. We will return later to this point concerning criteria.

Several different kinds of attempts have been made to interpret these "impractical" sayings of Jesus in such a way as to escape the dilemma. We will outline four such attempts.

One interpretation takes the sayings of Jesus as eschatological. Jesus speaks not only about a new age which has already arrived but also about a future time when he will return and complete the establishment of the Kingdom of God. Might it be the case that these sayings of Jesus, which sound so impractical in the context of the present age, are meant to apply to the very different mode of life in the age to come?

There are several difficulties with this interpretation. First, it has little or no support in the texts of the Gospels. The "impractical" sayings of Jesus are grouped together with other sayings. They are not set apart and there is no indication given that Jesus has switched from challenging his listeners about how to live this life to explaining the nature of a future life. Furthermore, it is not clear to whom these sayings would apply in a future age when the judgment of God is completed and the sheep have been separated from the goats (Mt 25, 31–46). Will either the sheep or the goats have use for a precept that states that if your eye causes you to sin, you should pluck it out?

A second interpretation would explain the "impractical" sayings of Jesus as part of an interim ethics. According to this interpretation, Jesus expected that his second coming and the full realization of the Kingdom of God would take place quite soon. Accordingly, the rules he gives constitute an interim ethics suited for life during a short and critical period of turmoil. Once it is discovered that the second coming of Jesus is not necessarily imminent, then certain rules of the interim ethics—the "impractical" sayings of Jesus—are no longer relevant because they make sense only in a period of waiting for an imminent coming. In support of this interpretation it might be pointed out that in 1 Corinthians 7, 25–29 Paul explicitly refers to the shortness of the time (before the second coming) as a factor determining behavior with respect to marriage. If it was a factor for Paul, then, it might be argued, it could easily be a factor in the ethics of Jesus.

To what extent does the expectation of an imminent second coming influence the teachings of Jesus? We will not try to settle that general question here. However, this expectation, even if we grant that it was present, does not seem to help make sense of some of the "impractical" sayings of Jesus. Does the fact that the second coming is expected to occur within a very few years provide a basis for plucking out an offending eye or cutting off an offending hand? It is not clear that it does. Many people can reasonably expect to live only several more years or perhaps only a few more weeks. To pluck out offending eyes and cut off offending hands seems to make little more sense for them than for others.

A third interpretation is that the ''impractical'' sayings of Jesus indicate an ideal way of acting, but one which is too demanding and difficult for weak mortals to attain. A fourth interpretation is that these sayings point out works of supererogation. That is, they point out more perfect ways of acting, but if one fails to choose these ways one is not sinning. One is simply less perfect.

The difficulty with both of these interpretations is that they suppose that the ''impractical'' sayings point out more perfect but difficult ways of action, whereas in fact these sayings seem to be impractical not simply because they require what is difficult but because they seem to require what is wrong. Far from being more perfect, plucking out one's eye just seems to be wrong in most cases.

One or more of these interpretations of the ''impractical'' sayings of Jesus could be right, at least insofar as the arguments against them are not completely conclusive. But all of these interpretations present serious difficulties. There is another interpretation which seems to avoid any serious difficulty, and it is this interpretation which we will adopt.

According to this interpretation[7] the ''impractical'' sayings of Jesus are not to be taken literally, but are figures of speech, just as are the parables of Jesus. The parables are not literal history but stories which express or dramatize some lesson. So some sayings of Jesus are not rules to be followed literally but figures of speech which express and dramatize some quality of Christian life. ''If your right eye causes you to sin, pluck it out and throw it away'' is a figure of speech which could be translated in literal form approximately as follows: Whatever prevents you from seeking God's Kingdom, even if it be something as precious to you as your eye, get rid of it. ''Do not seek what you are to eat and what you are to drink'' figuratively means that food and drink, important as they are, should command very little of your attention compared to the concern you should give to the Kingdom of God.

An obvious objection to this interpretation is that it does not avoid the problem of selectivity. We objected earlier to the practice of selecting some New Testament norms as practical and ignoring or modifying those that strike us as impractical. Now, it seems, we have been willing to select and keep certain norms because they seem to us to be practical, and to modify those that strike us as impractical. Our attempt to answer this objection will help clarify the meaning and the limits of our interpretation.

Three points should be explained. First we must focus on what criteria are used in deciding which sayings are to be taken literally and which are figures of speech. If my criteria are my feelings at the time, or my moral beliefs arrived at in any random way, then my selection is not legitimate. In selecting some sayings as figures of speech I am simply modifying the New Testament teaching to suit myself. Suppose, however, that my criteria are taken from a careful and critical reading of Scripture? In that case I am following an age-old principle of scriptural interpretation, namely that individual passages of Scripture are to be interpreted by using the rest of Scripture. The presupposition is that what the inspired word of God teaches in one text will not be contradicted by what is taught in another text of Scripture.[8] If I find that a saying of Jesus, if taken literally, goes against some other teaching of Scripture, then I am justified in searching for some figurative quality to this saying.

A second point is that some sayings of Jesus have a quality about them which makes them apt to be figures of speech and other sayings do not. Two examples may illustrate this. In Matthew's account of the Sermon on the Mount Jesus says: "If you forgive men their trespasses, your heavenly Father also will forgive you; but if you do not forgive men their trespasses, neither will your Father forgive you your trespasses" (Mt 6, 14–15). Upon reading this one is not likely to suppose that the forgiveness mentioned here is a figure of speech pointing to some other kind of behavior that is being recommended. One easily sees that one is simply being instructed to forgive. On another occasion Peter asks Jesus: "Lord, how often shall my brother sin against me, and I forgive him? As many as seven times?" Jesus replies: "I do not say to you seven times, but seventy times seven times" (Mt 18, 21–22). Here again, the forgiveness does not appear to be a figure of speech, but the number "seventy times seven" is almost certainly a figure of speech meaning literally "an indefinite number of times," as often as you are offended." We know that it is a figure of speech for two reasons. First, its literal "sense" would really be nonsense, for from what Jesus says about forgiveness there is no reason why it should continue for four hundred and ninety times and then stop. This first reason, the fact that the literal sense does not agree with other verses of Scripture, alerts us to the likelihood that it is a figure of speech. Secondly, the number, seventy times seven, or any large number in similar contexts, is likely to mean "a large number" or "an indefinite number," as we can illustrate in literature generally.

A third point is that interpreting some sayings of Jesus as figures of speech need not, and should not, be a watering down of the sayings of Jesus to fit one's own disposition. One can be challenged by figures of speech as much as or more than by literal statements, provided one tries to honestly accept the meaning that is there in the text. To pluck out one's eye is, admittedly, very painful and a great loss for the rest of one's life. To get rid of all that stands between oneself and full acceptance of the Kingdom is at least as demanding, however, and much more comprehensive. It calls for lifelong conversion and, if necessary, the sacrifice of life itself.

Why did Jesus choose to put some of his moral norms in figurative form? One might answer that he did it for the same reason that motivated him to use parables. Beyond this, however, we can see several reasons why the figurative form is a very apt form for expressing Christian morality. In explaining this we will be explaining several important points about Christian morality.

There are two characteristics of Christian moral life[9] which make it appropriate that in some cases moral norms should be stated figuratively. One such characteristic is that rules applied mechanically cannot capture the fullness of Christian life. Here "rules applied mechanically" refers to situations in which once it is decided that a rule is to be applied in a particular situation, then it is obvious precisely what behavior is required. Applying the rule requires little deliberation about how the rule is to be applied.

Consider the situation of a night watchman at a building site. He sees his responsibility as the protection of the property by using force if necessary, but without endangering life. The commandment "Thou shalt not kill" will be applied in all cases in which only property loss or damage is at stake. Two youths break into the building site with the apparent intention of stealing. If the situation involved only the matter of life and death, then the commandment "Thou shalt not kill" could be applied mechanically, because it would be obvious what kind of behavior is ruled out. However, the concrete situation is not as simple as that. The watchman has an obligation to protect the property. He must then deliberate, consider what course of action can best protect the property while causing minimal risk to the lives of the two intruders. The watchman must grasp the different factors in the situation, consider the likely results of certain courses of action, and choose the best.

In other cases, especially in applying positive commands, a mechanical application of rules is even less satisfactory than it would be in the case just mentioned. Consider the commandment: ''Honor your father and your mother.'' The type of behavior which best fulfills this commandment varies widely from situation to situation. Among young children, honoring parents normally involves obedience. For an adult, honoring one's parents may mean giving them financial support, or living with them, or visiting them often, or allowing them to help one with one's work. Toward some parents, kindness may best be expressed by good-natured joking. For other parents, kindness may require patient listening. One might try to write down in a book all of the things which honoring parents may mean. The book could never capture the fullness of the parent-child relationship. The most the book could do is to suggest what kind of behavior might be appropriate in certain typical situations and for certain typical kinds of people. These types, however, never fully express the reality of any one situation or any one person.

This means that applying moral norms often requires imagination and creativity. Good moral decisions frequently require a grasp of the situation, sensitivity regarding which elements in the situation are most important, imagining different possibilities, calculating probable results of possible courses of action, deciding which course of action best achieves various goods while minimizing evils. Moral decision making in many cases is rather like the process by which a creative artist discovers how to express himself in a beautiful work of art.

Let us return to the use of figures of speech to express moral norms. As far as the conceptual content is concerned, whatever is expressed figuratively can be stated in a norm which can be applied literally. What is the advantage of the figurative statement? The figurative form can help to stir the imagination, prod one to the kind of creative application that is necessary. Jesus could have said: ''Whatever keeps you from full acceptance of the Kingdom of God, get rid of it.'' If this moves me at all it is likely to move me to a rather conventional review of my life. Jesus says: ''If your right eye causes you to sin, pluck it out.'' I am startled.

The image gets me thinking of possibilities which habit and convention have hidden from me. It provokes me to look at myself in a different way.

This creative aspect in moral judgment is important. General rules, applied literally, are necessary, of course. But applying the rule is only the first step. Beyond that is the fullness of life, a new life poured forth by the Holy Spirit, a mystery too rich to be captured even by the best possible set of rules. The freshness and attraction of the Gospel, and of a life based on the Gospel, comes especially because of this richness of life which cannot be expressed in rules.

It is not enough for the Christian to extract some literal rules from the New Testament and follow them. The Christian must return to the words of the Gospel over and over again and let those words stir up in him or her this creative insight and response.

A second characteristic of Christian life is that it is open-ended. One never reaches a stage of perfection beyond which further growth is impossible. For example, one never loves so wholeheartedly, generously and intensely that one could not develop a greater love. The same is true of such other qualities as faith, hope, devotion in prayer, joy and peace. It is not simply that one happens always to have faults. The very meaning of love, and of other Christian qualities, is such that no finite development exhausts all of their possibilities, so further growth must always be possible.

The further one progresses in these qualities the more clearly one is able to see still further possibilities for growth. This accounts for the curious fact that those whom the Church has recognized as saints frequently call themselves sinners. This is not false modesty on their part. Rather, their sanctity makes them better able to see how God's grace makes even greater things possible, and according to this standard they still fall short.

Here again, it is helpful to have some moral norms put in figurative form. When a norm is expressed in literal form we easily become used to it and begin to interpret its demands in a customary way which no longer challenges us. A figurative expression of the norm, by prodding us to imagine further possibilities, helps us to remain open to further growth, to that continuing conversion which should remain a quality of all Christian living.

Many of the parables of Jesus may be classed along with certain of his sayings as figurative expressions of moral norms. The parable of the good Samaritan, for example, is a figurative expression of the call to love of neighbor. The parable of the treasure hidden in the field is a figurative expression of the call to wholehearted devotion to the Kingdom of God.

3. The Example of Jesus

Another way in which the New Testament provides criteria for discerning what comes from the Holy Spirit is by presenting the example of Jesus. Jesus does only the work of the Father (Jn 5, 19–21). He is fully docile to the Spirit, is filled with the Spirit, is led by the Spirit (see Mt 3, 16; Lk 4, 1; Acts 2, 33; 10, 38). In Jesus then we may expect to find a portrait of what a life fully in accord with the Spirit will look like.

In using the example of Jesus as a criterion for what is in accord with the Spirit we must take steps similar to those outlined in section A above. We need not go into these steps in detail again. A couple of points should be noted, however. In determining as closely as possible the meaning of the text itself we must refrain from hasty conclusions about the manner of acting of Jesus himself. For example, reading of passages in isolation might give the impression that often Jesus was rather peremptory in manner. A reading of Matthew 4, 18–22 (or Mark 1, 16–20) in isolation could suggest that Jesus acted quite suddenly and without deliberation in choosing his disciples. This impression may be due to the fact that the evangelists here are giving only a brief outline of the facts. The account in Luke 6, 12–16 of Jesus praying before choosing the apostles and the description in John 1, 35–42 suggest that the choice of the apostles was a longer and more gradual process.

In determining how widely to apply the example of Jesus as a criterion, we must realize that it would not be proper to try to imitate Jesus in all details. For one thing, what was proper for Jesus in one situation may not be proper in the different situations we encounter. For example, Jesus for the most part confined his own preaching to the people of Israel. This is not a norm for the later preaching of the Church. Especially should we be aware that the qualifications of Jesus were quite different from our own, and because of this what was proper for him to do may not be proper for us. Jesus apparently felt at liberty to reinterpret the sacred traditions of his people, and people marveled at the authority with which he spoke (Mt 7, 28–29; Mk 1, 21–22). It does not follow that every Christian may assume for himself or herself a similar authority.

In some cases the New Testament itself specifies aspects of the life of Jesus which are to be imitated. In the previous chapter we have seen how the New Testament makes clear that Christians are to have a love like that of Jesus. The evangelists in other passages quote Jesus himself as presenting certain aspects of his action to be imitated. It is especially his lowliness, sacrifice of self and service of others that are so presented (see Mt 11, 29; 20, 25–28; Jn 13, 12–17).

Our imitation of Jesus should be less a copying of isolated actions and more a matter of personal qualities. When we get to know a person well we discover that though this person's actions may be materially very different in different situations, yet the actions all express similar personal qualities such as kindness, humor or cynicism. If by prayerful reflection we come to know the person of Jesus we discover that his varied activities all express similar personal qualities. It is these personal qualities rather than material details that should be the principal focus of our imitation of Jesus.

There are other persons in the New Testament whom the Christian can use as examples of what is in accord with the Holy Spirit. These others are, of course, secondary and imperfect models for imitation. Nevertheless, in varied ways the New Testament itself indicates that certain aspects of their lives are to be imitated. Paul, for example, explicitly recommends to the Corinthians that they imitate him on a particular point, as he imitates Christ (1 Cor 11, 1). Elsewhere he describes his own behavior in terms which make it clear that he is commending it for imitation (see, for example, 1 Cor 4, 8–13). In various passages in the New Testament the actions of people are described in terms which make it clear that they are good, and products of the Spirit (see, for example, the description of the common use of goods in Acts 4, 32–37).

4. Statements with Moral Consequences

Some statements in the New Testament are not explicitly moral but they have moral consequences. Some statements are in reality moral statements but do not show this by their form. For example, Paul tells Philemon that the latter has been enabled to receive back his slave, Onesimus, as a brother (Phlm 15–16). This takes the form of a statement of fact. However, the word "brother" here should probably be taken to mean: "One who is to be loved and cared for." This being the case, it is really a normative statement, a declaration that Philemon should receive his slave back with love and care. Other statements are truly statements of fact, but when combined with norms they have moral consequences. For example, in various passages the New Testament states that God loves us. This is in itself a statement of fact. It is closely associated with several normative statements, however, and in combination with these it has moral consequences. One might express this in the form of a syllogism. God loves us gratuitously. We should be grateful to one who loves us gratuitously. Therefore we should be grateful to God. Of course we normally do not put it in a form of a syllogism because we experience the goodness of gratitude more or less spontaneously, and as a result we spontaneously perceive God's love as something calling for gratitude.

In some cases one statement in isolation may give only uncertain guidance concerning what is in accord with the Spirit. In many such cases one may achieve greater certainty by using several statements, either to reinforce each other or to give a more complete and nuanced picture of what is in accord with the Spirit. It is also helpful to combine different categories of statements. Using only literal statements one may lose the dimension of imagination and creativity. Using only figurative statements may leave one with criteria that are too indefinite and open to personal bias. Using both kinds of statements from the New Testament will give one's moral judgment both required dimensions.

Discernment must include, of course, the action of the Spirit who transforms us inwardly and gives us the appetites by which we can appreciate what is good. If one tries to discern what comes from the Spirit but one does not have the Spirit-caused appetites which allow one to appreciate what is good, one can have only a very imperfect grasp of the meaning of the norms which one accepts. One who does not have *agape*, for example, can have only a very imperfect knowledge of what it means to love one's neighbor as oneself. Proper discernment involves the union of the two dimensions: first, the subjective disposition, the appetites of the discerner which cause him to appreciate what is good; second, the scriptural criteria by which the discerner can check whether his subjective appreciation conforms to what truly comes from the Spirit.[10]

Of course discernment is also a work of intelligence. To formulate norms requires not only the raw materials, the scriptural criteria and the appetites, but also the activity of intelligence, sifting evidence, comparing, and generalizing only as far as the evidence justifies generalization.

The more one becomes adept at discerning what is of the Spirit, the more one goes beyond mechanical formulation of rules to recognize spontaneously those pervading personal qualities which mark the lives of those who live by the Spirit. In a sense one learns to recognize the personality of the Holy Spirit, the personal presence of God, in the lives of persons who live by the Spirit.[11]

C. Conclusion

The basic law for the Christian is a life written in the heart of the believer by the Holy Spirit. This life is first of all an active faith, a living awareness of God's love and the salvation he offers in Jesus Christ. The Christian responds to that love and that offer of salvation by his own act of love and of hope. From this core of faith, hope, and love flow the various Spirit-formed appetites which both motivate and guide Christian moral life.

While there is an active "interior" life of faith, hope, and love, exercised in prayer and action, the moral rules of Christianity are experienced as formulations of what the Christian wants to do. When the inner life wanes, the moral rules remain, but they are experienced as burdens, as something imposed from outside, as what one has to do. Christians may continue in this way, conforming to rules which no longer express their inner life. At a certain point, however, when the inner life is sufficiently weak and the opposite pressures sufficiently strong, the conformity breaks down. Then the people will revolt against Christian morality as being too demanding; or they may quietly ignore it and drift away from Christianity; or they may reformulate a new morality more to their liking, and call it Christian. They find it easier to conform the Gospel to their own inner life than to conform themselves to the Gospel.[12]

Chapter Thirteen

THE RELATION OF SCRIPTURAL ETHICS TO NON-SCRIPTURAL ETHICS

A. The Problem

One might ask the question: What is the relation between natural ethics and supernatural ethics? The answer to that question would require a definition of "natural" and "supernatural," a task that will not be undertaken in this book. Here we will pose the question in different terms: What is the relation between an ethics based on the Christian Scriptures (scriptural ethics) and ethics based on human experience apart from the Christian Scriptures (non-scriptural ethics)?[1]

The terms of the question must be made more precise. "Scriptural ethics" here does not refer to every Scripture-based ethical doctrine developed by various authors. It refers to the Scripture-based ethics described in the preceding five chapters of this book. "Non-scriptural ethics" here does not refer to all of the non-scriptural ethical systems developed by Aristotle, Bentham, Marx, and any number of philosophers. It refers to the ethics described in Part One of this book. Accordingly, this chapter discusses the relation of the ethics set forth in Chapters One to Seven to the ethics set forth in Chapters Eight to Twelve.

This question can be discussed on the level of norms or on the level of how norms are applied in particular situations (the topic of Part Three of this book). This chapter considers the question on the level of norms.[2]

Comparing scriptural and non-scriptural ethics on the level of norms, two distinct problems arise: the first, in the area of method, concerns how one discovers the norms; the second, in the area of content, concerns what kinds of things are morally good or morally evil. Section B of this chapter considers the problem of method: How is the method of discovering norms in non-scriptural ethics the same as or different from the method of discovering norms in scriptural ethics? Section C will consider the problem of content: To what extent do the norms of non-scriptural ethics agree with or disagree with the norms of scriptural ethics?

The answers to these problems have practical consequences. To what extent should a Christian expect to find non-Christian allies in working for such moral goals as just wages or family stability? To what considerations should a Christian appeal in order to convince non-Christians to pursue such moral goals? In a pluralistic society composed of Christians and non-Christians, are there common public moral values which can serve as goals of a common effort, or must morals become either a private matter or a subject of public conflict? To what extent can Christians learn ethical truths from those who do not accept Sacred Scripture?

B. Methods of Scriptural and Non-Scriptural Ethics

Both non-scriptural and scriptural ethics use two methods of discovering moral norms: personal appreciation and authority.

First we will consider personal appreciation. Part One of this book developed the idea that we know something is morally good or evil if we have an appetite for or against it. Our appetite gives us a personal appreciation that something is good or evil. Part Two has set forth the idea that the Holy Spirit instructs us inwardly that something is morally good or evil by giving us an appetite for it or against it. In this way, scriptural ethics too are based on personal appreciation.

Both non-scriptural and scriptural ethics make use of authority. Part One of this book has argued that it is not advantageous to take only one's actual appetites as a basis for moral judgment. One should take account of potential appetites. If one has not actualized a potential appetite in oneself, one can become aware of the appetitive potential by recognizing that it has been actualized in other human beings, and concluding that the same potential may exist in oneself. This discovery of the basis for moral norms therefore involves learning from others. One attributes authority to the other because of the other's superior knowledge of good and evil based on the superior development of his or her appetitive potential. The authority of the other may be accepted voluntarily by those who realize that it is advantageous to learn from another. In other cases authority may be imposed upon those (e.g., young children) who do not realize that it is advantageous to learn from others in this respect.

In scriptural ethics, too, authority plays a significant role; and again, the basis for authority is the fact that an individual has actualized only part of his or her appetitive potential, and so it is advantageous to learn from others who have further developed their potential. The use of authority in scriptural ethics has distinctive features, however. First, Christians attribute a quite unique authority to Jesus Christ. He developed human appetitive potential to a unique extent. Accordingly, his example and his words indicate not merely one of many good directions for human development but the one best way. Christians attribute a further special authority even to those parts of Sacred Scripture which do not deal directly with the example and words of Jesus. These parts of Scripture, especially of the New Testament, help to show what are the greatest appetitive potentials of human beings, what brings us the greatest happiness, what is the fullest development of human beings by the operation of the Holy Spirit.

In spite of this, the Christian does not have a static model of morality which can be adopted mechanically and literally in every case. What each individual personally appropriates from the words and example of Jesus, and from all of Scripture, will depend to a great extent on the individual's inner development, his or her appetites formed by the action of the Holy Spirit.

For both scriptural and non-scriptural ethics, a general rule applies: the less developed one's appetites, the more one needs authority; but because one never in this life reaches a state of perfect development of one's appetites, so one remains always in need of learning from others concerning moral norms.

C. Contents of Scriptural and Non-Scriptural Ethics

To what extent do the norms of non-scriptural ethics agree with the norms of scriptural ethics? On matters of sexual ethics, for example, or property rights or honesty in speech, should we expect non-scriptural ethics to agree with scriptural ethics?

There are two distinct questions here. The first concerns what is morally good or evil according to what is true absolutely.[3] The second concerns our actual and imperfect knowledge of ethics.

The first question is: To what extent does non-scriptural ethics agree with scriptural ethics concerning what is morally good or evil absolutely? For the sake of simplicity we will discuss this matter from the point of view of the moral good, leaving for the reader the task of applying this thinking to the area of moral evil.

According to the explanation of non-scriptural ethics in Part One, the moral good involves: (1) the development of one's positive appetites (likes) insofar as it is possible to satisfy those appetites, and (2) the actual satisfaction of those appetites while avoiding where possible the object of negative appetites (dislikes). Achieving this goal constitutes happiness.

Scriptural ethics too must accept this as a valid description of the greatest moral good. Were scriptural ethics to reject this description it would imply that God in Sacred Scripture does not direct human beings to the most complete happiness possible. This would not be consonant with the teaching of Sacred Scripture.

From this agreement on the abstract definition of the greatest moral good, can we conclude to an agreement about what concretely constitutes the moral good in particular cases? (Notice, we are still speaking about what is true absolutely, not about the actual state of knowledge.) To examine this question we must distinguish two factors: first, the appetitive potential, which determines what things are good as ends (as desired for their own sake); second, the means to attain those ends.

Regarding appetitive potential, if it is the same human beings who are involved in both types of ethics, then the appetitive potentials are the same in either case. Regarding means to the end, both types of ethics seek the most effective means possible. Theoretically, therefore, the means are the same for either type of ethics (though they may differ widely in their ability correctly to identify those means).

This brings us to the second and more realistic problem. To what extent do the norms actually held by non-scriptural ethicists agree with the norms held by scriptural ethicists? There seem to be great discrepancies between the two types of ethics as they are actually propounded, given the imperfect state of our actual ethical knowledge. The question of the agreement or disagreement of the two types of ethics becomes very complex, because we are speaking of many individual ethicists of either type who vary greatly in their ethical views.

One type of variation, i.e., variation in ethical theory, we are eliminating from this discussion. We are not considering any and every ethical theory. We are considering non-scriptural ethics according to the theory set forth in Part One, and scriptural ethics according as it is set forth in Part Two. However, agreement in theory does not necessarily mean agreement on all ethical norms.

In non-scriptural ethics, those who accept the theory in Part One might still differ from each other concerning particular moral norms because they have developed their appetites to different degrees or in different ways, and so they appreciate values in differing ways. Such differences may be the result of differences in culture or in personal experience and background. Further differences arise because different people discover different means to achieve ends.

In scriptural ethics, those who accept the theory given in Part Two might still differ from each other in the moral norms they claim to get from Sacred Scripture. Partly this would be the result of differences of appetite, which lead to differences in interpretation of texts or the selection of texts or the weight given to texts. Partly the difference could result from disagreements in scholarly interpretation of texts.

Clearly, to trace all the possible differences between individual scriptural ethicists and individual non-scriptural ethicists would be an endless and not very satisfying task. Nor has it been possible for this author to spell out a few simple principles according to which certain classes of moral truth are assigned to scriptural revelation only while other classes of moral truth can be known both by reason and Scripture, while a third class can be known by human reason alone. Rather, it is a matter of examining ethical truths one by one.

Such an examination reveals a sort of continuum. At one end are certain ethical truths revealed in Scripture which people cannot know, explicitly at least, without Sacred Scripture. For example, the New Testament makes clear that in order to achieve the supreme good one must have faith in Jesus Christ, through whom there is forgiveness of sin and the gift of God's grace.[4] There are some ethical truths which are taught in Scripture and may also be discovered by people without Scripture, but these truths will probably be recognized explicitly only by a few, and then often unclearly, with uncertainty and a mixture of error. For example, Scripture teaches that our complete happiness involves personal union with the one omnipotent and loving God. People who base their ethics on human reason and experience without Scripture do not commonly accept this truth. We should not conclude, however, that human experience can give no indication that this is the goal of life. Such an awareness, even if it does not come through Scripture, would still be the work of God in the person. Another moral truth in Scripture is that we are to love others unselfishly, for their own sake. Though this contradicts a certain "worldly" attitude, yet some people who do not accept Sacred Scripture seem to have discovered that this is the proper way to act. The Holy Spirit can cause this special kind of love in people who do not accept Scripture.[5]

Certain ethical truths given in Sacred Scripture are also commonly (though not universally) accepted by those who do not accept Sacred Scripture. Such moral truths include the condemnation of murder and theft and the duty of honoring parents.

Finally, certain ethical principles are more or less generally held by people but are not taught by Sacred Scripture. Among these are the conviction that slavery is wrong and the belief that people have a right to participate in the choice of their government. It might be claimed that these ethical beliefs are based on principles found in Sacred Scripture. Even if this is true, nevertheless acceptance of these ethical beliefs involves some sort of appreciation of particular values besides the principles given in Scripture.[6]

D. The Christian and Non-Scriptural Ethics

To what extent should Christians use non-scriptural ethics? Advocates of the *Sola Scriptura* school of Christian ethics reject any use of non-scriptural ethics. For them, human reason is corrupted by sin and unable to know either the true end or the proper means of human life, and is therefore an unreliable guide for Christian conduct. On the other hand, some Christian ethicists of the natural law school seem to use non-scriptural ethics as a source quite separate and independent of Scripture. Neither of these positions presents the whole picture.

Christians who approach Sacred Scripture for moral guidance bring with them certain personal qualities which are involved in ethical judgment. They have developed certain appetites which enable them to appreciate certain values. They may have formulated certain moral principles, based on their own appreciation, or on authority, or on conformity to some group. They bring personal and cultural biases, insights, habits, and past experiences, all of which affect their moral judgments.

Christians do not, and I dare say cannot, leave behind all of these personal qualities when they come to Sacred Scripture for moral guidance. They use these personal qualities in understanding the ethical message of the Scriptures. Without the appropriate personal appreciation, for example, one can understand "Thou shalt not kill" in a certain way, but one cannot appreciate the rightness of it. Indeed, had readers of Scripture no previous experience of good and evil they would not even know what the words mean when Scripture uses the terms "good" and "evil."

However, these personal qualities which people bring to the study of Scripture are far from infallible guides to moral conduct. On the other hand, one should not suppose that they are all completely wrong. Therefore one must discern which of these personal qualities are reliable and which are not. Part Two of this book has indicated how the New Testament may be used in this process of discernment. Scripture does not come to a vacuum in the human person and then build a completely new moral structure. It comes to an actually operating moral agent and allows that agent to discern what of the existing structure is sound, what is to be discarded, and what new elements must be developed.

On some ethical issues Scripture either gives little or no guidance or gives guidance of such a general sort that it does not by itself determine the issue. The prohibition against slavery, and the wrongness of using addictive drugs which impede the exercise of personal freedom, are examples of such issues. The Scriptures give basic principles or norms relevant to these issues, but some further perception of values seems to be required in order to arrive at these particular norms.

In cases where Scripture does not give adequate criteria to settle the issue, we should still use our human resources to make as good a moral judgment as we can. Our human resources for moral judgment are fallible, it is true, but our human minds are fallible in many areas, and this does not mean that we need not use them as well as we can.[7]

The Christian seeks not only to elaborate a system of ethical rules but also to undergo a development of a more personal kind. Gradually the person should learn which types of urges, wishes and intuitions are reliable and which are not. With the proper development the unreliable urges, wishes and intuitions become less frequent, or weaker, or are more quickly recognized as unreliable.

There is a feature of scriptural ethics which may seem to distinguish it further from non-scriptural ethics. However, further investigation suggests that the two types of ethics are quite similar even on this point. This feature concerns the motive for pursuing some good for which at the moment one has little or no appreciation. According to non-scriptural ethics one pursues such goods in order to learn to appreciate them, and having learned to appreciate them one can attain greater happiness. Scriptural ethics provides further motives. For example, suppose that you do not have a sufficiently strong love of neighbor to appreciate the value of patience with a very difficult person. What motive is there for being patient with him anyway? Non-scriptural ethics can argue that being patient with him will help you gradually to become a patient type of person who will appreciate more the value of other persons, and this will allow you to become a happier person. Scriptural ethics can add that if you love God and you know that God wills you to be patient, you will wish to be patient. On a less generous level, in this situation you may be patient out of fear of punishment for going against God's will.

Further consideration shows, however, that non-scriptural ethics can provide similar motives for seeking a good which one does not yet appreciate. A love for someone can move one to pursue certain goods which one does not yet appreciate but which the other person desires. In other cases fear of punishment, e.g., by parents or by the state, will move one to choose certain goods one does not yet appreciate.

Having discussed the central question of this chapter we will return briefly to the related practical questions posed in Section A.

First, to what extent should Christians expect to find non-Christian allies in working for such moral goals as just wages or family stability? The amount of agreement possible will depend on the particular moral goal and on the dispositions of the particular people whom the Christian seeks as allies. The degree of agreement possible must be discovered empirically. Non-Christians can in fact have those dispositions and beliefs which enable them to appreciate and agree with a wide variety of goods which Christians may seek as moral goals for society. Whether in fact a particular population has these dispositions and beliefs will be discovered from the results when one appeals as rationally and convincingly as possible to their "better instincts."

To what considerations should a Christian appeal in order to convince non-Christians to pursue such moral goals? Again, the answer must be discovered empirically. Some non-Christians may have a rich appreciation of values held by the Christian. A clear explanation that these values are at stake in the situation will ordinarily be enough to convince them. Other people may have only a very imperfect appreciation of these values. In that case the Christian can focus their attention on that part of their experience which opens them to these values. Many people will pursue a goal which they appreciate only imperfectly if they know from past experience that the people who advocate this goal are trustworthy. Focusing on the goal and actually pursuing it will ordinarily increase one's appreciation of the goal. Other people will have little or no appreciation of the values in question. Toward them the Christian still has two courses of action which may be effective. For the short run the Christian may be able to give these people extraneous reasons for cooperating in seeking a goal which they do not appreciate in itself. For example, people may be moved out of self-interest to seek justice for others in order to prevent civil unrest. For the long run, the Christian can continue to witness to the values which others fail to appreciate. This witness will keep alive in society the possibility for people to learn to appreciate these values.

In a pluralistic society composed of Christians and non-Christians, are there common public moral values which can serve as goals of a common effort, or must morals become either a private matter or a subject of public conflict? In substance this has already been answered in the discussion of the previous questions. A note may be added on the political aspect of the matter. Public conflict may arise if a government enforces a law which is based on an ethical belief which is accepted by many but not accepted by many others. A law against abortion might be an example. Governments may attempt to avoid such outcry by refraining from passing a law unless the overwhelming majority accept the moral principles underlying the law. This makes the moral issue a private matter only. Public action tends then to be guided only by a lowest common denominator, those (perhaps few) ethical principles accepted by nearly all. (In fact governments do not refrain from legislating on all issues which involve ethical differences among the people, but only on those deeply-felt issues where a public outcry is likely to be greatest.)

This following of a lowest common denominator in setting public goals has serious drawbacks. If a government refuses to support an ethical value dear to a considerable part of the population, that part of the population may be quite disturbed, and so the government will not even achieve the goal of avoiding public conflict. Furthermore, to reduce the ethical content of law means to fail to pursue many worthwhile public goals. In addition, the law is itself an instrument of education. If the law upholds certain values it reminds people of the importance of those values. If it fails to uphold those values some people will conclude that those values are not important. Christians therefore have a duty to use the means available to help others come to an appreciation of certain values, so that the law can support solid moral values.

To what extent can Christians learn ethical truths from those who do not accept Sacred Scripture? In those areas in which the guidance of scriptural ethics is insufficient in itself to give precise moral guidance, Christians can certainly learn about moral values from non-Christians. Non-Christians are certainly capable, as are Christians, of developing their appetites, appreciating certain goods, and telling others about them. Even in areas covered by scriptural ethics Christians can learn from non-Christians. Christians may be ignorant of, or ignore, certain values taught in Scripture. The example of non-Christians can recall Christians to these values. For example, the example of non-Christian social reformers can remind Christians of their own, perhaps neglected, heritage of justice taught in Sacred Scripture.

PART THREE

Practical Moral Judgment

Suppose that your neighbor's child has caused considerable damage by starting a fire in your garage. Several alternative courses of action are available. Because you want to do what is morally good you reject several violent alternatives which come to mind, and try to think about the matter rationally. Several general moral norms or rules relevant to the case might be formulated, such as: respect the property of others; take responsibility for your actions; seek peace and friendship between neighbors; do not seek revenge; respect the bodily integrity even of delinquents.

Your task, however, is not to remain on the level of general norms but to judge what is the morally good thing to do in this concrete situation. Should you take legal action against your neighbor and/or his child? Should you adopt a mild and lenient approach? Should you try once more to urge on your neighbor the necessity of controlling his son's behavior? If several alternatives are morally good, which one is morally best?

Part Three will examine the process by which one makes these moral judgments in particular situations in the light of general moral norms. Before proceeding, however, we must deal with ethical particularism. Ethical particularism denies the validity of using general norms in making moral judgments in particular situations. This position will be evaluated in Chapter Fourteen. Chapter Fifteen will analyze the process by which moral judgments are made concerning particular situations. Chapter Sixteen will discuss situation ethics.

Several terms should be clarified. "Conscience" here means the capacity of a person to make rational judgments about whether a course of action in a particular situation is morally good or morally evil. Conscience in this sense is not a feeling but an ability to judge.

By "prudence" we mean the habit or virtue which gives us skill in making moral judgments in particular situations. Many people can play tennis but not all of them have developed the ability to play tennis well. Similarly, of all the people who have the capacity we call "conscience," not all have developed the ability to use it well. The prudent person has learned to exercise conscience well. "Prudence" for some people suggests caution. This is not the meaning we attach to it here. In some cases the prudent judgment—the correct judgment—will dictate a cautious course of action, but in other situations it may recommend daring or a calculated risk.

The judgment of what is morally good or evil in a particular situation we will call "the judgment of conscience."

Chapter Fourteen

ETHICAL PARTICULARISM

A. The Meaning of Ethical Particularism

"Ethical particularism" here denotes the position that general ethical norms are useless and misleading in making moral judgments in particular situations.[1]

The ethical particularist need not be an ethical relativist, as the latter has been described in Part One. The ethical relativist holds that no moral judgment can be true absolutely. The ethical particularist, on the other hand, may hold that some moral judgments (i.e., judgments of conscience at least in certain cases) may be true absolutely. He denies the validity of general rules of morality. In the example given at the beginning of Part Three, the ethical particularist may believe that your moral duty in that particular case at that moment is to try once more to persuade your neighbor to control his son's behavior. The particularist may believe that this moral judgment is true absolutely. He claims, however, that neither in this nor in other situations is it useful or valid to use general rules to make particular judgments of conscience.

Ethical particularism should be distinguished from situation ethics, which will be discussed in Chapter Sixteen. Situation ethics holds that one can formulate valid general moral rules which are helpful in making moral judgments in particular cases.[2] The situation ethicist refuses to consider these general rules to be universal, allowing of no exceptions.[3] While using these general rules to help make judgments of conscience, he is willing to make exceptions to any of them, or almost any of them, in particular circumstances.

B. The Arguments for Ethical Particularism

There are several possible arguments for ethical particularism. One argument rests on the philosophical view that each situation for moral action is so unique that it cannot be validly included under a general rule; what constitutes an act as morally good or evil in a particular situation is always something so unique that general rules about what is morally good or evil are not useful.

A theological argument for ethical particularism holds that the correct judgment of conscience is always the product of the special guidance and inspiration of the Holy Spirit in the particular situation and is not reached by applying general moral rules. According to this view, the moral good is always the will of God, and to insist on general moral rules is to imply that there are rules which God must follow. Where would such rules come from? Do they arise independently of God and impose themselves on God? Such a proposition would deny that God is omnipotent and would suppose that God is subject to something outside of himself. Might general rules arise from within God himself? Must God follow some general rule because of some necessity within himself? Such a proposition seems to deny God's freedom. If God's will is not bound by general rules, and if the moral good is always in accord with God's will, then the moral good cannot be stated in general rules.

We will now evaluate ethical particularism, first from a philosophical and then from a theological point of view.

C. Philosophical Evaluation

At this point we should note the distinction between moral good and pre-moral good, as well as the distinction between moral evil and pre-moral evil. A pre-moral good is any object of liking. As stated in Chapter Six, a moral good for a person in a particular situation is the good reckoned with a view to the whole of what is good for that person. A pre-moral evil is any evil which is the object of dislike. A moral evil for a person in a particular situation is the evil reckoned with a view to the whole of what is good or evil for that person.[4]

To see how generalization enters into moral judgment it is helpful to distinguish two phases in making a judgment of conscience.[5] First, one recognizes that particular things are pre-moral goods or evils and one recognizes how great or how small a good or evil each is. In the second phase one compares the pre-moral goods and evils in order to decide whether a particular course of action is morally good or evil. In this second phase one must judge whether the choice of particular goods or evils contributes to the whole of what is good for the person or whether it detracts from the whole of what is good and contributes to the whole of what is evil for the person.

We will examine first why we can generalize concerning pre-moral goods and evils. If the actual and potential likings of each person were in no way similar to the actual and potential likings of other people, and if each liking were directed only to one unique object, then generalizations about pre-moral goods would not be valid. However, our likings are usually not of this kind. A liking for food, for example, usually is not directed only to one particular morsel. Normally it can be satisfied by any of a large number of foods, so a large class of objects is good for a person who likes food. Again, one person's actual or potential liking for food is similar to the actual or potential liking of many other people for food. For this reason one can generalize that many foods are good for many people.

A similar generalization holds for pre-moral evils. Our actual and potential dislikes usually are directed not to unique objects only but to general classes of objects. Furthermore, the actual and potential dislikes of one person are usually similar to the actual and potential dislikes of other people. Accordingly we can generalize that certain classes of objects are evil for a large number of people.

One must grant to the ethical particularist that it is not legitimate to generalize about moral goods and evils to the same extent that one can generalize about pre-moral goods and evils. A reality which is a pre-moral good in many situations may not be a moral good in all of those situations. Sexual relations, for example, are objects of liking and therefore are pre-moral goods in many situations. In some of those situations, however, sexual relations may preclude certain other, greater goods and so detract from the whole of what is good for the person. In such cases sexual relations would be pre-moral goods but not moral goods.

A similar conclusion must be drawn concerning evils. Pain is an object of dislike and is therefore a pre-moral evil in all situations in which it occurs. In some cases, however, the pain may be an unavoidable accompaniment to some important good. In such cases the pain, though a pre-moral evil, may be chosen as part of a morally good course of action. The fact that one can generalize that things in a certain class are pre-moral goods or evils does not mean that the same generalization may be made that they are moral goods or evils.

Nevertheless, one can validly generalize about moral goods and evils. One can state validly that certain classes of things are generally morally good and certain classes of things are generally morally evil. (Whether, and to what extent, these generalizations admit of exceptions will be discussed in Chapter Sixteen.) These generalizations may be formulated in a simple or in a more complex way.

A simple type of formulation can be made concerning certain very important goods and evils. Certain classes of pre-moral goods are so important that in most cases at least, the choice of such a good will contribute to the whole of what is good for the person. In most cases, at least, such a good will be a moral good. "Feeding the hungry is a moral good" is a valid general moral rule. Some classes of the pre-moral evils are so great that in most cases, at least, they detract from the whole of what is good and contribute to the whole of what is evil for a person. "To kill a human being is morally evil" is a valid general moral rule.

By adding nuances one can formulate a rule which admits of fewer exceptions than would the rule in unnuanced form. "To kill a human being is morally evil" admits of exceptions, according to most moralists. They would make exceptions in cases when the only way to preserve the life of oneself and of others is to kill an unjust attacker. Foreseeing this exception we can formulate the rule in a more nuanced way. "To kill an innocent human being is morally evil."

Another form of a valid general moral rule specifies that it applies only to situations in which the only significant goods or evils are those mentioned in the rule. One such rule might be: "Other things being equal, it is morally good to choose loyalty to friends rather than the pleasure which comes from telling secrets." The term "other things being equal" means that the rule is meant to apply only in situations in which the two factors mentioned in the rule are the only two significant goods or evils.

The generalization about moral rules which we have discussed thus far is based on generalizing about things which are good in themselves (i.e., liked for their own sakes) or evil in themselves (i.e., disliked for their own sakes). Another source of generalization concerning moral rules concerns the means to achieving or avoiding things which are good or evil in themselves. Judgments of conscience frequently require generalization from past experience concerning means. For example, a father must decide how to respond to his young son's misbehavior. He needs to know what means would be effective in producing a better attitude in the boy. This requires that he, or someone who will advise him, learn from past experience with this child or others. To apply past experience to a particular case one must first generalize.

In summary, we must grant to the ethical particularist that particular situations for moral action are to some extent unique. However, situations for moral action contain sufficient similarities with each other to serve as a basis for the formulation of some valid general moral rules.

D. Theological Evaluation

The theological argument for ethical particularism was that positing general moral norms does not seem to be consistent with God being both free and omnipotent. We must admit that part of the argument which states that no general rule to which God is bound can arise independently of God. What of the other part of the argument, which claims that if God is free he cannot follow any general moral norms arising from within himself? The validity of this argument is far from obvious. Fortunately, here we do not have to solve the matter by looking into the mind of God. It will be sufficient merely to look at what God has established for the human race. Insofar as God has established human beings with certain appetites and an intelligence by which to guide activity, he has provided for a certain amount of generalization in moral thinking, as we have just argued. Insofar as God has made his will known to human beings through Sacred Scripture, here again he has given a basis for some generalization concerning morals. Many of the norms given in Sacred Scripture must be supposed to apply as general rules, not merely as precepts covering single cases.

We have argued here only that a certain degree of generalization is possible, and even necessary, in making correct judgments of conscience.

We have not tried to show whether or not moral rules are sometimes universal, allowing for no exceptions. That topic would bring us to the question of situation ethics. Before discussing that question we will first analyze more closely the process by which we make judgments of conscience.

Chapter Fifteen

THE JUDGMENT OF CONSCIENCE

A. The Starting Points for a Judgment of Conscience

A judgment of conscience requires two kinds of starting points: knowledge of facts and knowledge of norms. One kind of starting point without the other cannot yield a judgment of what is morally good or evil in a particular situation.[1]

The knowledge of facts that is required is not simply a record of sense observations. There must be interpretation or understanding of the facts.[2] There are various systematic ways of understanding facts, the methods of the different positive sciences, for example, or the methods of different philosophies. There are unsystematic ways of understanding facts, ways which carry us through our daily lives, and these ways too may be quite complex. My observation that my traveling companion is impatient, for example, is not only an awareness of certain sense perceptions but also an interpretation of their meaning. Different kinds of systematic and unsystematic ways of understanding facts help in making moral judgments. We value things, like them, or dislike them, not merely insofar as those things are perceived by the senses, but also insofar as they are understood in various ways.

The knowledge of facts which is a starting point for judgments of conscience includes not only knowledge of what actually is at the present, but also a knowledge of what is likely to happen and what might possibly happen, and knowledge of the appropriate means by which certain effects can be produced or avoided.

The second kind of starting point for making judgments of conscience is knowledge of norms. Parts One and Two of this book have dealt at length with knowledge of norms; we will deal with them only briefly here.

There is a knowledge of norms which comes from the actual appetites of which we are aware at a particular moment. I perceive that something is good because I like it and I perceive that something is evil because I dislike it. This is a knowledge which we possess by ourselves, without depending on anyone else. (Of course we may in the past have depended on someone else to help us develop these appetites.)

As Chapters Three and Four argue, the appetites of which we are aware at a particular moment may not be adequate guides in our pursuit of the greater good. One subordinate rule given in Chapter Three is that we should choose not in accord with the appetites of which we are aware at a particular moment, but in accord with the whole range of our likes and dislikes. In this kind of knowledge of norms we basically depend upon ourselves, but others may help us by pointing out certain elements which we might otherwise overlook.

Another subordinate rule given in Chapter Three is that one should choose not in accord with the likes and dislikes of which one is capable at the time of choice, but in accord with one's likes and dislikes during the whole time affected by the choice. In knowing norms in this way, we may depend on our own calculation of what our likes and dislikes will be during the time of choice. Others may be very helpful, however, if their experience allows them to calculate better than we ourselves what may be our likes and dislikes in the future. Of course others can help in this case also in the way pointed out in the previous paragraph, by pointing out something that we may have overlooked.

Chapter Four argues that one should act in such a way as to develop the greater potentialities for likings which can be satisfied. For this kind of knowledge of norms we are necessarily dependent on others. To follow this norm we need to know which potentialities are great. We find out about potentialities by seeing them actualized. Since they have not yet been actualized in us, we must learn about them from others in whom they have been actualized.

We have spoken of knowledge of norms according to the position outlined in Part One, non-scriptural ethics. With scriptural ethics we do not scrap all of this and start over. We begin with our moral experience and use scriptural criteria to discern which of our appetites are reliable guides and which are not, and what new appetites should be developed. In scriptural as in non-scriptural ethics, we have a type of knowledge which we get from our own appetites, products of the Holy Spirit, and we have a knowledge we learn "from the outside." In scriptural ethics, however, this knowledge from the outside comes from the word of God and so carries a very special authority.

B. The Process of Making Judgments of Conscience

There are two stages in the process of making judgments of conscience. We will call them the stage of recognition and the stage of weighing.

1. Recognition

This stage involves a step beyond understanding the facts. Having understood a fact one then identifies the realities involved as good or evil, and one recognizes each as a relatively great or small good or evil. At this point we are speaking of good and evil in general, pre-moral rather than moral good and evil.

In some cases this recognition occurs so quickly and spontaneously that we are hardly aware of it as an intellectual process. A boy comes home from school and announces, plausibly, that he is hungry because he forgot to bring his lunch to school. Having been made aware of the fact, the mother gives him something to eat, without having to deliberate about whether this is a good thing to do. Her recognition that this is a good thing is spontaneous because she appreciates the good. She loves her son and she appreciates that food is good for hungry people. Her desires cause her to make a spontaneous judgment that this concrete act is good, and she doesn't have to refer to any general rule, though a valid general rule could be formulated.

In some cases when a person does not appreciate the good or evil the stage of recognition may have to be slower and more deliberate. A man is angry at a neighbor who has offended him. He has little or no spontaneous appreciation for an act of forgiveness. He can recognize it as good only by relating it to the general rule which requires Christians to forgive.

This first stage in making a moral judgment must include not only recognition of goods and evils which exist in the present but also recognition of goods and evils which might come into existence. A considerable creativity, not unlike artistic creativity, can occur at this stage when a person combines several abilities: an ability to recognize the potentialities or possible results of a situation; an ability to identify the right means to cause or to prevent these results; a sensitivity to the goodness or evil of the results.

An example of this kind of creativity is the life in L'Arche homes founded by Jean Vanier. Many people observing the plight of retarded persons and seeking a good solution might think of providing better facilities and better custodial care in institutions. Vanier, however, discovered that when retarded people live with well-motivated and balanced "normal" people in small communities, both types of people profit from the experience. The retarded people are helped by the attention, by the degree of responsibility given to them, and in other ways. At the same time they teach the "normal" people about such things as emotional honesty, simplicity and the appreciation of everyday goods.

2. Weighing

A judgment of conscience is a judgment about what is morally good or evil in a particular situation. Attaining one good may preclude attaining another, and so one must decide which is the greater good. Choosing a certain good may produce an accompanying evil. One must decide whether the good is sufficiently important to outweigh the accompanying evil.

In some cases generalizations help to indicate that one type of good is preferable to another type, or one type of evil is to be avoided even at the cost of accepting another type. For example, in choosing between human life and property, life should be chosen because it is a prerequisite for the enjoyment not only of property but also of many other goods.

In some cases general rules are of less help in deciding which goods or evils are to be chosen or rejected. Consider the case of a thirty-three-year-old mother of four children whose husband is an irresponsible alcoholic. She is close to a nervous breakdown. There are several goods and evils among which she must choose: her own physical and mental health, her husband's physical and mental health, the emotional well-being of her children, money on which to live. Should the point come when she must sacrifice one good in order to attain another, the general rules will not at all determine a solution. One cannot say that the good of one's spouse is always to be chosen ahead of one's own good. It depends upon what good of the spouse is in question and what good of oneself. One cannot say that mental health is always more important than physical health. It depends on what kind and degree of mental or physical health is in question.

In these questions when one must consider exceptions to general rules or choose between general rules, one must weigh the particular goods and evils in comparison with each other. To do this properly one must have developed a proper appetite which gives an appreciation of the good and evils, or else one must depend on the better judgment of someone whose appetites allow him or her to appreciate the goods and evils properly.

An important principle can be summed up here. When people do not have properly developed appetites they cannot properly weigh particular goods and evils in comparison with each other. Therefore they must depend on others. This help from others may come in the form of general rules about what goods and evils are to be given preference in cases of conflict. In cases where such general rules are not helpful, the individual with poorly developed appetites must depend on the judgment of others concerning the particular case.[3] Because with all of us it is the case that our appetitive development is far from perfect, we do well to seek outside help at least in important decisions.

Because of our limitations in knowing the facts and norms and in weighing goods and evils in comparison with each other, Christians should seek the special help of the Holy Spirit in making judgments of conscience. The judgment of conscience concerns what is good in view of the whole of what is good for the person. For the Christian this whole embraces both this life and the life hereafter. It involves not only the good of one individual or of one small group but the good of the Kingdom of God and the building up of the body of Christ. To judge the good in this context requires more than human wisdom.

The Holy Spirit guides judgments of conscience by producing in us those appetites which enable us to appreciate what is best. The Holy Spirit helps us also to recognize the possibilities of good which can come out of a situation. A life which falls into routine, which repeats the same pattern over and over again, misses the possibilities for fuller life which are present in everyday situations.

A question arises at this point. Have we denied God's freedom by binding him to an ethical system? Are there not occasions when God calls individuals to very special actions which are justified not by an ethical system but by the fact that God so wills?

A proper response to this question involves several points. First, God's freedom does not mean that he could contradict himself. Having constituted a human being with a particular appetitive potential, God thereby constitutes certain things as good for him. God does not then arbitrarily determine that the person's good is something else which contradicts the orientation of his nature.

Within the general orientation of a human being toward certain goods, there remains a variety of forms which the attainment of those goods may take. Within the general orientation of a human being's nature, God is certainly free to determine that one rather than another form is to be chosen. For example, a particular person may be fulfilled by a life of contemplation, or by a life of works of mercy, or a life of ministry of God's word. God may determine that for this person the life of preaching God's word is the primary thing to be chosen. God could communicate this choice to the person by direct revelation, bypassing the normal process of making judgments of conscience. Such a revelation falls outside of our ethical system, and we will not presume here to construct a systematic ethics to cover this possibility. However, God may communicate his choice through the normal process of making judgments of conscience. He could, for example, give the person a special appetite and appreciation for this way of life, or a special understanding of the facts leading to a clear recognition of the needs of the people.

Another factor relevant to this question is the fallibility of human judgments of conscience. The number of facts and norms pertinent to a particular judgment of conscience may be beyond the capacity of most human beings to grasp. For this reason God's judgment may differ from the consensus of human beings. The Holy Spirit may, in these cases, communicate God's correct judgment by direct revelation, bypassing the normal process of judgments of conscience. However, the Holy Spirit regularly communicates God's right judgment by strengthening the individual at the various stages of the process of making judgments of conscience. The Holy Spirit may do this by giving the person special appetites and appreciation for goods, for example, or by giving a special understanding of the facts. If God's right judgment communicated to a person differs from human consensus it may seem that God's judgment goes contrary to any ethical system. In fact, however, God's judgment coincides with the decision of a true ethical system used with full knowledge.[4]

Finally, each and every situation calling for a judgment of conscience is in some way unique and special, even when that situation falls under a general rule, so we cannot make a simple distinction between special and regular types of calling from God. Consider, for example, a particular situation in which telling an untruth would allow me to escape an embarrassing situation. The judgment of conscience is quite straightforward and similar to the proper judgment in many other similar situations. I should not tell this lie. However, this situation is still special and unique in the sense that, though I may be in similar situations later, this individual act will not be repeated, and although I am applying a general rule, I am responding to a particular call of God in this particular time and place.

C. Intermediate Moral Norms

Among the general rules used in making judgments of conscience, one can distinguish general moral principles from intermediate moral maxims. General moral principles are moral rules which are self-evidently true to any person who has properly developed appetites. The good which is commanded or the evil which is forbidden in the general principle is sufficiently apparent that the person with properly developed appetites will spontaneously recognize that the rule is to be followed. For example, anyone with a reasonably developed love of neighbor will recognize that torture of another human being is an evil to be avoided. (He will spontaneously recognize it as a *general* moral principle. Whether he would recognize it as a *universal* rule, admitting of no exceptions, is a matter we need not settle here.)

Different authors attach slightly different meanings to the term "intermediate moral maxim." In our usage, an intermediate moral maxim is a moral rule which is general but is not self-evident to all people who have reasonably developed appetites. These rules are not self-evident to all because an individual, even though appreciating the end goods or evils which are involved, may lack factual knowledge about means. Over a certain period of time one may learn that a certain type of behavior, although not evil in itself, yet tends to lead to evil consequences. Out of this experience an intermediate maxim is formulated stating that one should not act in this way.

An example of an intermediate maxim is: "Parents have primary responsibility for the welfare, rearing and education of their young children; neither the state nor any other agency should take on this primary role except in cases of grave necessity." To see the rightness of this rule requires not only properly developed appetites but also a knowledge of the likely consequences of following this maxim and of disobeying it.

Intermediate maxims contain wisdom acquired over many years, perhaps over many generations. In some cases people accept these maxims not because they have had the experience and knowledge of consequences which originally led to their formulation, but because these maxims are taught with authority or because the people have learned to feel guilty about disobeying them. Because these intermediate maxims are not self-evidently true they may be scrapped by "reformers" who wish to get rid of all rules whose value they do not grasp, viewing such rules as irrational relics of the past. Individually, we may be overly willing to make exceptions to such maxims because we lack the experience which led to their original formulation.

D. Sin and the Ideal

Part One has defined the moral good in a situation as a good reckoned with a view to the whole of what is good for the individual. In a particular situation there may be several alternative moral goods, several alternatives which contribute to, rather than detract from, the total good of the individual. Some of these moral goods may be greater than are others. We have not reserved the term "moral good" only to the greatest possible good in a situation, because it goes against common usage to say that a person has not done a morally good thing simply because something better was possible.

Our usage, however, obscures an important point. In choosing a small rather than a great good in a particular situation one is failing in a significant way. Especially is this true in a Christian religious context.

God calls us not to mediocrity but to choose great goods. Most fundamentally, we are called to choose God, *the* good, not one good among many. To be satisfied with lesser goods is not only to lose a greater good but also to reject God's call.

We must discuss this in terms of sin. Sin is not only a moral failure but an offense against God. Furthermore, sin involves not only the objective factor, the goods or evils which are chosen or rejected, but also the subjective disposition of the person turning toward God or away from him.[5]

Shall we say that to choose anything less than what we judge to be the greatest good in a particular situation constitutes not only failure, but also an offense against God, a sin? Human nature is open-ended. In this life we never reach perfection, never love God or neighbor fully, without room for improvement. Are we to say that in this life even the best we do is still sinful, because it falls short of the greatest good, the ideal?

Some thinkers answer ''yes'' to that question. To argue with their position is to a certain extent to argue above the use of words, and such arguments are not always fruitful. However, even if we accept their position one must still distinguish several different states of a person in this respect.

One state is that of the person who does approximately the best that is possible for him at the time. This is not the attainment of ideal perfection. It may not be as good as the actions of other people in similar situations. Nevertheless, this person is not responsible, at this time, for failing to choose a greater good. This person may be said to be acting sinfully, insofar as he falls short of the ideal. Those who associate the term ''sin'' with a failure for which one is responsible will not call this action sinful.

A second state is that exemplified by Mrs. Green, who works with a well-meaning but not very likable woman. In a particularly trying situation Mrs. Green becomes angry at her co-worker. With some difficulty she refrains from saying the harsh things which she would like to say. Instead she does a little bit extra to help her annoying associate. She realizes that it would be even better if she would spend more time helping her co-worker, and use this as an occasion to discuss the difficulty in order to prevent similar problems arising again. Mrs. Green does not do this extra good deed. Her response might be called sinful insofar as she fails to do the best thing possible to her at the time. However, what she did was good and was motivated by love of God. Many Roman Catholics would call her action an imperfection, and would reserve the term ''sin'' for the following state.

The third state is that of a person who in a particular situation does something evil or omits some good, and the action or omission is not motivated by love of God but simply contradicts it.[6] Mrs. Brown, in a situation like that described in the last paragraph, does not try to restrain her anger, but lashes out verbally at her annoying co-worker. Her action does not proceed from love of God, but contradicts it, and so is a sin in a stricter sense than are acts involving the first or second state.[7] Even the ''imperfections,'' however, fall short of the fullness of life to which God calls us. The Christian should regret them and ask God's forgiveness for them.

To hold that the goal for the Christian is the best possible alternative in a situation is not to recommend an anxious scrupulosity about possible failings. God invites us to a wholehearted response to his love, not to anxiety about our performance.

Chapter Sixteen

SITUATION ETHICS

A. The Meaning of Situation Ethics

"General moral rule" here denotes a moral rule which states that a certain class of things is morally good or evil. The term "general" indicates that the rule does not apply only to a particular individual person, action or thing. "Universal moral rule" here denotes a general moral rule which admits of no exceptions. If "Do not kill human beings" is a general rule which is not universal, that means that killing human beings is generally morally evil but in certain exceptional cases it is not morally evil.

This chapter does not examine the details of the thought of particular situation ethicists. It discusses one central proposition of situation ethics. That proposition is that all (or nearly all)[1] general moral rules or laws admit of exceptions when applied to certain unusual cases. Unlike the particularist discussed in Chapter Fourteen, the situation ethicist believes that general moral rules are useful, even necessary, in making correct judgments of conscience. The situation ethicist, however, accepts none, or almost none, of these general moral rules as universal.

Several terms are used to denote ethical theories which resemble situation ethics in varying degrees. Consequentialism, proportionalism and contextualism are such terms. This chapter will not discuss these ethical theories except insofar as they may espouse the one central proposition noted in the previous paragraph. An adequate treatment of other aspects of these theories would require a discussion which would expand this book well beyond its intended length.

B. The Apparent Case for Situation Ethics

The ethical theory given in Part One might seem to lead to situation ethics. That theory refrained from defining any class of things as morally good or morally evil apart from a situation in which they might become the object of choice.

Consider first the possibility of a universal rule concerning moral good. In Part One, part of the definition of the moral good for a person in a particular situation is that it is a good reckoned with a view to the whole of what is good for the person. Universal rules concerning moral good take the form: "X is always morally good." Apparently for this rule to be valid X must represent a good or a class of goods the attainment of any one of which would contribute to the whole of what is good for the person, in every possible situation, regardless of what other goods might be precluded by this attainment, and regardless of what evils might be caused by or accompany or be necessary means to this attainment. Will there be many, or any, such classes of goods?

In Part One, part of the definition of moral evil for a person in a particular situation is that it is an evil reckoned with a view to the whole of what is good or evil for the person. Universal rules concerning moral evil take the form: "Y is always morally evil." Apparently for this rule to be valid Y must represent an evil or a class of evils the causing of any one of which would detract from the whole of what is good for the person and contribute to the whole of what is evil for the person, in every possible situation, regardless of what goods might be caused by or accompany this evil and regardless of what further evils might be averted by choosing this evil. Will there be many, or any, such classes of evils?

C. The Gospel and Situation Ethics

Does the New Testament give us any guidance in this area? Situation ethicists have appealed occasionally to the words and example of Jesus to support their position. They point out that Jesus criticized certain Jewish leaders of his time for their legalism, and was attacked by them for his willingness to make exceptions to laws. Does Jesus in fact support situation ethics? We must examine the relevant texts.

Two parallel passages (Mt 23, 23–24; Lk 11, 42) describe the criticism by Jesus of the Pharisees who attended to certain details but neglected more important matters of the law. One may hold that this implies that the rules governing these lesser details must admit of exceptions. The text does not say this. Even if one were to use the texts as support for making exceptions to lesser rules, one can find there no support for exceptions to the rules which constitute the weightier matters of the law. Furthermore, the lesser details appear to be matters of positive law. If Jesus made exceptions to positive law or to moral laws of lesser importance, this would not make him a situation ethicist.

Three parallel passages (Mt 9, 14–17; Mk 2, 18–22; Lk 5, 33–39) present the defense by Jesus of his disciples against the criticism that they failed to fast. Here Jesus is stating that the rightness of fasting depends upon the context. Few people suppose that there is an obligation to fast at all times and in all circumstances. One need not be an advocate of situation ethics to believe that there are times and circumstances when it is not obligatory to fast. Jesus here is simply spelling out certain circumstances in which it is appropriate to fast or not to fast. He is not making an exception to any law which would be upheld by serious moralists as universal in the sense of being binding at all times.

Two parallel passages (Mt 15, 1–20; Mk 7, 1–23) describe the criticism by the Pharisees and scribes that the disciples of Jesus did not wash their hands before eating food. In his defense Jesus does not advocate making exceptions to the rules such as those governing the washing of hands. He rejects the rules outright. Mark 7, 8 makes clear that the rules Jesus rejects are a merely human tradition.

There remain the texts concerning the sabbath rest. These texts can be divided into two groups. One group consists of three parallel passages (Mt 12, 1–8; Mk 2, 23–28; Lk 6, 1–5) concerning the disciples picking and eating corn on the sabbath. In these texts Jesus justifies making an exception to the law of sabbath rest because of need. According to Mark he enunciates the principle that the sabbath is made for man, not man for the sabbath.

Can these texts be used to support situation ethics? An argument might be made as follows: Jesus not only makes an exception to the sabbath law but implicitly appeals to the principle that laws are made to serve the good of persons, and when they fail to serve the good of persons one may make exceptions to them. Therefore one may make an exception to any moral law if in a particular situation it should prove that following the law does not serve the good of persons.

Jesus would be a situation ethicist only if he accepted two propositions: first, that moral laws are made to serve people and when they do not serve the good of people one may make exceptions to them; second, that in the case of all, or nearly all, moral laws, the observance of the law in some situations does not serve the good of persons. The text gives reason to suppose that Jesus accepted the first proposition. It gives no indication of whether or not he accepted the second. The fact that he thought that observance of the sabbath law in some cases does not serve the good of persons does not indicate that he thought the same to be true of all or nearly all moral laws.

A further point should be noted. Each of these three texts concludes with the statement of Jesus that the Son of Man is master of the sabbath. This suggests that here he is giving an interpretation based on his special authority as Son of Man. (Elsewhere in the Gospel Jesus assumes a special authority to interpret the law. See, for example, the Sermon on the Mount in Matthew, where he uses the formula: "You have heard that it was said. . . . But I say to you. . . .") It seems that the exceptions made by Jesus do not prove that he intended all people to take upon themselves the same responsibility in interpreting other laws.

A second group of texts describes healings by Jesus on the sabbath. In one text (Jn 9) Jesus offers no justification for his action. Other texts do give his justification: the cure of the man with the withered hand (Mt 12, 9–14; Mk 3, 1–6; Lk 6, 6–11); the healing of the dropsical man (Lk 14, 1–6); the healing of the crippled woman (Lk 13, 10–17). These texts do not prove that Jesus was a situation ethicist any more than do the texts about the disciples picking corn. It is clear that Jesus believes that following the letter of the law of sabbath rest in certain cases does not serve the good of people. These texts do not indicate that Jesus held the same to be true of all or nearly all moral laws.

In summary, although the Gospel texts picture Jesus as clearly opposing certain legalistic characteristics of some prominent Jews, they give no evidence that Jesus was a situation ethicist.

On the other hand, it is difficult to find in the New Testament an explicit rejection of situation ethics. For the most part, when the New

Testament lays down moral rules it does not state whether or not exceptions might be made to those rules.

In the absence of clear scriptural teaching, can ethical theory give us a basis for evaluating situation ethics?

D. Intrinsically Morally Good or Morally Evil Conduct

The term "conduct" here refers either to deliberate action or to deliberate omission. "Action" here includes not only externally observable actions but also actions which cannot be observed directly. Accordingly, acts of remembering, understanding or intending to do something are actions in this sense, and constitute conduct.

Conduct which is intrinsically morally good is conduct of a type which by its nature would be morally good in any situation. If conduct B is intrinsically morally good, then "B is always morally good" is a valid universal moral norm.

Conduct which is intrinsically morally evil is conduct of a type which by its nature would be morally evil in any situation. If conduct C is intrinsically morally evil, then "C is always morally evil" is a valid universal moral rule.

It is easy to establish universally valid moral rules by using tautologies. If one defines murder as immoral killing of a human being, then the rule "Murder is always morally evil" is certainly valid and universal. This rule, however, simply states that immoral killing is immoral and leaves the really significant task undone—i.e., discovering what types of killing of human beings are immoral.

Ethicists have pointed out that there are certain "purely formal" moral rules which bind universally. "Do not act unjustly" is an example of a purely formal moral rule. This rule does not by itself provide sufficient normative criteria to determine what is morally good or evil in a particular situation. Suppose that I must decide whether I shoud pay damages to my neighbor because in a windstorm a tree in my yard fell on his garage and caused considerable damage. The rule "Do not act unjustly," while undoubtedly correct and applicable to the case, does not provide a sufficient norm for a moral judgment. I need further criteria to determine what is just in this situation.

Many purely formal moral norms appear to be tautologies. Justice is commonly defined as giving to another his or her due. The term "due" here, if it is to give meaning to the definition, must mean something like "that which belongs to a person rightfully," or "that which one is bound to render to another." The rule "Do not act unjustly," therefore, means something like "Do to your neighbor that which is morally right to do to your neighbor."

Purely formal moral rules can be useful. These rules point generally to moral duties and encourage people. The fact that they do not provide sufficient normative criteria for judgments of conscience does not make them useless.

Are there universally valid moral rules, either purely formal or otherwise, which are not tautologies? In other words, are there intrinsically morally good classes of behavior, classes of behavior which can be defined without using the notion of moral goodness and which would be morally good in any possible situation? Are there intrinsically morally evil classes of behavior, classes of behavior which can be defined without using the notion of moral evil, and which would be morally evil in any possible situation?

At least a few moral rules can be defended as universally valid. "Do not prefer any created good to God" is one such rule. Any exception to this rule should be justified only by the attainment of some greater good or the avoidance of some greater evil. There is no greater good than God, however, and the greatest evil would be the loss of this infinite good.

Other moral rules which Christian ethicists generally would agree to be universally valid are: "Love God and love your neighbor with an *agape* form of love"; "Do not hate anyone with a hatred opposed to *agape*"; "Do not choose evil as an end." Other such rules might be cited.

The four universally valid moral rules we have just set down are not purely formal rules. Equipped simply with one of these rules and the knowledge of the relevant facts, one will have sufficient criteria for making certain important and far-reaching judgments of conscience.

Besides these rules which deal with very fundamental orientations of Christian life, there is another type of moral rule which is universally valid. This type of rule is formulated to apply only to quite specific situations. An example of such a rule is: "Other things being equal, when one must choose between causing the death of a human being and causing the death of an animal, one should cause the death of the animal." The phrase "other things being equal" specifies that the only two morally significant factors in the situation are the two specified in the rule. In the case of certain types of goods or evils, any instance of a good or evil of one particular type is greater than any instance of a good or evil of another particular type. For this reason, in situations in which these are the only morally significant factors, a moral rule can apply universally.

As we have seen, a few classes of behavior can be shown to be intrinsically morally good or intrinsically morally evil. This leads to a few moral rules which can be defended as universal. However, a large majority of the moral rules we commonly use in making judgments of conscience are not self-evidently universal nor can they be shown to be commonly accepted as universal. Must we say that for this large majority of moral rules, the situation ethics approach should be used?

E. Further Questions

Before trying to answer that question, a further analysis of the problem will be helpful. We will begin with an example of a general moral rule: "To kill a human being is immoral." Most ethicists would hold that there is an exception to this rule when the only way to preserve one's own life or the life of another is to take the life of an unjust attacker. Some might wish to allow exceptions in the case of punishment for certain crimes. Some would allow killing in war, even in some cases the killing of innocent people when this is an indirect, unintended effect of an attack on crucial military targets. To take account of these exceptions we can reformulate the rule: "Directly to kill an innocent human being is immoral." Here "innocent" does not refer to the general state of worthiness of the person, but indicates that the person is not an unjust attacker or guilty of a capital offense.

If one accepts this reformulated rule as universal, then one has not adopted a situation ethics approach in this area. If one holds that there are exceptions even to the reformulated rule, then several further questions can be asked.

Let us ask these further questions of a would-be situation ethicist, Mr. Smith. Who should make the exceptions? Should any adult individual be willing to make exceptions according to his or her own views? Would it be proper to make an exception only if some higher authority (a civil authority such as the police or the courts, or an ecclesiastical authority) judges that exceptions should be made? If Mr. Smith accepts this latter alternative, is he still a situation ethicist in this matter?

Perhaps we can judge whether Mr. Smith is a situation ethicist only if we know what criteria he would use in judging whether an exception should be made. First, whether it is an individual or some higher authority deciding about the exception, are the criteria used for making this decision formulated in a general way into sub-rules? (One could conceive of such sub-rules guiding police or courts or ecclesiastical authority.) If Mr. Smith believes that the criteria are formulated into sub-rules, then he is still not a situation ethicist in this area. True, he holds that there are exceptions to the rule when it is formulated as follows: "Directly to kill an innocent human being is immoral." However, one could reformulate the rule to include the sub-rules, and in that case the rule would be universal.

Perhaps, however, Mr. Smith believes that the criteria used in deciding whether to make exceptions are not formulated into general sub-rules. In that case, we can ask why they are not formulated into sub-rules. Could they be so formulated? Is it simply a matter that the sub-rules could be formulated but they would be so numerous and so complicated that it is not practical to formulate them, so we trust in people's judgment to make decisions according to these criteria although they have not yet been formulated into sub-rules? If Mr. Smith agrees that this is the case, is he being a situation ethicist in this area of killing of human beings? The answer to that, presumably, will depend on exactly what one means by "situation ethics."

Perhaps Mr. Smith adopts the other alternative, that the criteria for making exceptions could not be formulated in a general way, being quite unique to the particular case. Such an answer establishes Mr. Smith's credentials as a situation ethicist regarding this area of ethics. However, it leaves a further question. Are the criteria purely subjective, with no reference to an objective truth about the matter? If Mr. Smith believes this to be the case he is not only a situation ethicist but also an ethical relativist. As such he would run into the objections to ethical relativism laid down in Part One.[2]

Perhaps Mr. Smith believes that the criteria are not purely subjective. In that case, one final set of questions can be asked. Having used these criteria to decide to make an exception to the rule, would one be able to defend that decision in a convincing way before fair-minded people? If so, how is this possible if the criteria are not able to be stated in a general form? Alternatively, perhaps the criteria are so tied to individual insight that they do not admit of public discussion. If that is the case, is there any way of knowing whether or not they are purely subjective?

This chapter will not attempt to answer all of these questions in detail. However, the questions form a context for further analysis of the problem. It is ironic, perhaps, that situation ethics, which purports to lay such stress on the concrete situation, has often been discussed in abstraction from any thorough consideration of who decides to make an exception and how the criteria for such a decision are formulated or known.

F. Judgments of Conscience and Limitations of the Individual

Who is qualified to decide when exceptions to general moral rules should be made? A consideration of that question can begin with an examination of the limitations in the resources which individuals possess for making such decisions. Some of these limitations are found more or less commonly in all individuals. Other limitations are found only in some.

1. Knowledge of Facts

Frequently one's knowledge of the facts relevant to a judgment of conscience is quite inadequate. "Knowledge of facts" here involves not only familiarity with the phenomena but also an understanding and interpretation of them. In many cases even the resources of the whole of society put together will arrive at only a very imperfect knowledge of the facts.

One obvious area of ignorance of facts involves consequences. It is often said that the moral quality of an action depends upon its consequences. Normally, however, an action sets in motion a series of consequences, some predictable and some not, some immediate and some in the remote future, some localized in one or a few people and others bearing on society in general. No one merely human person can know all of the consequences of an action.

Frequently the knowledge of facts comes only from long experience. This is particularly true when the fact concerns the likely outcome of a type of behavior. An inexperienced army officer may suppose that a particular practice will lead to an enhancement of his authority among the troops. A more experienced officer may have learned that this is not true. The experience of some urban communities has shown that the building of expressways had not only the intended effect of moving more automobiles in a limited time, but also some unintended effects such as the erosion of the tax base for the maintenance of needed services in the core of the city.

Some kinds of facts, especially some kinds of consequences, can be known only after much intelligent research. Before deciding on the morality of capital punishment one should know the extent to which it is likely to deter crime. This knowledge is not available by casual observation or from unsystematic anecdotal evidence. Before introducing massive technological change into a "primitive" culture one should know what the likely effects will be. Even experts do not always agree about what the effects might be. Knowledge of the full societal effects of adultery, of various courtship patterns, of certain forms of entertainment, or of pornography is not easily available even to experts. At the present time it is questionable whether one could find general agreement even concerning the methods of research which would lead to adequate knowledge in these areas.

Ignorance of facts may involve failure to understand the phenomena which have been observed. One may observe a series of actions but fail to grasp that they constitute the exploitation of a person or a reversion to childish behavior or a refusal to face reality.

In summary, adequate knowledge of the facts relevant to a judgment of conscience frequently is very difficult to achieve.

2. *Knowledge of Norms*

In a conflict situation when one must decide about making an exception one may be guided by a rule which says that when value A conflicts with value B, value A prevails. Such an exception is not the stuff of situation ethics, since the decision follows a rule. Situation ethics enters when an exception is made without the guidance of a rule which determines the decision. In making exceptions in these cases one may follow the advice of someone else. This merely makes it someone else's problem. One may make the decision based on one's own appreciation of the goods or evils involved. This point is important: If a judgment of conscience does not follow a rule, the person making the judgment can base it only on his or her own appreciation of the goods or evils involved.

Parts One and Two have shown that our appreciation of goods and evils is always imperfect. None of our human appetites has been developed perfectly, and often we are far from properly assessing the importance of goods and evils. Not only is our appetitive development imperfect. To a greater or lesser extent, we are all prone to sin.

Often the goods and evils which conflict in a situation are incommensurable, at least according to our finite knowledge. That is, often we have no solid basis for saying which of several conflicting goods or evils is greater. For example, it may be impossible to say with solid reasons whether causing a certain intense emotional distress is a greater or a lesser evil than causing a physical ailment to go untreated for an extended time. It may be impossible to know whether it is better to improve the intellectual life of a community by spending on liberal arts education or to spend the money helping poor but not destitute people to live more comfortably.

3. Bias

"Bias" here refers to the tendency of a person who has knowledge of facts and norms to allow his or her practical judgment to be determined not by that knowledge but by some other factors. Usually one hides the irrational nature of this process by rationalizing—that is, by giving reasons (either facts or norms) to support a decision which really is held for non-rational reasons, while ignoring facts or norms which would discredit one's decision. Frequently the process of rationalizing is more successful at convincing the rationalizer than it is at convincing others.

Some factors produce bias in all or nearly all people. For example, all or almost all people tend to attach importance to things in direct proportion to the extent to which these things affect them personally. In assessing candidates for office and their policies, for example, people tend to attribute considerable importance to the fact that their own incomes have not kept up with the rate of inflation, and somewhat less importance to the fact that in other parts of the world people are starving. All or nearly all people tend to attach greater importance to things in the immediate future than to things which will happen only after a year or two. Our defense of our egos often causes bias. Through carelessness a worker allows his employer's equipment to be damaged but then makes the excuse that too much was being asked of him to attend to several things at once.

Many factors which cause bias are peculiar to particular people, or to people in particular moods. An angry mother may punish her child rather severely and justify it as being what the little brat needs. In a more mellow mood the next day she has rather different views of the needs of the child.

Such factors as social class, peer group, professional identity or economic status can cause bias in judgments. Politicians recognize this when they formulate their messages to particular groups.

The element of bias becomes particularly strong when there is vagueness concerning facts or norms. The vagueness allows us to fasten on certain facts or norms which support our predisposition and to ignore facts or norms less agreeable to that predisposition.

4. Traditional Moral Rules

Some moral rules which have been followed in the past receive considerable support in the present in spite of the fact that most people (perhaps nearly all) do not explicitly understand or appreciate the reasons for them. There may have been a time in the past when the factual and normative reasons for these rules were generally understood and appreciated. Some rules may embody intuition, learning from trial and error, and a sense of propriety without many people ever having reflected much upon or formulated the underlying reasons. Because these rules have been a part of a more or less integrated way of life, one must presume that they have served some purpose, even if that purpose is not obvious to many people today. These rules have stood the test of time, and this itself may constitute a sort of empirical evidence which may be almost impossible to find in any other way.

There is a tendency to discard moral rules as outdated or irrational if one does not understand and appreciate the reasons for them. To discard them, however, may be to discard valuable and perhaps irreplaceable wisdom based on long experience. This is not to say that traditional rules should never be discarded or modified. Simply evaluating such rules is an immensely difficult and sensitive task if it is to be done well.

G. Effects of Situation Ethics

In view of the limitations in the resources individuals possess for making judgments of conscience, we can reasonably expect that if people begin to act "on their own" in making exceptions to general moral rules, their decisions are likely to reflect their own subjective pre-dispositions rather than objective truth. But are people left to their own resources in making exceptions? When making judgments of conscience people constantly use factual and normative information supplied by others. Can they not use help from others when making exceptions to general moral rules?

They can. However, much of the help which society gives to individuals for making moral judgments is given in the form of general moral rules. Knowing and following the rule, the individual often does not have sophisticated knowledge of the facts and appreciation of the values which lie behind the rule. Once one considers making an exception to the rule, however, one must depend on one's own knowledge of facts and appreciation of values, and help in this area is often not easily obtained.

In some cases no one in the society has adequate knowledge of the facts or appreciation of the values relevant to a particular judgment of conscience. It may be that the consequences are very unpredictable, for example, or there may be a conflict of two incommensurable values. One might be tempted to say that in such cases any isolated individual would be well equipped as anyone else to decide about an exception. In theory this is true. In practice, however, the isolated individual is likely to focus on certain facts or values, to take these as *the* relevant facts and values, and to act as though he had adequate knowledge. This is a weakness not of uneducated people only, but of some professional ethicists.

For example, individual A sees individual B suffering from an apparently incurable and painful disease. Individual A wonders whether an exception should be made here to the general rule against killing persons. Having left behind the guidance of the general law, he must make this decision based on his own knowledge of the facts and appreciation of the values. In truth, no one with whom he might consult knows enough about the factors in the situation to judge whether it is better for an individual to live or to die. However, certain aspects of the case, the pain and the unlikelihood of recovery, strike individual A forcefully. He takes these to be the relevant factors and acts as though he had adequate knowledge.

In other cases some people in a society may have more or less adequate knowledge of the facts or values relevant to a judgment of conscience. Often, however, it is difficult for this knowledge to become available to a person trying to decide about making an exception to a law.

Consider first the knowledge of facts. A refugee is traveling through unfriendly territory. He can reasonably presume that most of the local residents are not willing to help him. If he steals from them he will be able, with luck, to get along without suffering from hunger, and within several weeks he will cross the border into friendlier territory. The alternative to stealing is begging. This will very probably provide him with enough food to survive, but he is likely to suffer from hunger and his progress toward the border will be slower. The people in the area are undergoing a food shortage because of the war. Is he morally justified in stealing from people things which he can reasonably judge they are unwilling to give?

Society provides the generally accepted norm that one should not take from people what they are unwilling to give. Society also sanctions at least one general exception to this rule. It sanctions taking property when it is the only way to save one's life, so long as disproportionate harm is not done to the people from whom one steals. The case of the refugee does not fall under this general exception. His seems to be a borderline case, as far as generally formulated societal rules are concerned, so he must use his own resources in deciding whether to make an exception to the general rule.

Certain general facts are relevant to this judgment of conscience. What are the societal effects of people taking property according to their own judgment about whether it is right or wrong? Perhaps some people in the world have knowledge about this, but our refugee is going to have difficulty getting that information, even if he has access to a well-stocked library and two or three weeks to sort out and compare the different views. Certain particular facts are relevant. What are his chances of not reaching the border if he must slow down in order to beg? On this point he may be as good a judge as anyone available. How much will this family suffer if he steals one of their chickens? A good estimate might be forthcoming from the mistress of the household, but she is not likely to be consulted. Factual knowledge, even if someone possesses it, often is not easily available to a particular individual when he or she needs it.

In most cases people will not spend a long time learning all of the relevant facts. An "objective" study of the facts may not even be considered as a duty or as a real possibility. People will simply base their judgments on facts which at the time seem important to them.

With regard to help from others concerning values, any general knowledge concerning values is communicated in the form of general rules. Once one goes beyond the rules to judge whether exceptions should be made to them, one foregoes any further help of a general nature. Help concerning particular values in a case is available by consultation. An advisor with a well-developed appreciation of values can give opinions concerning the relative importance of the particular goods and evils in a situation. Some help is available too in the discussion by moralists of typical cases. Such a discussion can give one a better feeling for how to judge similar cases.

To sum up, help from others concerning facts and norms often is only partially successful in countering the tendency to follow one's own subjective predispositions rather than objective truth when one makes exceptions to moral rules. Because of this, in society as a whole the practice of making exceptions to a rule can erode both observance of the rule and appreciation of the value which lies behind the rule, and can lead to improperly subjective judgments which may cause serious harm to individuals.

What is involved here is the social learning of morals. Not only do children learn their moral principles from others; adults as well, to a great extent, learn to follow the prevailing rules of a society. For example, the changing of laws concerning abortion and its legal acceptance, along with recent advocacy by certain groups, has been enough to create a very different climate of opinion on that subject. One of the main ways in which social learning of morals takes place is through the prominence given to certain moral rules. Once exceptions according to an individual's private judgment are seen as legitimate, and the number of exceptions increases, individuals may cease to take seriously the value behind the rule.

One might object that exceptions will erode a rule only if the exceptions are not legitimate. If the original rule is based on a legitimate value, and the exceptions are made only when they are justified, then the observance of the rule will not be eroded.

The question, of course, is how we can assure that the exceptions will be limited to those which are justified. A further question concerns the criteria by which we might judge whether an exception is justified or not. If these criteria are stated in general terms, then we are not concerned with situation ethics but with refinements of the original rule. If the criteria are not stated in general terms, then the erosion is likely to take place.

In certain crucial matters the erosion of observance of a rule becomes a matter not only of bad moral decisions but of violations of justice and even a breakdown in society. Human beings bear within themselves not only the resources for generosity and kindness but also a tendency to sin. Most of us are not so much virtuous as civilized. That is, our observance of certain crucial rules in living together is based less on profound nobility of character than on conformity to prevailing mores because of peer pressure and a sense of shame in doing what is disapproved by others.

Our tendency to sin, to meanness, hatred, etc., normally causes a great deal of suffering among those with whom we live, and results in failure to reach full human potential. However, so long as people more or less unquestioningly accept certain rules and structures, civilized life remains possible. So long as certain rules of respect for life are observed in a society, then even unvirtuous people usually do not express their sinfulness in killing. So long as certain principles governing family life are observed, even people who are ungenerous in many ways will continue to expend energy on the good of their children, and to that extent they provide for the good life of those who follow them. Once they begin to question these rules and structures, and to make the observance of them conditional upon their own dispositions, grave injustices and perhaps atrocities and a breakdown in society will follow.

The notion that our safety and the welfare of society is assured by the moral quality of the population is an illusion, and a dangerous one. It makes us think that ''those kinds of things couldn't happen here'' because we are not that kind of people. It can even cause us to refuse to admit an atrocity is present when it does appear. After all, we are good people, and if we allow abortion, then abortion can't be that bad, can it?

The argument here is not that people are uniformly or basically evil. The argument is that human beings who are both prone to sin and capable of heroic virtue need more or less unquestioning conformity to certain basic principles if society is to operate in a way conducive to justice and human growth.

Accordingly, a special concern to situation ethicists should be the effects of that practice on the attachment of people to certain structures and rules which confine the more sinful tendencies of people and allow their more generous tendencies to prevail in certain critical areas of life.

Possible effects of situation ethics can be suggested by the history of the just war theory. The Catholic Church in a sense has adopted a situation ethics stance on the question of war. The prevailing teaching on war in the Church has been that in certain situations a war may be just and morally permissible. Theologians have insisted that for a war to be just, certain conditions must be present. However, some of these conditions seem to have been sufficiently vague to allow a variety of conflicting views in particular situations. The historical effects are revealing.

Though the New Testament does not explicitly condemn all war, there is no doubt that the general spirit of the New Testament is against violence of this kind.[3] Jesus insists on forgiveness of those who have offended, on loving one's enemies, on turning the other cheek when offended. Paul even criticizes certain Christians for bringing others to court to assert their rights. The early Christians seem generally to have interpreted the New Testament in a pacifist way. Gradually, however, pressure grew to allow Christians to go to war. Some soldiers who converted to Christianity in the earliest times felt it necessary to leave the army, and some were persecuted for their failure to fight. As more and more of the Roman Empire became Christian however, the notion grew that defending the empire against barbarian invasions was a good work and a proper work for Christians. When the Emperor Constantine himself opted for Christianity he was far from supposing that this required him to lay down his arms and surrender to his enemies within or outside of the empire. In fact it appears that he considered his victory in an important battle to be due to his fighting under the sign of the cross.

Various Church Fathers discussed the question of whether and why Christians might wage war. St. Augustine's resolution of the problem is more convincing than most. He argued that if Christians are not allowed to go to war a sort of international outlawry results. If those who are intent on a just way of life are not allowed to defend themselves against the vicious, then the vicious will have their way in society. The innocent will be killed or persecuted, the products of hard work and intelligent planning will be plundered, destroyed or stolen, and a civilized life will be impossible. If states intent on a just way of life may not defend themselves against unjust attack, the same results follow on an international scale.

Pacifism is a wonderful ideal, but a simple-minded attempt to implement it in our sinful world will give rise to terrible consequences.

Augustine's is as effective a situationist argument as has been made on this point. The theory itself is not based on a biased selection of some norms or facts while ignoring others. In the absence of precise and certain knowledge of the consequences, a good case can still be made that in the long run the consequences of never going to war (domination of society by the most vicious, etc.) are worse than the consequences of the use of war as a last resort.

In spite of an apparently sound theory, an obviously wrong practice has resulted. In innumerable wars Christians on both sides have been convinced that their own side is justified. In reality, at best only one side can be in the right. Because each side has judged the case in a subjective way, the theory is unable to control war in practice. The recent clash between England and Argentina over the Falkland Islands is an example of how both sides, and Christians on both sides, judge their own cause to be just. So common did wars become under this theory of the just war that gradually Christians lost the whole non-violent spirit of the Gospel, and have in some centuries reintroduced the notion of the Holy War, a notion which owes nothing to the Gospels.

If people, including responsible leaders, and including well-meaning and virtuous people, have been rather consistently deceived on so serious and terrible a matter as war, it seems naive to suppose that they will usually be more objective regarding lesser issues.

In conclusion, situation ethics in practice leads to judgments of conscience which reflect people's own subjective pre-dispositions rather than objective truth. Must we, therefore, reject completely the position of situation ethics? Is the only reliable solution to follow the general moral rules in all cases? Such a position has at least one intrinsic difficulty. Following general moral rules can lead sometimes to erroneous judgments of conscience. A situation may be such that following a particular general moral rule will lead to serious harm to persons, harm which could be prevented by a prudent exception to the law.[4]

We need ways of allowing for exceptions when they are needed while at the same time avoiding, as far as possible, the bad effects of making exceptions. There are such ways, some of which are already in use both in the Church and in secular society.

H. Making Responsible Exceptions to General Moral Rules

1. Public Defensibility

A moral judgment is publicly defensible in the sense intended here when a group of impartial and informed judges with a better than average ability to appreciate the relative importance of goods and evils would generally agree, upon hearing the defense, that the judgment does not merely express the subjective pre-dispositions of the subject, and that it is at least plausible that it is the objectively correct judgment. For public defensibility we do not require that one be able to convince all such judges that the decision is certainly correct. This would require the kind of certitude which often is not possible in judgments of conscience.

Publicly defensible exceptions are more likely to reflect objective truth and less likely to reflect mere subjective dispositions than are exceptions which are not publicly defensible. Accordingly, exceptions which are publicly defensible are less likely to erode social awareness of certain values than are exceptions which are not publicly defensible.[5]

How can we help assure that judgments of conscience are publicly defensible? Public defensibility is assured primarily by actual public discussion and debate. One could conceive of this happening in the form of a public discussion on the rightness of a particular judgment of conscience. However, in order to grasp how public defensibility is assured in unusual situations, we should begin by looking at how it takes place first of all on the level of general rules.

Consider the general rule: "To kill a human being is immoral." This rule can be publicly defended as generally valid (not necessarily as universally valid). That is, in a public discussion, convincing reasons can be given in support of this rule. As in any rational public argument, resolution of the issue is sought by searching for some commonly accepted principles or starting points from which one can demonstrate that one or other conclusion is correct.[6]

It is generally conceded that there are exceptions to the general rule: "To kill . . . is immoral." However, we do not at this point turn the matter over to an individual's private judgment to make whatever exceptions he or she deems fitting. Rather we make sub-rules to cover exceptions, and these sub-rules, general in form, can in turn be publicly discussed and their public defensibility ascertained. One sub-rule would allow killing of an unjust attacker when that is the only way to save one's own life or the lives of others. Other sub-rules allowing exceptions in the cases of capital punishment or a "just war" might get considerable support but be less publicly defensible than the first sub-rule mentioned. The sub-rules themselves may, after discussion, be found to be too general, and more refined formulations will be made.

To this point, the rules and sub-rules are general in form, and their public defensibility is ascertained by ethical arguments about the correctness of general formulations. Beginning with the most general rules, one adds rules which are still general in form, but less general, applicable to narrower classes of cases.

At some point, however, this effort to give more particular but still general rules must end. It may be that at a certain point it would be possible to give further general rules which are even more particular, but the effort becomes impractical. As the rules become more numerous, applying to narrower classes of cases, active public debate of so many rules may be extremely time-consuming, and the rules become so numerous that no normal citizen is likely to learn them. At a certain point one may go beyond all generalities and one is confronted by two concrete, particular alternatives and no available general rule resolves the issue.

At this point, in the matter of killing human beings, we still do not turn the matter over entirely to the private judgment of the individual. In our society there is public scrutiny in any such case. Sometimes the public scrutiny comes before the action, as when police may be authorized in some situations to shoot to kill when necessary to protect the lives of others. In other cases the public scrutiny follows the action. An individual in an urgent case may kill to save life, but such conduct, if it beomes known, is reviewed by the police, and if there is doubt concerning whether it falls within publicly accepted norms, it will be reviewed by the courts. Little is left to private judgment in this area. Similarly, many matters of property, bodily harm and the preservation of one's good reputation are subject to public legislation, scrutiny and control.

We would not want public legislation, scrutiny and control in every area of morality. However, in every area of morality, if we want objective and correct moral judgments, we must have some means to assure public defensibility.

On the level of general rules and sub-rules, this public defensibility was the purpose of the casuist tradition in Roman Catholic moral theology. By the discussion of cases the casuists tried to elaborate rules, sub-rules and types of exceptions in a publicly defensible way. They brought into the domain of public disputation the whole matter of exceptions to general moral rules. In that discussion authors criticized each other's opinions, drew on insights of past and present experts, passed on the accumulated practical wisdom of a tradition, and tested their own opinions in a community of scholarship.

The practice of casuistry in the Roman Catholic Church has to some extent acquired a bad reputation. It has been accused of hair-splitting about trivialities while losing sight of the basic themes of Christian life. It has been accused of bad ethical theory. Some of the criticism has been deserved. However, the effort of casuists to give people extensive and publicly defensible help in making judgments of conscience is praiseworthy and important.

On the level of particular judgments of conscience, public defensibility can be assured in a large majority of cases insofar as these cases fall more or less clearly within general rules and sub-rules which are publicly defensible. Unusual cases, however, may seem to fall outside of the available general rules and sub-rules or require exceptions to them. Even in such cases there are methods to help assure public defensibility of judgments of conscience. One method involves the discussion by experts of typical cases. Such discussions may suggest solutions for similar cases in real life. A second and very important method is consultation with prudent people who can give objective and informed opinions concerning the moral quality of particular actions in particular situations.

2. The Direct-Indirect Distinction

In some cases an evil may be be foreseen and result from a deliberate choice and is intended either for its own sake or as a means to some further result. According to the terminology used in this section, such an evil is said to be done directly. In some cases an evil results from one's deliberate choice but it is not intended either for its own sake or as a means to some further effect. Even if such an evil is foreseen, according to our terminology it is said to be done indirectly. [7]

It is sometimes said that the end does not justify the means, or that one may not do evil as a means to a good end. In our terminology, this

would mean that one may not directly do evil. This notion has been incorporated into the principle of double effect in Roman Catholic moral
theology. According to that principle, one may cause an evil effect only
if certain conditions are fulfilled. One such condition is that the evil must
not be used as a means to the intended good.[8]

In order to evaluate this statement that one may not cause an evil as
a means to a good end, we must consider more precisely what type of
evil is being considered. There seems to be no reason to believe that the
formulators of the principle of double effect were speaking of moral evil.
Were they speaking of moral evil, it is difficult to see how they would
be willing to allow the causing of evil in certain situations. Indeed, the
purpose of the principle of double effect is to help one decide what is the
morally good or morally evil alternative. Were it speaking of moral evil,
it would presume that one had already decided what was morally evil
before using the principle.

Certainly from the point of view of the moral theory presented in
this book the principle of double effect would make no sense if the evil
in question were either objective moral evil or subjective moral evil. Objective moral evil in any situation, as we have defined it, is evil reckoned
with a view to the whole of what is good or evil for a person. In any
situation, therefore, in deciding what is morally evil one would already
have considered any good ends intended and any evil means or other evils
which would result. It makes no sense to add another rule specifying when
this moral evil may or may not be caused. Subjective moral evil is the
choice of what one judges to be objectively morally evil. Subjective moral
evil presumes a judgment about what is objectively morally evil. Having
made that judgment, it makes no sense to introduce a further rule specifying under what conditions one may not cause a subjective moral evil
(i.e., specifying under what conditions one may not do what one judges
to be objectively morally evil) and under what conditions one may cause
subjective moral evil.

The evil considered by the principle of double effect, therefore, must
be a pre-moral evil. In that case, however, the principle ceases to be valid
in a considerable number of cases, according to common opinion. For
example, if the only way to save a person's life is to cause a person some
pain and disability by amputating an arm (a pre-moral evil) this is justified. If the least drastic way of training a child to behave properly includes
an occasional spanking, again this pre-moral evil is justified.

As stated without qualification, therefore, the notion that one may never do evil as a means to a good end does not hold according to the ethical theory presented in this book. This does not mean that we can ignore the matter. A notion which has engaged the attention of serious moralists over a considerable period of time is likely to have some basis in reality. What follows is an attempt to incorporate what seems to be that basis in reality into the ethical theory presented in this book.

First, when there is solid evidence that the good to be achieved is greater or more important than the pre-moral evil which is used as a means, and other things are equal, one may cause the pre-moral evil as a means to the good.[9] (In the expression "as a means to the good" we include cases when the means is used to avoid another evil, since the avoidance of evil can be seen as a good.) This in fact is the practice generally approved both by secular and Roman Catholic ethics, at least in very many cases. It makes sense according to the ethical theory of this book. The moral good is what is good reckoned with a view to the whole of what is good for a person. A use of a pre-moral means to achieve a greater good contributes to the whole of what is good for the person, and therefore is morally good. In accordance with this rule, one may amputate a hand to save a person from greater pain and disability later.

Second, when there is solid evidence that the good to be achieved is less than, or less important than, the evil which is used as a means, and other things are equal, one may not cause the pre-moral evil as a means to the good. This in fact is the practice generally approved both by secular and Roman Catholic ethics. It makes sense according to the ethical theory of this book. To use a greater evil to produce a lesser good detracts from the whole of what is good for a person, and therefore is morally evil.

There remains a third category of cases, those in which there is no solid evidence that the good intended is greater or less than the evil used as a means.[10] This may be because the good and the evil appear to be equal in importance. It may be because of ignorance of facts. For example, one may be so uncertain about the actual results of a course of action that one does not know whether the good intended and achieved will be greater or less than the evil used as a means. In still other cases the lack of solid evidence is the result of lack of knowledge of norms. Even after one's best effort to weigh alternatives, it may be impossible to judge whether a particular good is greater or less than a particular evil.

Certain goods or evils are incommensurable, at least according to our imperfect appreciation of goods and evils.

In cases in this third category one should not cause evil as a means to the good.

At first glance, this rule may seem to be unjustifiable. If there is no solid evidence one way or the other, then in acting one is as likely to cause more good than evil as the contrary. Such being the case, the action seems to be morally neutral, and one should be allowed to act.

However, if in cases in this third category we cause evil as a means to a good end, we produce a further evil, the erosion of the moral quality of life and action. This further evil is the reason why it is wrong in these cases to cause an evil as a means to good. The meaning of "erosion of the moral quality of life" should become clear as our discussion progresses.

This erosion of the moral quality of life and of action occurs on two levels, on the level of the individual and on the level of society.

We will begin with the individual level. Suppose that a person follows the practice of causing pain in situations in which it is not clear whether this pain accomplishes a good which outweighs the evil of the means. Some cases of torture to get valuable information or of punishment to secure a reform of behavior could fall into this category. (Normally this category would not include situations in which painful operations are used to secure a cure of a disease, because the pain, while it accompanies the means, is not the means to the cure.) Given the imperfection of our knowledge both of facts and of values, such situations are likely to be quite frequent. Particularly among irascible and impatient people, but also for average people under pressure, there will be a tendency to act according to one's pre-dispositions at the time and to become less sensitive to the evil character of causing pain. One's character is thereby affected. Partly this is because we tend to be biased and to rationalize decisions which are less than admirable. Even apart from bias and rationalization, the very act of directly causing evil forms one's character. Causing pain to others makes us less sensitive to the evil of causing pain. Telling untruths forms us into untruthful people. Pursuit of sexual pleasure outside of a particular context makes one sexually undisciplined.

There is a type of situation in which the preceding argument does not apply. In *some* cases in which the evil means is suffered by oneself and is clearly and vividly recognized as a loss to oneself, the use of an evil means to accomplish a good (which is not clearly greater or less than the evil) would not erode the moral quality of life. If one assumes a painful burden to relieve another of some evil which is not clearly greater or less than the evil of the burden assumed, such an action is not likely to erode the moral quality of life. This seems to be implicitly recognized in the common attitude of approval of people when they assume such burdens. When the evil to oneself is not clearly and vividly recognized as a loss to oneself, however, the use of the evil means in such cases will erode the moral quality of life. For example, if the evil one assumes is a loss of freedom which one does not immediately recognize as important, then the use of such an evil means to achieve a good which is not clearly greater or less than the evil of the means would erode the moral quality of life.

We have discussed how the direct causing of evil, even for a good purpose, forms our characters by forming dispositions or habits. There is another factor in the erosion of the moral quality of life and action which can result. Often even a single action, even if no habit is formed, can constitute a person in some sense as a particular kind of person. If one fails to live up to a commitment to a friend, even for a good reason, and even if one does it only once, one in some sense becomes a betrayer. One who commits adultery once, even intending some good effect, must still see himself marked by infidelity, at least if he has any strong sense of fidelity. One act of prostitution, even if the money earned is intended for a good cause such as paying the rent, still marks a person as a prostitute. This argument does not by itself prove that all such acts are immoral in every situation. It is simply an argument that a person is marked by the actions he does. To the evil of the means considered in its immediate context, therefore, we must add this erosion of the moral quality of life and action.

By being "marked" by an action I do not mean any social stigma, nor any enduring quality of character. (The latter has been discussed in preceding pages.) I mean that by a certain kind of human action one constitutes oneself as a person of a particular kind for the very moment of the action. There is no inner being of the responsible person which is constituted solely by the good intentions toward the end and is immune to the quality of the means chosen to achieve the end.

The erosion of the moral quality of life and of action occurs also on the level of society. Our moral beliefs and behavior are greatly influenced by our human milieu. If the quality of life is eroded on the individual

level, people see their peers acting with little appreciation for particular
moral qualities. Children see their elders acting against certain values as
a commonplace practice; and there is no particular sentiment against it
because, after all, you usually don't know whether or not the evil of the
means is justified by the good intended. In such a society, progress in
appreciation of the higher and more noble values is not likely to be fostered. The appreciation of the most truly human values involves discipline
and the formation of character over an extended period. Where sexual
relations are sanctioned whenever it is not clear that the good achieved
is less than the evil involved in the means (considered in its immediate
context), few people will come to appreciate the full meaning of sexual
fidelity. When stealing is allowed without censure whenever it is not clear
that the evil outweighs the good, respect for property is not likely to flourish. When killing is allowed on the basis of one's ignorance of whether
it is better or worse in the long run for a person to be dead or alive, not
many lives will be safe.

To summarize, when there is no solid evidence whether the good
intended is greater or less than the evil used as a means (that evil being
considered in its immediate context), if one proceeds to cause the evil,
one produces another evil, the erosion of the moral quality of life and
action. This erosion is the reason why, in such cases, we must refrain
from causing the evil means.

If this erosion of the moral quality of life occurs in this third category
of cases would it not occur also in cases when evil is done as a means to
a greater good? The answer is that erosion does occur in such cases. In
some cases this erosion is a sufficiently serious matter that one should
refrain from causing the evil means, even if that evil, considered in its
immediate context, is not so great as the good which is intended. Our rule
was that when the good intended is greater than the evil of the means
considered in its immediate context, one may cause the evil if other things
are equal. Now we are saying that, in some cases at least, other things
will not be equal, because of the erosion of the moral quality of life and
action.

It should be noted, however, that when the good outweighs the evil
of the means, this normally reduces, if it does not always eliminate, the
erosion of the moral quality of life. One who takes the property of others
only when it is clear and publicly defensible that the good achieved
outweighs the evil of the means does not constitute himself a thief

and is unlikely, by that kind of act, to become insensitive to property rights.

We have discussed situations in which one may or may not directly cause an evil as a means. Might the same conditions apply to causing evil indirectly? That is, may one cause an evil only if there is solid evidence that the good results outweigh the evil results? Does it really make any difference whether an evil is caused directly or indirectly? To many, the distinction between direct and indirect causing of evil seems to be insignificant, and its use in Catholic moral theology to be more hindrance than help.

However, the direct-indirect distinction should not be so easily set aside, for two complementary reasons. First, although the indirect causing of evil may in some instances erode the moral quality of life and action (and in such cases this erosion must be balanced with other factors in making a moral judgment), yet this erosion is not built into the indirect causing of evil. Suppose, for example, that a doctor gives a patient a drug to ease pain, not knowing whether in the long run more good than evil results will follow. The moral quality of his life and action are not shaped so much by the evil he causes indirectly as by the good he causes directly.

There could be exceptions to the conclusion drawn in the previous paragraph. When the good caused directly is to oneself, and is immediately and vividly appreciated as good, and the evil result is an evil to others, or is an evil to oneself that one does not vividly appreciate as evil, the element of bias and rationalization might enter and erode the moral quality of life. In such cases one might be justified in acting only if special precautions are taken to assure that one's decision is publicly defensible.

There is a second reason why the direct-indirect distinction should not be set aside. If we were to apply to the indirect causing of evil the same restrictions as we apply to the direct causing of evil, we would be practically paralyzed in decision making in many areas of action. Given the limitations in our knowledge of facts and norms, frequently we do not know whether a course of action will cause more evil than good in the long run. A father moves to a certain city to get a better job and give greater financial security to his family, but he risks his health because of the air pollution in that city. In taking care of the health needs of a sick member of the family, parents jeopardize the family finances. Were we not allowed to act in favor of the proximate good in such situations, in fact, the moral quality of our lives would be harmed.

In many cases, therefore, the direct-indirect distinction is relevant in determining whether one may cause evil. Concerning the indirect causing of evil the following rules seem to be defensible. When there is solid evidence that the evil indirectly caused by one's action is greater than the good achieved, one may not cause the evil. When there is solid evidence that the evil indirectly caused by the action is less than the good achieved, one may cause the evil. When there is no solid evidence whether the evil indirectly caused by one's action is greater or less than the good achieved, considering the evil more or less in its immediate context, (see note 10 in this chapter) one may cause the evil unless for some special reason such a choice will erode this quality of moral life. The point here is that in the indirect causing of evil considered as such there is no built-in tendency to erode the quality of moral life, but such erosion may occur because of the special factors present in the case.

3. Goods and Evils Considered Concretely

We have considered how the direct causing of evil may be significantly different from the indirect causing of evil. We turn now to an aspect in the weighing of goods and evils more generally.

Some people in trying to consider goods and evils concretely in fact consider them only in their immediate context, and thereby miss something important. We may call this a false concrete consideration of goods and evils. It considers the goods or evils as particular, but it considers them in abstraction from factors important for their proper evaluation.

For example, a man and woman live together and raise a family in a loose, quasi-marital relationship. They say that their relationship helps them and causes no harm to others. However, in judging what is helpful or harmful they depend mainly on their immediate experience. This causes them to neglect certain relevant factors. What effect do such unions have on family life and the training of children? A plausible hypothesis has been put forward that the main reason why certain people become trapped in ghettos and unable to cope with many aspects of modern life is precisely the failure of many families such as this to raise children properly. Another sort of inquiry might show that this type of relationship makes it unlikely that people will grow in appreciation of fidelity. Our point here is not to try to prove in a few lines that such relationships are wrong. Our point is that a certain kind of concrete consideration of goods and evils by considering only the immediate context can fail to consider relevant factors.

Several factors can lead to a false concrete consideration of goods and evils. For example, one may fail to consider all of the results of an action. Such results include the effect on the character of the person and the effects on society, especially the effect of creating a milieu and of helping people to learn or to fail to learn to appreciate certain values.

A false concrete consideration of goods and evils may result because one considers actions outside of the contexts which give them meaning. The significance of an act of generous loyalty or an act of betrayal can be understood only in the context of the long-term friendship of the two persons involved. The significance of an act of adultery can be understood only in relation to the long-term personal relationship of the spouses and to the still wider context of the role of the family in society.

A false concrete consideration of goods and evils may result from the failure to recognize the root cause of a problem. A factory worker feels dissatisfied with his job. The personnel officer pacifies him by making certain concessions, changing his working conditions slightly, and giving him more free time. The solution seems to be admirably concrete because it deals with this person's feelings at this time. However, precisely by focusing only on those feelings, the "solution" really hides the fact that the work is really dehumanizing and a much more radical change is needed.

Aspects of the false concrete evaluation of goods and evils can be seen in the matter of telling the truth or telling an untruth. A situation ethics approach would hold that in certain situations in which harm would follow from telling the truth or remaining silent, telling a falsehood is not only morally permissible but obligatory. In each case in deciding whether to tell a falsehood one must weigh the evil against the harm that would follow from an alternative course of action. The question arises: How does one weigh the evil of telling a falsehood? Is the weight to be calculated by one's awareness of damage done by the falsehood? Or are other aspects to be considered?

One aspect in evaluating the importance of telling the truth and the evil of falsehood is the role in human life of knowing the truth. As intelligent beings, the fundamental meaning of our lives is to know the truth. To be deceived, to live in an illusory world, contradicts the very meaning of being intellectual beings. Were illusion as good as truth ("so long as they are happy'') then madness would be equal to sanity; absurdity and making sense would have the same value.

A second aspect in evaluating truth telling and falsehood is the importance of communication in human life. Communication, especially by speech, has obvious practical importance in achieving goals and functioning smoothly in society. Beyond this, communication is fundamental to all interpersonal life. Equally important with communication is the trust which allows people to receive any communication for what it is.

We have spoken in general terms of the significance of knowing the truth, of communication and trust. A certain kind of situation ethicist would be quite impatient with this general and "abstract" consideration. After all, he would insist, in telling a falsehood one has not destroyed all truth, communication and trust.

One must grant this latter point. One might want to point out, however, that if one has not first grasped the fundamental nature of knowing the truth, of communication and trust in human life, one can hardly evaluate the importance of telling a falsehood.

A further question arises. Our particular type of situation ethicist seems, by implication, to have divided truth-telling into parts. He seems to have offered certain parts of it for a price, supposing apparently that the rest remains intact. Do truth and truth-telling admit of such division? Are truth and truth-telling composed of individual parts which added together form a total? Can one give up to two percent of the truth and keep ninety-eight percent intact? If one tells falsehoods in ten percent of the cases, does ninety percent of truth and truth-telling remain intact?

Whether or not such a division of truth and of truth-telling is possible in theory, it certainly will be difficult in practice. Let us begin with an example. Was the Richard Nixon camp justified in telling falsehoods about the Watergate break-in? A number of situation ethicists would be impatient at the mention of this example. They would remind us that in allowing falsehood in certain cases they are not intending to sanction every sort of shoddy and self-serving deceit.

However, let us look more closely at the case. *From the point of view of the Nixon camp,* the incumbent president was more intelligent, more experienced, less naive, than his opponent in the presidential election. The re-election of the president was extremely important, perhaps crucial for stability in the world and the maintenance of freedom. They had, from their point of view, excellent reasons for false speech.

One may disagree with their assessment. What does this mean, however, about the morality of falsehood? Does it mean that false speech is all right when it is done by us, but not all right when those others do it? Does it mean that falsehood is all right if one is not biased? Who then would qualify as proper speakers of falsehood? Or does it mean in this case that one can conceive of oneself being the victim of false speech, and this gives one an unusually objective and therefore less lenient view of the practice?

The problem is not simply that people are biased and nasty and are liable to abuse a good thing (i.e., the making of exceptions). The problem is that the criteria for measuring the evil of speaking falsely against the other goods and evils in such cases are vague and inevitably decisions are shaped by the subjective dispositions of the decision makers. The criteria for moral judgment cease to be publicly defensible.[11]

Our discussion of truth and falsehood has not included the dimension of social milieu and the learning of values. If falsehood for a good reason is morally justified in certain cases, either one should set forth those cases in the form of further rules (which would not be a situationist approach) or one should admit that it is up to individuals to decide. If this latter is the case, we must get rid of any sense of shame or blame about speaking falsely simply because in following one's own judgment about false speech one acts contrary to the judgment of another. In such an atmosphere it would be difficult to cultivate a strong devotion to telling the truth.

Another example may bring out another aspect to be considered in evaluating false speech. Would it be all right for Catholic historians to write false history in order to hide certain less than edifying episodes in the lives of certain highly placed members of the clergy? The reason would be the very great good of avoiding scandal to some persons, with possible great spiritual loss. Or should we not say, as a recent Pope has said, that God has no need of our falsehood? And if not here, precisely where might God have need of our false speech?[12]

The point is not merely rhetorical. Every Christian, in pursuing particular goals, is called to be God's instrument in building his Kingdom, and the Christian is not supposed to pursue any goals apart from the Kingdom of God. Are there certain means which are effective in bringing about important goods, means which in isolation seem not to cause very great harm, but which are not apt means for one who is God's instrument in building the Kingdom? There are certain goals very attractive in themselves which can only be attained by the use of such means. Must one not say of some ends, this victory in battle, that satisfaction of human need, that if they can be attained only by such means, then they must not be part of the Kingdom of God, even in the imperfect and incomplete form that Kingdom takes on this earth while we await the return of the Lord?

4. Practically Exceptionless Norms

Section D of this chapter considered certain moral rules which apply universally, without exceptions. To see that these rules apply universally it is sufficient to know the meaning of the terms and to relate the rules to the basic truths of moral life. In this section we will consider another type of universal moral rule, the practically exceptionless moral rule. There are certain classes of behavior which in theory in certain cases might be morally good, but, given the actual state of our knowledge of moral norms and facts, the rules forbidding such behavior should be treated in practice as universal. To see that these rules admit of no exceptions it is not sufficient to know the meaning of the terms and to relate the rules to the basic truths of moral life. It is necessary also to understand these rules in relation to the actual state of our knowledge of moral norms and facts.

There are several categories of practically exceptionless rules. The first category consists of rules which fulfill both of two conditions. First, they forbid the causing of a particular kind of evil. Second, although in theory the evil in question in some cases may be less than the good produced, in fact because of the limitations in human knowledge we can never know this.[13] The point has been made earlier that one may never do an evil as a means to a good unless there is solid evidence that the good is greater than the evil. Since we do not have this solid evidence in the case of these rules, they apply universally.

An example of this first category of practically exceptionless rule is: Human beings may never be killed for their own good. Whether a person is sick or well, in pain or experiencing pleasure, unless one has a special revelation from God one cannot know whether, from the point of view of the whole of what is good for that person, it is better for him to live or to die.[14]

A second category of practically exceptionless moral rules consists of rules which fulfill both of two conditions. First, like those in the first category, they forbid the causing of a particular kind of evil. Second, in theory the evil in question may in some cases be less than the good produced, and to know this is not beyond human power, but in fact because of the vagueness and imperfection of human knowledge and our tendency to bias and self-deception one is always more likely to be correct if one follows the general rule than if one makes an exception.

There is likely to be much controversy about which moral rules should be placed in this category, because it will involve assessment of the kind of certitude one can get in a certain type of case against the likelihood of bias and self-deception in such cases. Normally before placing a moral rule in this category one should see whether it requires refining. In certain cases a rule formulated simply requires exceptions. If moralists consider what types of exceptions should be made, according to publicly defensible criteria, it will be possible to reformulate the rule in a more refined way so that it will not allow of exceptions. The preceding discussion has shown that this author is impressed with the significance of bias and self-deception in making judgments of conscience. Accordingly, I believe that many of the rules which the approved Roman Catholic manuals of moral theology by general consensus set forth as universal should be placed in this category.[15] The manualists over several generations did this work of refining the formulation of rules which made it possible to make the rule universal. To go beyond this and state which rules should be classed in this category would be to go into the content of moral norms, which is beyond the scope of this book.

There is another category of moral rules which should be mentioned here although they are not exceptionless rules. These are rules which in theory allow of exceptions, and in fact some people are properly qualified by knowledge and objectivity to make exceptions; however, if there is no mechanism for assuring public defensibility, once it is generally perceived that these rules allow of exceptions most people will make exceptions which are not well founded. This will lead not only to incorrect judgments of conscience on their part but a general erosion of people's appreciation of the values involved. Such rules represent an enormously difficult pedagogical problem not only for the Church but for society generally.[16]

5. *Discernment*

Discerning what is truly morally good, what is truly from the Holy Spirit, is a large topic which involves many elements discussed in earlier parts of this book and elements which will be discussed in Part Four. One aspect should be noted here. Judgments of conscience are more likely to be objective and unbiased if they are accompanied by qualities which we can recognize as coming from the Holy Spirit, qualities such as peace, joy, gentleness, generosity and patience. Such qualities show that the Spirit is active in this person's life and is likely to be influencing moral judgments. If a person is filled with impatience, bitterness, anger or contempt, these factors rather than the movement of the Holy Spirit may be determining his or her judgment.

6. *Conclusion*

The risk of subjectivism in making judgments of conscience is less if one is prudent, open to the action of the Holy Spirit, with properly developed appetites. No one, however, is so prudent, so virtuous, so in accord with the movement of the Holy Spirit, as to be beyond the risk of subjectivism. Therefore exceptions to general moral rules are to be approached with caution, with serious effort to be honest, with a strong presumption in favor of the general rule until it is shown that the exception is justified. Above all, judgments of conscience are to be approached with prayer. Discerning the will of God requires special openness to God's help.

Another defense against subjectivism is authority. This is the subject of Part Four.

PART FOUR

Individual Conscience
and the Church

Chapter Seventeen

A CRISIS OF AUTHORITY
IN THE CATHOLIC CHURCH

Catholics in our day are vividly aware of dissent from the Church's official teaching on moral issues. Many Catholics, including priests and theologians, disagree with the traditional teaching of the Church concerning artificial contraception. In 1968 Pope Paul VI issued the encyclical *Humanae Vitae* repeating the Church's official rejection of artificial contraception. Far from stopping dissent, the encyclical seemed to provide an occasion for louder and more insistent disagreement with the official teaching.

The contraception issue may be only the tip of the iceberg. Many Catholics now disagree with official Church teaching on divorce and in some areas of sexual ethics. Some challenge the Church's teaching on abortion. There is an increasing gulf between traditional Catholic moral teaching and popular opinion in our society. We should not be surprised if, on more and more issues, some Catholics will conclude that popular opinion is right and that the official Church, holding on to its traditional views, is out of date.

The dissent leaves many Catholics perplexed. Their perplexity is particularly strong because the present dissent seems so different from earlier practice. In the "good old days" remembered by those of us middle-aged and over, moral questions seemed to be settled by a clear hierarchical structure. Parents taught their children what was morally right or wrong. They used catechisms officially approved by Church authorities.

Occasionally cases would come up not covered by catechisms. Then one could consult a priest. A priest, not being omniscient, occasionally might have to consult one or more "approved authors," that is, books of moral theology to which Church authorities had given the *imprimatur,* which indicated that nothing in the book contradicted Church teaching. On particularly complex or unusual problems, where the approved authors seemed not quite to cover the case, the priest might consult the bishop. The latter might confer with specialists in moral theology before deciding how the official Church teaching applied to this case. Occasionally very difficult problems were referred "to Rome," which meant that one of the Vatican congregations would be asked for a ruling. Very important points might elicit the intervention of the Pope himself who, like the Vatican congregations, had the services of expert advisors. Alternatively, very important controversial matters could be submitted to the judgment of an ecumenical council of the Church, although the relative infrequency of such councils prevented them from being useful for settling questions needing prompt attention.

The general impression given by this system was that for any moral question an answer would be given from somewhere within the Church hierarchy. There was little visible dissent from these official answers.

With dissent becoming common and the hierarchical system seeming to be breaking down, many Catholics are distressed. For some, the certainty with which they have held to a code of ethics is shaken. Others, who hold fast to the traditional teachings, are pained by the spectacle of many Catholics rejecting some of these teachings. Is a sort of lawless individualism to become the common practice? Some who disagree with the Church's moral teaching leave the Church by a definite decision. Others drift away. The Church seems to have lost much of its power to affect consciences.

One school of thought explains this distress and disruption as an inevitable part of Catholics reaching a state of maturity in our day. The hierarchical teaching, they explain, was paternalistic, handing down ready-made answers from pulpits or in catechisms or in decrees from Rome. The hierarchy decided what people's moral judgments were to be. Catholics by and large accepted the moral rules laid down by the Church without necessarily understanding or appreciating the reasons behind the rules.

Especially was this the case in sexual morality, according to this school of thought. When a person does not understand or appreciate the reasons behind a moral rule, how can you get him to accept the rule? You can use disapproval and guilt, appealing to or building up a super-ego. Parents have impressed on children the notion that certain sexual actions are dirty and shameful. Children have accepted this without either the parents or the children understanding or appreciating the reasons behind the rules.

This school of thought would admit that conformity to this old hierarchical system has its rewards. The security of clear authoritative answers is comforting. To leave this system may mean to discover one's lack of real understanding and appreciation for the moral rules. One may be thrown into doubt and confusion. To act against the hierarchical system may mean risking condemnation by one's super-ego, suffering feelings of guilt.

Nevertheless, according to this school of thought, Catholics should leave this security. They should free themselves from domination by the super-ego, and they should make moral judgments on the basis of their own authentic appreciation of what is good or evil. They should free themselves from dependence on outside authorities and should assume responsibility for making their own moral judgments based on their Catholic beliefs.

There is much truth in the position of this school of thought. Paternalism treats people in a way appropriate to children. This prevents people from developing toward full freedom and responsibility. It takes initiative away from individuals. They wait for the hierarchy to tell them what to do before they act. Of course the hierarchy cannot be present to make all of the decisions, nor does it have the expertise to decide all of the issues which arise on the various levels of the social, political, economic, intellectual and professional life of society. As a result, many opportunities for Christian action, and for a Christian impact on society, are lost. Not only is greater responsibility and the emergence from paternalism a good thing. It is inevitable. Catholics now live in democratic and pluralistic societies which presuppose that people will take responsibility for their own judgments. Some Catholics, at least, will demand or assume the right to do the same in the Church.

The assumption of responsibility, however, requires more than the decision to become responsible. It requires knowledge. If I decide to be responsible for my own health, I do not suddenly come into possession of medical expertise. This leaves two viable alternatives. I can choose a

good physician, and trust his judgment, within limits; or I can study medicine for enough years to enable me to diagnose and treat at least those
ailments I am most likely to experience.

The decision to be responsible for my moral judgments does not
automatically give me the required moral knowledge. A reading of this
book and a few others on similar topics will convince most readers that
a firm grasp of the basis for ethics is not easy to acquire. A reading of a
dozen books in some special area of ethics (sexual ethics, medical ethics,
economic ethics) will show the complexity of the problems to be considered before making a moral judgment on any particular question. We
should not be surprised that moral truths are sometimes difficult to discover. Ethics is like other areas of knowledge in that a deep and comprehensive knowledge takes years of study.

It is safe to say that few people make moral judgments based upon
sophisticated ethical knowledge. What factors influence our ethical judgments? The media certainly do. The message of the media is not always
designed to convey moral insight. The advertising industry spends billions of dollars to give us certain images of success, of happiness, of the
good life. These billions are not being spent primarily to promote critical
ethical thinking. Our economic system conditions us daily, rewarding
some types of behavior and punishing others. The rewards and punishments are not assigned exclusively in view of the moral quality of the
behavior. Our moral judgments are influenced by our appetitive development, a development which is often quite mediocre and perhaps more
perverted by sin than we would like to admit. We are subject to bias and
rationalization. Millions can starve and not arouse the moral sense of
many. Crucial matters of human life are discussed by some with no more
depth than that found in a soap commercial. Business can be transacted
in a "dog eat dog" atmosphere that is taken for granted.

Our society spends billions of dollars on technology, on building
effective means. It spends little, and apparently thinks less, on the ends
which should govern the use of those means. As the changes come more
quickly we are left with less time to consider the ethical implications
before we are swept along on a course of action dictated by economic
forces, by the demand for technical efficiency, or by political expediency.
Once we are caught up in the practice, once the decision is made, perhaps
we will find moralists to justify what has happened. They will tell us that

what we are doing is right, just as there were always court prophets to tell the Israelite kings what they wanted to hear.

All of this is not an argument that we should remain in a paternalistic Church and shun responsibility. It is an argument that assuming responsibility means more than just deciding to be responsible.

Some who dissent from the Church's moral teaching seem to adopt an unjustifiable individualism. They imply that they may dissent from the Church's teaching whenever they find unconvincing the reasons the Church gives for the moral teaching. This seems to take away all authority from the Church on moral matters. If I agree with the Church only when I find convincing the reasons it gives for a teaching, then I am attributing to the Church no more authority on moral matters than I would attribute to any stranger I meet on the street. In a Church with so little authority, each individual member goes his or her own way. Is such a collection of individuals really a Church?

One can elaborate a theology of Church authority which makes it not only possible, but commonplace, for individual Catholics to dissent from Church teaching on such questions as artificial contraception. In the process one may have eroded any ability of the Church to challenge consciences on the great issues of social justice. If one looks at the authority problem from the point of view of social justice, might it not seem that the problem is that too few Catholics have heeded the official Church teaching? If the Church loses its authority to take stands on moral issues, does it not lose its ability to be prophetic as an institution?

These questions are posed in a rough form, without precise analysis of the problem. They are not intended to settle the issue, but rather to show the need for further examination of the relation of the individual conscience to the Church. The question of authority in the Church in moral matters should be seen in the wider context of the role of the community in aiding the individual to reach sound judgments of conscience.

Chapter Eighteen

SOCIETY AND THE LIMITS
OF INDIVIDUAL CONSCIENCE

In order to understand how the community can aid an individual in making moral judgments, one should first look at the limitations to the resources of individuals for making such judgments. Chapter Sixteen dealt with three factors which may cause an individual to make moral judgments in a subjective rather than objective way. These factors are ignorance of facts, ignorance of norms, and bias. It was pointed out that this tendency to subjectivism can be countered by an appeal to general norms. These appeals constitute the use of societal resources to supplement the individual's resources. This discussion need not be repeated here. This chapter will elaborate further on the limits of the resources of the individual in making moral judgments[1] and how these limits call for help from society.

A. Culture and Conscience

"Culture" here is used in a wide sense to denote all socially learned aspects of human life. Culture in this sense is so comprehensive that it becomes easier to say what is not cultural than to say what is. Certain physical functions such as digestion and breathing are not cultural because they are not learned. Certain learned things are not cultural because the learning is not social. One can learn from personal experience, without using a social context, that hot objects when touched cause pain. The area of social learning, of culture, remains vast. It is much wider than the fine arts, which constitute culture in a narrower sense. Culture in our wider sense includes the family, state, school, grocery stores, banks and all of the institutions which structure our behavior. It includes technology, sciences, philosophy and intellectual pursuits generally, emotional reactions, physical skills, habits of work and recreation, behavior toward strangers, toward elders, toward children. It includes language itself, which not only provides a means of communication but shapes the concepts by which we think. Culture does not only influence external behavior. It shapes thoughts, emotions, attitudes.

We listed three factors which can cause subjectivism in moral judgments: ignorance of facts, ignorance of norms, and bias. In listing these we supposed an already existing individual with knowledge (albeit a limited knowledge) and certain biases. We must now note that this individual has already been shaped in many ways by culture. His or her biases and knowledge of facts and norms are products of an interaction between the "raw material" of the person's nature and the social environment.[2]

This means that it is impossible to make moral judgments apart from one's social milieu. One may think of oneself as a rebel, making moral judgments in the face of opposition by a hostile society, but the knowledge and attitudes underlying those judgments have already been profoundly shaped by some society. Our question is not whether we should be influenced by society in our moral judgments. We are so influenced. On that point we have no choice. Our question is how one may use the resources of society to aid the individual to make correct, objective, moral judgments.

B. Scripture

The Christian uses Sacred Scripture as a basis for moral judgment. Part Two of this book pointed out that this use of Scripture is not a matter simply of imposing an external norm on an individual. The individual's appetites can develop, allowing him or her correctly to assess certain goods and evils. This development of appetites is a special work of the Holy Spirit. Insofar as one's appetites are properly developed one can spontaneously appreciate the moral norms given by Sacred Scripture. Scripture can then be used as a criterion to determine to what extent one's appetites are rightly developed and as a reliable guide for moral judgment. In spite of one's appetitive development, Scripture remains necessary for moral guidance for two general reasons. First, no individual lives fully by the Holy Spirit, and so no one may take his or her spontaneous reactions as sufficient guides to what is good or evil. Second, Scripture contains revelation of certain facts which are relevant to moral judgments.

Any use of Scripture places one immediately in a position of dependence on others, in several ways.

In the first place, the Scriptures come to us in and through the Church. Both the Old and the New Testaments were written as expressions of the faith of believing communities. The believing communities then put their stamp of approval on various books of the Bible by accepting them as the divinely inspired expression of the faith of the communities. It has been the enduring communities of believers which have preserved the Scriptures, continuing to identify them as the inspired work of God and presenting them as such to succeeding generations.

Catholics are especially aware that the Scriptures continue to be read and understood within a believing community. To some extent the influence of the faith community on the individual's understanding of Scripture is inevitable and more or less automatic. One's ideas and one's sensitivities inevitably are influenced by the people with whom we associate. On the other hand, some of the influence of the faith community on the individual's understanding of Scripture is quite deliberate and planned. When two people read the same text of Sacred Scripture and arrive at two incompatible interpretations, both cannot be right. It is not enough for each to hold to his or her private understanding, unconcerned with other opinions. There must be ways in which, through communion with a faith community, one's limited understanding can be corrected and supplemented by the help of others. This may occur informally, by discussion. It may occur in more formal ways by which one is in touch with the *sensus fidelium*, the general consensus of the faithful. One can also be in touch with the insight and critical thinking of the great thinkers of one's own or earlier ages.

There are two elements in the help others give us in grasping the moral message of Sacred Scripture. One element is intellectual. The logic, insight and analysis of great minds aids our understanding of Scripture. Another element is appetitive. Holy people of our own and other generations gain a "co-natural" understanding of the moral message of Scripture because of their superior appetitive development. The contributions of St. Augustine, St. Thomas Aquinas and St. Teresa of Avila to our understanding of divine truth come not only from their intellectual qualities but also from their holiness of life.

C. Creativity

Chapter Fifteen pointed out that, beyond the possession of sound general norms, the discovery of what is the best course of action in a particular case may require creativity. Some people are much more creative than are others. Often the creativity of one person in a community can be a resource for others.

An example of this creativity is the founding of the hospice movement to care for the dying. People such as Mother Mary Aikenhead, a nineteenth century Irish Sister of Charity, and Marie Curie in England in this century, realized that regular hospital procedures do not provide ideal conditions for care of the dying. They set about establishing better facilities and methods. Their creative discovery of better alternatives has led to the establishment of hospices in various parts of the world. Creativity need not be remarkable or famous in order to be valuable. It may be communicated by casual advice about how to deal with particular problems, or by instructions of an expert to new recruits on a job.

D. Catholicity

Clearly, one cannot avoid subjectivism simply by an indiscriminate appeal to the resources of society. Particular societies and particular groups within society share certain biases and limitations in knowledge of facts or norms. The capitalist who needs to overcome his bias against labor may find little help in appealing to his business associates, just as the worker who needs to overcome his bias against capital may not find the correct balance in his union. During wars, contact with one's national society will increase rather than moderate one's bias against the enemy.

One needs contact, beyond one's particular group, with a wider society which can supplement the limited resources of one's particular group. To go beyond the limitations and biases of one's social class one can appeal to the larger society which includes several social classes. To make up for the limits of one's national society one can appeal to international society. To overcome the limitations imposed by one's century or culture one can use the insights of thinkers of other centuries and of other cultures.

"Catholic," according to its Greek roots, indicates that which is "according to the whole." This catholicity involves two factors. Doctrine is catholic and "according to the whole" when it includes the various aspects of the truth on a particular point, not merely one aspect of it. Doctrine is catholic and "according to the whole" also when it is accepted by a wide community of believers over a long period of time. These two factors are complementary. Doctrine is more likely to include the various aspects of the truth when it takes account of the views of a wide circle of communities over a long period of time. By seeking to integrate the views and insights of varying groups one is less likely to leave out some aspect of the truth.

We have been speaking of catholic with a small "c" to indicate that we are discussing an ideal. The Catholic Church, by its name, professes this ideal. It does not embody the ideal equally at all times and in all of its members. Catholics offend against the catholic ideal especially in two ways. Among the "liberal" Catholics there are some who offend by taking some particular modern view as normative, and neglect or even contradict whatever in traditional doctrine does not fit that view. For them, attachment to what is fashionable causes them to narrow their grasp of the truth. Among "conservative" Catholics there are some who offend against the catholic ideal by taking one of several limited traditional views as exclusively normative, specifying it as the only permissible way of expressing the truth.

How the community[3] which is the Catholic Church can operate to foster a catholic grasp of the truth in moral matters is the topic of the next chapter.

Chapter Nineteen

THE CATHOLIC CHURCH
AND MORAL TEACHING

A. Unity, Catholicity, and the Holy Spirit

In doctrine there is need both for unity and for diversity in the
Church. In more than one passage the New Testament makes clear that
the followers of Jesus Christ are to accept and live by the truth handed
down through the apostles. Christians are not free to accept or reject doctrine according to their whims. Historically the Church has sought to
maintain fidelity to this truth by framing statements of the one faith. Some
of these statements are made in a solemn way and are infallible. Other
statements, while not infallible, are highly authoritative and are meant to
express the common faith of the believing community. This unity of belief
leaves room for considerable diversity. Different theologies can use different intellectual tools to understand and explain revealed doctrine. On
certain non-essential points some people may hold views quite incompatible with the views of others and yet be united to those others in belief
in the essentials of the faith.

Because our focus is not on the general area of doctrine we need not
go beyond this rather obvious summary on the issue of unity and diversity.
We need some more specific treatment, however, concerning unity and
diversity in the area of ethical teaching.

A divergence of opinion on a serious ethical issue should be a cause
for real concern, because it is a sign that some people, at least, are mistaken on this point, and by acting with a sincere but mistaken conscience
they will cause harm. There is a divergence of opinion, for example,

concerning whether a nation may stockpile nuclear weapons in self-defense. Presumably there is a correct answer to this question, either one of the answers currently being supported or some variation which has not yet come to light. There is no reason to rejoice that the present diversity of opinion leaves us "free" to think and do what we like on this issue.

Diversity of opinion on serious moral questions is a fact. Allowing many views to be heard in public discussion may help us discover the right answers. Nevertheless, the diversity is a state of imperfection, of uncertainty, of at least some people being wrong. It is a state one should try to overcome. A comparison with medicine may be useful. A difference of opinion about how to treat a particular disease is a state to be overcome, because we want general acceptance of the best method to treat the disease.

Some moralists seem to miss this point and to be attached to pluralism in ethics as though it were something valuable in itself. Their failure seems to be the result of a sort of lingering legalism, although they might be surprised at being accused of legalism. A sort of legalism, derived from voluntarist and nominalist sources, sees moral norms as rules imposed more or less arbitrarily from the outside. In this view one likes to interpret moral laws as narrowly as possible, leaving more room for individual freedom. With such a view of morality one might rejoice because a pluralism of moral opinions seems to leave the individual more free to do what he or she likes.[1] The view of this book, however, is that valid moral norms are guides and insights concerning what is truly good and beneficial. In this view, pluralism of opinion may be a useful tool in seeking truth, but it is also a state of ignorance which leads to harmful action in ethics as it does in medicine, engineering or navigation.

In summary, pluralism in ethical opinions is a fact, and allowing a discussion of differing views rather than stifling it is normally an aid to arriving at the truth; however, a responsible person will not rest in this pluralism, but will seek as far as possible to resolve differences by reaching conclusions which can command general assent and stand up under criticism. Institutionally, the Church should not rest in pluralism, but should foster a critical effort to integrate the insights of various parties into as full and as accurate an expression of the truth as is possible.[2]

With respect to unity in doctrine generally (including in ethical teaching) the approach of the Roman Catholic Church has been rather different from that of most Protestant Churches. The Roman Catholic

Church has tended to stress unity. It sees that disunity can easily lead to many people setting aside some of the essentials of the truth entrusted to the Church. Disunity can lead to a form of subjectivism in which individuals pick and choose elements of Christianity which they like. Such a Christianity becomes an individualistic human creation, not a faith which challenges and raises people above themselves. The Roman Catholic Church has tended to use authority to preserve unity and to preserve the truth entrusted to the Church.

Protestants for the most part recognize the value of unity as well as the importance of preserving the truth entrusted to the Church. Many of them, however, have great difficulty with the exercise of authority in the Roman Catholic Church. To them, the pervasive appeal to authority restricts freedom, seeks to impose beliefs regardless of the dispositions of the subject, and in fact may be very uncatholic by imposing the narrow view of one group as though it constituted an adequate statement of the truth. We see a certain amount of ''protestantizing'' within the Catholic Church itself, insofar as some Catholics insist on ''making up their own minds'' rather than follow official Church teaching. This protestantizing element combines with something Catholic to form an anomalous sort of attitude in those Catholics who shop around among priests until they find one who will, in effect, give them permission to act against the official teaching of the Church.

This conflict between the need for unity and preservation of the truth, on the one hand, and the need for freedom, authenticity and open discussion, on the other, seems to lead to a dilemma. It is a dilemma which should be a grave concern to both Roman Catholics and Protestants. Both sides should be alarmed at the bad results which are proven possibilities arising from their positions.

This dilemma can be overcome only by the Holy Spirit, the Spirit of truth, who makes us free. The Holy Spirit by working within Christians produces a unity of love and of belief which is not imposed from outside. Both Roman Catholics and Protestants can agree that the ideal is this unity produced by the Holy Spirit. The differences arise concerning how one should act in a sinful world in which people go their disparate ways rather than living fully the life of the Spirit. One cannot dismiss the dilemma by pointing to the ideal. The world in which we live will not cease to be sinful and divided. However, the necessity of living in a sinful world should not so accommodate us to the world that we begin to think that the ideal has no practical relevance. Insofar as people are sinful, the exercise of authority will have unhappy consequences and the lack of exercise of authority will have unhappy consequences. People, however, can be more or less sinful, less or more open to the Holy Spirit. We know the direction in which we must tend in order to lessen the dilemma, and we know that it cannot be dealt with adequately by mere human methods alone.

This author by conviction approaches this dilemma from the Roman Catholic side, holding that authority must have a crucial role in preserving unity and truth in a sinful world, while recognizing that constant openness to the Spirit, with all that this implies, is necessary to assure that the unity achieved is free and authentic and that the formulation of common belief takes account of the sensitivities and insights of widely varying groups.

There are several ways in which the Church community can help individuals to discover the truth in moral matters. Some help is informal, as when a person advises a friend casually about what to do, or when some individual provides an inspiring example of the possibilities for good in human life. There are more structured and formal ways in which several agencies in the Church help individuals discover what is morally good or evil. We will now consider the working of three of these agencies, beginning with the hierarchy.

B. The Hierarchy

The hierarchy in the Catholic Church, involving the Pope and bishops, exercises responsibility for the teaching of doctrine, including moral doctrine, in the Church. The teaching office of the hierarchy is often called the magisterium.[3]

It is easy to think of the teaching office of the whole Church as though it were a sort of pyramid. At the top are the Popes and the ecumenical councils. Below these are the Vatican congregations, local bishops, and national councils of bishops. Next come the priests, who share in the work of the bishops, and others who have responsibility for teaching Catholic doctrine. At the base of the pyramid are "the faithful" who are taught.

In contrast with this pyramidal model is a more or less democratic view[4] of the teaching office of the hierarchy. This democratic view points out that not all Catholic teaching comes to the "lower" levels of the

Church from the "higher" levels. All the faithful can read the Bible for themselves or listen to it being read. All can use their own intelligences. All can live intensely the life of the Holy Spirit, and thereby appreciate certain values correctly. For these reasons, they argue, the role of the hierarchy should be seen as formulating the common belief of the Church once it emerges, not as imposing a common doctrine from above.

This democratic statement of the case is too simple. The Bible which the faithful can read for themselves is to a great extent the product of authority. For the sake of brevity we will confine our comments here to the New Testament. The New Testament is based, first of all, on the authoritative teachings of Jesus Christ, and then on the authoritative witness of the apostles. Though we do not have detailed knowledge of the whole process by which the books of the New Testament were written and then accepted by the Church as inspired books, the process seems to have involved some exercise of authority in the Church, not merely a democratic consensus. The authority presumably did not exist apart from the common belief of the Church, but neither did the common belief grow up apart from authority.

Followers of the democratic view might admit that authority played a notable part in the establishment of the authoritative books in the early Church. Once that process was over, however, these democrats say, then the role of the hierarchy is confined to formulating the common belief of the Church once it emerges.

Again, the democratic statement of the case is too simple. First of all, a common belief does not arise in the Church without some teaching by someone. This teaching involves, first of all, a presentation of the Bible as an authoritative book along with ways of understanding the Bible. This teaching will involve also the development of theology, in an attempt to probe the meaning of revelation in terms adapted to different cultures. In morals it will involve the application of Gospel norms to new situations. Much of this teaching will be prior to, rather than consequent upon, common acceptance of the teaching by the faithful. There will be several agencies involved in this teaching—parents, school teachers, pastors, theologians, the hierarchy. Are we going to allow the other agencies a role creative of public opinion in the Church, but confine the hierarchy to formulating the consensus once it has occurred? Such a position certainly runs counter to what has been the case historically in the Catholic Church during its long history. Such a position is also inherently implausible. Teachers in general are called upon to use various intellectual tools to test any doctrine before they accept it, testing its faithfulness to Scripture and tradition, testing its inner coherence, its ability to explain data, and so forth. Are the members of the hierarchy to be the exceptions, contenting themselves as teachers with remaining uncritical and silent until a consensus emerges, and then formulating it? This would certainly narrow the scope for charismatic leadership by these supposed official teachers of the Church. Finally, although the Church, people and hierarchy acting together, often has difficulty reaching unity in the truth, it certainly shows more of a charism in this respect than does public opinion without the formative influence of the hierarchy.

We have outlined two extremes, the pyramidal and the democratic, which are more or less caricatures. These reflections on the caricatures may have value beyond simply the demolishing of straw men, however. They illustrate several elements which should go into a more balanced view of the magisterium. Such a view will leave the faithful in a more active role than they would have in the pyramidal model, and it will leave the hierarachy with a more active role than it would have in the democratic model. This view sees the hierarchy and the rest of the faithful playing roles which suppose the active contribution of the other. Just as the faithful do not come to a common belief apart from the ministry of an actively teaching hierarchy, so the hierarchy does not formulate doctrine apart from the belief and the many gifts of an active body of the faithful.

The hierarchy, of course, does not constitute moral norms as true because it states them. It must discover what is objectively true whether the hierarchy teaches it or not. To discover the truth members of the hierarchy must use the same methods as other people must use. God normally does not provide supernatural help to replace natural powers. For a member of the hierarchy to depend on the grace of office while neglecting other methods of discovering truth would be no more legitimate than for him to depend upon God's special grace to get him from one city to another without using normal means of transportation.

There are, of course, many elements in the proper method for reaching moral truth. Because it involves a truth handed down, there must be faithfulness to Sacred Scripture, studied by use of the best methods available. Because it involves an understanding of revealed truth by the use of various intellectual tools, and the discovery of what is morally good or evil in many different situations, it will involve many more intellectual skills. Because we learn from the best minds and the consensus of believers in other generations, there must be a properly conducted study of tradition.

At this point one might suppose that the work of the members of the hierarchy as teachers is simply that they become good academics. Such a supposition could easily lead to a misunderstanding. Certainly it is not enough for the hierarchy simply to ally itself with one or other of the schools of thought in universities. The divisions of opinion within university faculties, the shifting tides of opinion which make yesterday's common academic opinion to be today's outmoded theory, witness to the fallibility of academic beliefs. Often the opinion of academic specialists must be balanced by the ''common sense'' of people generally. In the matter of child rearing, for example, it is far from clear that the shifting opinions of ''experts'' have been more reliable than the views of common people. In the area of Christian teaching there are special reasons for balancing the views of academic experts by appeal to the sense of the faithful. The Gospel according to Matthew (11, 25) states: ''At that time Jesus declared: 'I thank you, Father, Lord of heaven and earth, that you have hidden these things from the wise and understanding and revealed them to babes.' '' ''These things'' in this passage are the lessons Jesus has been teaching, especially concerning the need to hear God's call to repentance. Sometimes the bias which is characteristic of academics prevents them from seeing simple truths which are obvious to other people. Academics may be too exclusively involved in the ''wisdom of the world'' which Paul sees as sometimes an obstacle to acceptance of the truth.[5] Certain truths are best recognized not by those who are learned but by those who are good. The faithful, on the other hand, are not a sufficient source of guidance in moral doctrine without the insight, critical judgment and systematic method of academics.

The hierarchy, we have argued, must use those methods which others must use to discover the truth.[6] What, then, is the special role of the hierarchy? There are many elements in the Church which contribute to a fullness of understanding of the truth. These elements do not function together if their operation is left to chance. Some order and structure are necessary. The hierarchy as teacher is a special ministry within the Church providing for a structure to help the Church to be united in the search for and discovery of the truth. This ministry can take place only if the hierarchy has a certain authority.

How in practice does the hierarchy perform its special task? We can begin by looking at the first teaching unit in the Church, the family. Parents teach their children. They are not the sole providers of moral knowledge to their children. The children, at least as they grow older, can read Scripture for themselves, use their own intelligences, learn from experience and from authors, and can live intensely the life of the Holy Spirit. The parents give the initial education. At first they are the almost exclusive sources of knowledge, and later recede to a less dominant but still important role.

If parents are to teach their children effectively they must also learn from them. They must listen carefully to their children to understand their questions and their way of thinking, and to recognize what is genuine and true in what their children already know. In trying to make moral teaching meaningful to their children, parents will learn something for themselves.

If the parents were simply following their own, partial version of the truth they would be of little help to their children. The parents, however, are in communion with the rest of the Church. They are in communion with the Church because they can listen to the pastor and consult with him, and they can read authors recognized as responsible teachers. The parents can easily check to see whether the version of truth they are giving is merely their own or represents the fuller view of the whole Church.

At each stage as one rises higher in the hierarchy a somewhat similar pattern is found. A priest does not teach people as though he were the only source for their moral knowledge. Rather, he can supplement what they learn from other sources while serving as an instrument by which they stay in communion with the universal Church. The priest can learn from the people as he teaches them. At the same time he must himself be in communion with the universal Church, through the local bishop and by reading authors who are recognized as responsibly setting forth authentic Church teaching.

A similar pattern holds for bishops. They are in communion with the universal Church especially by being in communion with the Pope, the bishop of Rome. Communion with the Pope as a private individual does not constitute being in communion with the whole Church. Communion with the Pope constitutes communion with the rest of the Church because the rest of the Church is in communion with the Pope. The Pope is not a mere passive recorder of the consensus in Church teaching. He takes an active role in forming the mind of the Church.

One can distinguish three distinct ways in which members of the hierarchy, bishops and Pope, are involved in moral teaching. The first way is by simple instruction. By oral or written communication they instruct people about moral norms, relating these to the basic meaning of a Christian life.

Other people can engage in this sort of instruction. What makes instruction by the hierarchy different is that it is official. When a parent, a theologian, or any other Catholic teaches concerning morality, the teaching may arise from within the Catholic tradition, but it remains that person's private view, not the official view of the Church. Of course any person can simply repeat the official teaching of the Church, but not every person can constitute a teaching as an official teaching of the Church.

What is special about official teaching, other than that it issues from someone who is authorized to teach officially? When private persons teach, their words have the authority earned by the person's learning, past performance, character, etc. An official teaching has the authority of the institution, presumably because it carries with it the resources and balanced view of the institution, and profits from the grace of office of those who speak. This does not mean that all official teachings are equally authoritative. They can range from solemn decrees of ecumenical councils to pastoral letters by local ordinaries. Nor need all members of the hierarchy always speak officially. They can give their own private views, but in doing so should make this clear, unless it is already clear from the context.

Priests share in a special way in the work of the bishop. What does this mean concerning official moral teaching? There seems to be little consensus on the details of the answer to that question. Some suggestions might be offered. First, a priest by his teaching on any point cannot constitute it as official teaching of the Church. Second, in many situations the priest is perceived as a spokesman for the Church. Normally this is the case when he preaches in church or when people consult him about Church teaching on some point. On such occasions priests must take care not to give the impression that their private views are official Church teaching. Suppose that a pastor believes that a certain economic measure by a government, or an industrialist, or a labor union, is unjust. In speaking about the measure he should carefully distinguish which elements in his teaching are official (e.g., certain principles taken from papal encyclicals) and which elements are his own views, carrying only the authority of his own reputation or the logic of his arguments.

What has been said of priests holds true in a general way for others who hold an official mandate to teach in the Church.

A second way in which the hierarchy is involved in moral teaching is by being responsible that proper teaching be provided by others. The members of the hierarchy cannot personally do all of the instructing. They have some responsibility, however, for the instruction done by others. This responsibility is exercised in different ways. Bishops may set up institutions, such as schools or colleges, to provide instruction. They may provide for experts in various areas of ethics, social ethics, medical ethics, etc., to be available where there is need. They may set up groups to study and provide guidance when serious new ethical questions arise. They may, in certain cases, declare that a certain teacher of ethics does not represent the authentic teaching of the Church.

In certain cases a writer or teacher may present a new or apparently new doctrine, one which may not seem to conform with the commonly accepted teaching of the Church. It becomes necessary to decide whether this doctrine is true or false. This involves a third way in which the hierarchy is involved in moral teaching. It must test new or apparently new doctrines before allowing them to be presented as correct formulations of Catholic doctrine. What this testing involves will be explained further when we discuss the prophetic role in moral teaching.

C. Specialists

Correct moral judgments may require knowledge possessed by specialists in such disciplines as economics, genetics, sociology, political science, medicine, philosophical ethics and moral theology. They may require the practical expertise of politicians, doctors, social workers and spiritual directors.

The proper relationship between the work of these specialists and the role of the hierarchy is not simple. On the other hand, the hierarchy is obliged to use the normal methods for attaining the truth. Therefore they are obliged to make use of specialists. This does not mean that they must accept the opinions of specialists uncritically, of course. Specialists are quite as fallible as are other human beings.

Specialists may be tempted to trust only their own judgment. They are subject, however, to the shortcomings and inadequacies discussed in the previous chapter. By trusting too much in their own expertise they may end up with a private view which is overly narrow, which has not taken account of other points of view, which is to some extent biased. There are, of course, scholarly methods by which the specialist can try to overcome this tendency. One great corrective, however, is attention to the teaching of the hierarchy, by which the specialist can be in communion with the teaching of the universal Church.

A special note should be included here concerning ethicists (including both philosophical ethicists and moral theologians). They, like others, perceive that certain things are good because they have appetites for them. Like others, the ethicists have only imperfectly developed appetites. Ethicists are prone to take their own perceptions of what is good as self-evident, unaware of the extent to which these perceptions rest upon imperfect appetitive development. This weakness can be countered if ethicists take seriously the perceptions of what is good of those who show by their lives that they live intensely the life of the Holy Spirit.

In the next chapter we will consider the situation in which there may be conflict between experts and the hierarchy.

The specialist and the bishop both have a teaching role, but the roles are somewhat different. The specialist can easily be more informed and learned concerning a particular question than is the bishop, who must devote his attention to a broad spectrum of affairs. The specialist is not an official teacher, however. The individual consulting the expert has the benefit of that person's learning, judgment, logic, etc., but does not have the assurance that the Church stands behind the expert's opinion.

The hierarchical system does not work perfectly. Bishops can make mistakes, either by not taking sufficient care to use all available resources before making a judgment, or by failing in judgment even after using all available means. The hierarchical system, however, provides one great advantage that individual expertise does not provide. It provides a structure by which individuals can be in communion with the universal Church.

D. The Prophetic Role

The prophet in the Old Testament was one who proclaimed the word of God. Frequently the Old Testament prophets proclaimed this word to an indifferent and unrepentant public, or to a hostile king. "Prophet" came to mean one who challenges the accepted thinking of a society or an age. In this chapter "prophetic" means challenging accepted views in morals in order to bring people to the truth.

Not all who challenge accepted moral beliefs are right. One person believes that the traditional rules favoring marriage permanence and fidelity are wrong. A second believes that people have neglected their moral obligation toward animals and would like to ban all hunting and slaughtering of animals for food. A third believes that the greatest good comes in the form of a drug-induced experience. Which of these are true prophets, and how can we tell? One can distinguish three types of situations.

In some situations the prophet calls upon others to repent and to recognize a truth which they would recognize if they were honest enough to consider the matter carefully. Testing the validity of the message of such prophets is a matter of examining one's motives, of striving for honesty, and looking to see if the message is true. This is not necessarily a complex process but frequently it is a difficult one. Not all truths are welcome.

In a second type of case the prophet can find some point on which there is general agreement, and then argue that if one accepts that point one should accept a series of sequences, leading to the conclusion proposed by the prophet. Discernment of the truth of the prophet's message in these cases is a matter of logical argumentation.

The third, and more difficult, type of situation occurs when there is no commonly accepted starting point for argumentation. The prophet has one type of appetitive development, which provides for certain starting points for his argument, and the people have a different type of appetitive development, providing a different set of starting points. How do we know whether a certain disturber of our peace of mind is a true prophet, with a superior appetitive development, or a false prophet, with inferior appetitive development? The question is difficult, but not impossible. There are three steps which can be used, none of them easy or foolproof, but all of them helpful.

The first step is to use our own appreciation of the good to test the credentials of the alleged prophet. Suppose I talk to a person and discover that she has quite a good appreciation of the goods which I consider important. She seems to have developed her appetites at least as far as I have. She tells me that there is something else that is good, something that I don't appreciate. It is reasonable for me to suppose that she is likely to be right. Certainly her valuing of this good does not arise simply from a failure to learn to evaluate anything worthwhile. Suppose, however, that in conversation I had discovered the opposite, discovered that she really had not learned to appreciate the things I have learned to appreciate. Then my reason for taking her opinion seriously disappears. Her attachment to this good which I do not appreciate is probably the result of her failure to learn to appreciate anything really valuable.

A second step in discerning who is a true prophet is to use the resources of the community. This means using the standards which the community in its collective wisdom has set down as moral norms. If a would-be prophet shows by his words that he has no appreciation for the values behind these norms, then his rejection of those norms is not a sign of any higher wisdom. However, if the would-be prophet shows a genuine appreciation of the communal values, then his desire to change the norms in some particular case may well be based in a higher moral wisdom.

In using the resources of the community to discern who is a true prophet we can use not only the codified and written norms, but also the living norms, i.e., the people who are the best judges because they have themselves developed their appetites properly. How do we identify such people? A comparison with another area of life can throw light on this question. I have not developed an appreciation for music to any high degree; yet I can make some sort of well-informed judgment about which people in our society have a more fully developed appreciation for music. The judgment of such people is authenticated by their peers, and if I do enough investigating to rule out the frauds, I can identify certain experts. If one such expert tells me that a new piece of music is beautiful, I have reason to believe him, and to wish that I had learned to appreciate that kind of music. In a similar way, one can identify certain people whose development of their appreciation of moral goods makes them more or less likely judges about the rightness of the message of a would-be prophet.

This use of community resources to distinguish true from false prophecy is by no means foolproof. It may happen, for example, that nearly all the people in a certain society share a certain narrowness or prejudice. It may be that the people who are recognized as experts in morals are themselves subject to narrowness and bias. This seems to have been the case in Israel at the time of Jesus. The experts in the law were, for the most part, less able to grasp the truth of Jesus' message than were the common people.

There is a third step available for discerning who is a true prophet. This step is to examine the life of the speaker. If he shows no sign of an intense life of the Holy Spirit, then there is no reason to believe that this person has a special wisdom based on properly developed appetites. If a person is arrogant and self-centered, lashes out angrily at those who disagree with him, and cannot recognize the limits of his own intelligence and knowledge, such a person is unlikely to have any special wisdom based on appetites formed by the Holy Spirit. A person who is patient, concerned for others, not interested in his own reputation, is quite likely to possess such wisdom.

Before any new, or apparently new, message is presented as a proper basis for moral judgment by Catholics, the hierarchy must test that statement to see if it is truly prophetic or not. By the interaction of the prophetic element and the hierarchy a balance must be sought between two extremes.

At one extreme is the simple repetition of the formulas of the past and the refusal to consider new ideas. Such an attitude fails the Church in several ways. It fails properly to apply moral principles to new situations. It fails to reformulate moral teaching so that the traditional principles can be understood in the contemporary world. It fails to use new insights to enrich the moral tradition of the Church. It may lead to legalism, because a group which is not constantly responding to new ideas and challenges easily takes refuge behind the repetition of formulas without fully understanding or appreciating the reasons behind the formulas.

The other extreme is uncritical acceptance of everything new. Such an attitude follows the current opinions in the world and allows large parts of the Gospel to be obscured because they do not fit the moods or biases of the times.

Usually the role of the hierarchy is not so much to reject what is new as to insist on the inclusion of the whole truth. Most heresies err by their one-sidedness. They fasten on one aspect of reality to the exclusion of other aspects. The hierarchy must insist on the integrity of the Christian message. It cannot allow the bias of this or that social class, this or that school of thought, this or that continent, to block out parts of the truth. It must not allow attention to certain New Testament texts to cause the neglect of others. A great help to the hierarchy in this matter is the long tradition of the Church. The great thinkers of the past have erred, of course, and they had their own particular biases. They can, however, give us an insight into aspects of the truth not appreciated by our own age.

The hierarchy at times is itself called to be prophetic. It may be prophetic by holding to the full breadth of the Gospel message even though parts of that message have become unfashionable. It may be prophetic by challenging the universal Church with a message which originated first in one group. Pope Leo XIII, for example, challenged the whole Church with the social teachings which first were elaborated by such thinkers as Bishop Emmanuel von Ketteler.

Inevitably there will be tensions between individual thinkers and the hierarchy. The prophets tell us that we have been neglectful, that we must change, that we have been wrong. We don't like to hear that message, and that is why prophets are not popular. Members of the hierarchy, laboring to fulfill their responsibilities, may be hurt by criticisms. The prophet, too, has sensitivities. No one likes his pet ideas to be criticized too thoroughly. What looks to the hierarchy like wise caution and necessary criticism before accepting something new, to the individual thinkers may seem to be indifference, faint-heartedness, or even expediency. Even when both sides are doing their jobs properly, tension is likely. When feelings of resentment, impatience or hurt take over they seriously hamper the search for truth.

A particular difficulty in our day is that disagreements on moral matters in the Church are discussed not only by carefully conducted meetings but also in the media. In the media, subtlety of thought may take second or third place, well behind the search for controversy and conflict and the need for attention-getting slogans. The public discussion may have some good effects. It does not always lead to calm and precise exchange of ideas.

E. Christian Community and Culture

It was noted in Chapter Eighteen that culture profoundly influences moral beliefs. We will now consider at more length this influence of culture, of the human milieu. The kind of people we are is influenced by the mass media of communication, by child-rearing practices, by formal education, by various institutions which organize our behavior, by economic and technological factors, and by all of the interpersonal relationships in which we engage. Our milieu shapes our ideas, our emotions, our aesthetic perceptions, manners, habits and patterns of behavior. Our milieu influences our moral beliefs on the level of articulated beliefs and on the level of appetitive development underlying those beliefs.

Our contemporary milieu is, to a great extent, non-Christian. Partly this is because many of our fellow citizens are not Christian or Christianity is not a dominant force in their lives. There is another significant reason why our milieu is not Christian. That reason is secularization. Secularized people have learned to live various parts of their lives more or less without reference to religion. Economic life, medicine, science, drama, sports, and other activities are carried on according to their own rules and meanings with little or no reference to Christianity. Secularized society does not forbid a person to be religious. However, it tends to push religion into a more or less private area of life, so that the public milieu has little religious reference. When the Catholic Church or the "moral majority" attempts to make any religiously based position a factor in politics, most people see it as an illegitimate mixing of politics and religion, an improper breaking down of the compartments which isolate religion from the public milieu.

In theory, secularization is religiously neutral. It allows people to have their own religion and it imposes none. In fact, however, the effect of secularization is not religiously neutral. Religion held only as a private matter begins to seem strange and irrelevant to the public world, the marketplace, government, school, etc. Eventually this religion comes to seem strange to ourselves, formed as we are by a public milieu which has no place for religion.

The moral beliefs and attitudes produced by a non-Christian milieu need not all be bad. Some are likely to be quite acceptable from a Catholic point of view. Some may contain elements which can enrich the Catholic tradition with insights which it has hitherto lacked. However, some of the moral beliefs and attitudes produced by a non-Christian view run counter to fundamentals of Catholic morality and should be rejected.

This presents a problem. A Catholic may attend Mass on Sunday, pray for a few minutes each day, and perhaps do a few minutes of religious reading each week. Many Catholics do less. For most of their waking hours they are subjected to the pervasive influence of a milieu which in many ways contradicts fundamental Catholic morality. The ideas of success, of happiness, of the good life presented by advertising and fostered by business practice or the entertainment industry are far from Christian. A Catholic formed by the public milieu will experience many Catholic moral norms as opposing some of his own perceptions and attitudes. He may resent these norms and be impatient with a Church which fails to update its moral teaching to be in tune with the modern world.

Can one live in, be continuously subject to, a non-Christian milieu while maintaining a lively appreciation for those Catholic moral norms which run counter to the ideas and attitudes fostered by the milieu? Some exceptional, inner-directed people may be able to do so. For the rest of us it will be extremely difficult.

Faced with this problem, one is led to consider the possibility of forming a counter-culture. Might people be able deliberately to create the kind of culture which will influence them in a way which they judge to be good?[7]

A comment might be interjected here concerning ghettos. During the 1950's American Catholics were often told to leave behind their Catholic ghetto mentality, to go forth and transform society. Whether in fact American Catholics of the time lived in ghettos is a matter that might be disputed. What is beyond dispute is that in the subsequent interaction between American Catholics and American society at large, Catholics have adopted the attitudes of the larger society much more noticeably than has society been attracted to Catholic attitudes. This should occasion no surprise. Catholics simply followed the general law of being profoundly influenced by their milieu. Ghettos can provide a milieu which allows a group to keep its identity rather than simply becoming a product of the surrounding culture.

This is not an argument for the preservation of ghettos. The ghetto, while preserving the identity of a group, also isolates its members from the surrounding society. This can have several undesirable results. It minimizes the likelihood of a Christian group influencing the society. The

Christian group in a ghetto is not likely to learn much from the surrounding world, and so the Christians are impoverished. It is not simply that Christians in a ghetto may fail to adopt effective technology or certain useful or worthwhile cultural elements from the wider society. God has used history to instruct his people. Often by wrestling with contemporary events and ideas Christians deepen their grasp of the implications of their faith. If Christians seek to preserve their faith and their piety by turning their backs on the real intellectual, personal and social problems of the contemporary world they begin to be less than fully honest intellectually and less than fully generous in their actions. Finally, ghettos in certain cases create a defensive posture by which members of an in-group begin to think of themselves as the elect. They may even seek to protect their own sense of worthiness by projecting evil onto outsiders, or at least blaming them for all evil, so that they come to be seen as the enemy. Such an attitude is hardly Christian.

There may be situations in which the better course of action for a Christian group is to remain in a ghetto, but such a stance does not recommend itself as the ideal course for the Church of the future.

Can one create a counter-culture which is not a ghetto? The creation of a culture of any kind is an extremely complex process. The creation of the kind of culture you want will not be accomplished in a couple of years in a commune. However, Christian churches have accomplished remarkable things in this respect at certain points in history.

A truly Christian culture will involve giving a Christian quality to many areas of life: to aesthetic activities of painting, music, poetry, fiction and drama; to intellectual pursuits, not only a theology or a philosophy existing in isolation, but a wisdom which both sees the limits and relishes the truth and the mystery in all discoveries of the human mind; to institutions; to patterns of behavior; to one's pace of life which allows for creative work and contemplation; to a mode of ownership which makes the economy serve persons, not persons serve the economy; to our attitudes toward the aged, the weak, the stranger.

Creation of a Christian culture requires a certain amount of withdrawal from the rest of society. One must say no to some of its influences and ways of acting or one is formed by it. This refusal by itself, however, does not create a Christian culture. The creation must be something positive. If the Christian culture is to avoid the undesirable qualities of a ghetto, this positive creation must involve honestly facing the genuine intellectual questions and social problems arising in the contemporary world.

Christian culture involves an actively creative, as distinct from a passive, manner of life. The secularized person has learned to live life in compartments, business, politics, medicine, recreation, etc. Each compartment tends to be autonomous. The rules and customs which govern economics or medicine, for example, are not integrated with religion or any other over-all system of meaning. This leaves the individual in a passive attitude. When one acts in any particular compartment one follows the rules and customs of that compartment, but one does not express any central meaning of one's own life, unless by way of departing from the normal mode of acting in that compartment. The rules of business, for example, require efficiency and acting according to the profit motive. The expression in business of any ultimate meaning of one's own life (presuming there is such a meaning beyond the search for wealth and economic power) might be tolerated if one is so good at the game of business that one can indulge in such luxuries, but it will not lead in itself to success in business. A Christian culture requires the rediscovery of integration in life, by which in each area of life one can express the central and primary meaning of one's life. Not all people will be equally creative in the sense of fashioning radically new modes of action. All, however, can be creative in the sense of expressing something personal in various actions; and when most people in a society are creative in this sense, creativity will increase also in the sense that more and more people will discover new ways of acting which provide new and deeper ways of self-expression.

A Christian culture will involve deliberate choices about ''input'' into one's mind and sensitivities. One cannot indiscriminately expose oneself to all of the movies, literature, advertising and other influences of secular culture without being formed by them. Again, this choice does not involve only a rejection. It involves deliberate cultivation of a better sort of input. It requires access to the rich but often neglected Christian cultures and creations of past ages. It requires fostering new artistic creations imbued with the spirit of the Gospel. Such creations will not flourish in a protected ''hot house'' atmosphere in which shallow works are praised simply because they are pious. There must be honest and bold addressing of contemporary questions and sensitivities.

A Christian culture requires a critical attitude. To be critical does not necessarily mean to complain. One must refuse to accept passively whatever is offered by the surrounding milieu. One must learn to subject everything to scrutiny according to the standards of faith. This has implications for how we should educate, implications not always brought out in the curriculum and pedagogy in Catholic schools. A Christian critical attitude will find a way politely to refuse rubbish, whether it comes from secular society or from the Christian community itself.

A Christian culture can exist only within a Christian community. A community is not simply an organization of people brought together to produce some goal extrinsic to the organization. The community life itself, the interpersonal relationships of its members, is a value to be sought for its own sake.[8] Among the most powerful forces by which a culture forms its members is the action of relating personally to another human being. The kind of persons we become depends to a great extent on the kind of interpersonal relationships we live. A community in which people relate to each other in a way inspired by the Gospel has already provided the basis for a Christian culture.

A Christian culture must have its basis in prayer and meditation. This is not a pious ornament added on to give a religious look to the process. Prayer and meditation are the basic acts of creating a Christian culture. They are the most radical acts by which we refuse to be formed passively by the prevailing culture and by which we open ourselves to the one central Meaning which we wish to form our lives.

Is this talk of creating a Christian culture naive and unrealistic? It is difficult enough to get a few parishioners to take time off from their busy schedules to attend a study group once a week during Lent. Where will we find people with the time, the energy, the conviction, the talent, to pursue the enormous task of creating a Christian culture?

Before deciding what is realistic, it may help to consider what is necessary. If a man must lose sixty pounds or risk death by heart attack, it may become realistic for him to lose the weight. If our alternatives are either assimilation into a non-Christian milieu, or retreat into a ghetto, or the creation of a Christian counter-culture, it is perhaps realistic to expect some Christians to try to create the Christian culture.

It is not as though we must start from scratch on such a project. Many religious orders and congregations in the past have functioned as Christian counter-cultures. Perhaps some may do so again. Certain other existing institutions, parishes, schools, and pious societies could be moved in this direction. New groups have arisen, base communities, certain social action groups and prayer communities, which work at providing a Christian milieu. Above all, we have the basic Christian community, the family, the strengthening of which requires the best efforts of Christians everywhere. There is certainly no easy and failure-proof road open to the creation of a Christian milieu, but there are possibilities of partial success, which is the only kind we will find this side of the parousia.

In a Church which is truly a community of communities, and whose members actively express a central Christian meaning in various activities, the problem of authority is not the same as in a Church whose members are pulled in various directions by social forces with no equivalent Christian influences. When in a true Christian community life people come together to discern what is morally good, what is the will of God, leadership and responsibility is not all in the hands of one or of a few. Each has a particular contribution to make, whether it is specialized knowledge, experience, compassion, organizational ability, or the capacity to listen. People contribute also by presenting their needs, eliciting the generous responses of others. The priest's special contribution in such a group will depend partly on his particular gifts, but always he should be one steeped in the knowledge of God's word, an official link with the universal Church, and a leader in prayer.

In a community one discovers that personal responsibility does not mean going off by oneself, being responsible only for one's own actions. Responsibility means learning from others and joining in a common life in which care for oneself is part of care for the whole community. People who are formed in such an attitude are allowing the Holy Spirit to do what is necessary to create unity in the Church.

Chapter Twenty

THE MAGISTERIUM AND DISSENT ON MORAL QUESTIONS

If an individual disagrees with the teaching of the Church's hierarchy on some point of morality, should that person follow the Church's teaching or reject it? There is no simple answer to this general question.

A. The Supremacy of Conscience

One is always obliged to follow one's conscience. Chapter One defined subjective moral goodness as choosing in accord with one's judgment of conscience. If I do not choose in accord with my judgment of conscience I am doing what I judge to be objectively evil, and I am subjectively guilty of evildoing. This holds true even if one's judgment of conscience is wrong. Suppose that a man, apparently in need, asks me for money which he says he needs to sustain him until his next paycheck. I judge that it is an objectively good thing to give him the money and that to refuse him would be immoral. In fact, however, he intends to use the money to help him commit an injustice against some third party. In reality, giving him the money is causing something objectively bad. Were I judging rightly I would judge that it is objectively morally wrong to give him the money. Nevertheless, if I refuse to give him the money I act in a subjectively immoral way because I act against my judgment of conscience.

Conscience is supreme, as far as subjective morality is concerned. To this we must add the complementary principle that the individual's conscience does not create the truth about objective morality. It should seek to conform to this truth. If, through no fault of one's own, one makes an erroneous judgment of conscience and acts in accord with it, one causes objective harm. If I kill an innocent person because I mistakenly judge that this is a good thing to do, I am not subjectively guilty, but the person is dead just the same. Along with the supremacy of one's conscience goes the crucial obligation to use all reasonable means to make a correct judgment of conscience.

Should one follow one's conscience if it goes against the teaching of the hierarchy of the Church? Yes. Subjective moral goodness, by definition, always means to follow one's conscience. In saying this, however, we have not addressed the really difficult issue. In arriving at a judgment of conscience, what weight is to be given to the teaching of the hierarchy of the Church?

The question must be broken down further, because the expression "the teaching of the hierarchy of the Church" covers many forms of teaching, from solemn definitions by an ecumenical council to a decree by the local ordinary. Several types of situations will be discussed.[1] No attempt will be made to give a simple formula for how to act in each case. Rather, certain considerations will be offered which are relevant for any prudential judgment about how to act in each type of situation.

B. Infallible Statements

Certain teachings have been solemnly defined by an ecumenical council or Pope as being true and as part of the Catholic faith. That such definitions are infallibly true does not mean necessarily that the formula used is the best possible. At some later time the Church may find a more perfect way of formulating the teaching. Nevertheless, the solemnly defined statement is true and is to be accepted by Catholics as true.

Few, if any, ethical doctrines have been defined in this solemn way. However, should circumstances make it advisable, there are ethical doctrines which could be defined in this way.

Suppose that an individual Catholic, after careful consideration, decides that he does not agree with a solemnly defined doctrine of the Church. Some other factors, apparently, have been weightier in this person's judgment than was the definition by the Church. How are we to judge this person's situation? Subjectively, the person must follow his own conscience. This much is clear. But there are other judgments to be made.

The Catholic Church judges that such a person is heretical, no longer belongs to the Church. Such a judgment does not imply that the person is sinning subjectively, or that this person is wicked, or to be rejected personally. It is a judgment that the person does not share in those fundamental beliefs which qualify one as belonging to the community of faith which is the Catholic Church.

Persons who do not accept the Church's solemn definitions should, in honesty, acknowledge that they no longer belong to the Church. They no longer accept the Church as a trustworthy guide to what is to be believed. For them to act as though they were members of the Catholic Church is to pretend to a unity which does not exist between themselves and the Church.

Besides issuing solemn definitions, the Catholic Church can also teach infallibly by what is called the "ordinary magisterium," as distinct from the "extraordinary magisterium" which is exercised in solemn definitions. If a teaching has been accepted as revealed by the whole Catholic Church, and the hierarchy has taught it unanimously, it can be presented as an infallibly true teaching of the ordinary magisterium. Frequently, however, it is difficult to determine whether the proper conditions have been fulfilled to constitute a teaching as infallible. For example, some writers have claimed that the Church's official teaching regarding artificial contraception is infallible.[2] Most writers on the subject say that it is not.

Certain teachings of the ordinary magisterium do fulfill the conditions for being infallible. For example, Christians are called to love God above all things, and to love their neighbors as themselves with a love like that which Jesus showed in his life, and this constitutes a fundamental norm for Christian life. There can be disputes and uncertainties about the exact nature of some things involved in this love, but the basic meaning of the teaching is clear. There is no significant dispute in the Church concerning the basic meaning of this teaching or about its truth.[3]

If after the proper investigation it is clear that a doctrine is presented by the ordinary magisterium as infallibly true, as part of the Catholic faith, then the individual stands in the same relationship toward such a teaching as toward a solemnly defined doctrine.

C. Consensus Statements

Some moral teachings are taught by the hierarchy, and there is a consensus among informed Catholics that they are true, although these teachings are not presented as infallible and part of the Catholic faith. The teaching on slavery is an example. Slavery is not condemned in the New Testament. In the letter to Philemon St. Paul presumes that slavery will continue, and he urges the master to treat his slave well. Over many centuries it became clear, however, both that society could get along without slaves, and that the practice of slavery goes against freedom to determine one's own life which is a right of every competent human being. That slavery is immoral is not, so far as I know, taught infallibly by the Church. It is taught by the Church,[4] however, and is not questioned by serious Catholic thinkers.

An individual Catholic may come to the conclusion that some people are better off as slaves because of their lack of prudence in running their own lives, and that slavery should be reinstituted to make profitable members of society out of a number of people who otherwise are likely to end up on skid row or become chronically dependent on welfare payments from the government. This pro-slavery opinion runs contrary to the consensus of opinion in the Church. What is the position of the holder of this opinion in relation to the Church?

Such a person is not a heretic. He has not denied anything which is part of the defined faith of the Church. He is not therefore automatically separated from the Church as a community of faith.

However, a reasonable person in this position must ask himself what chance he has of being right. Theoretically it is possible that he is right and all the rest of the Church is wrong. Practically, however, the chances of this being true are minuscule.

There is one situation in which the one (or a very few) people may be right and the rest of the Church wrong. The consensus in the Church may not be the result of careful and long consideration but be caused by lack of attention to a matter which is very new or which has not been considered worth serious study. The one person or a small group may be expert in this area and have come to an insight which the whole Church has not yet had a chance to gain.

If one thinks that this is indeed the case, one's first step should be to try to convince other intelligent people of the truth of one's position.

If one's position can stand up under criticism and is adopted by some intelligent and responsible people, the chances that one is right increase. If this does not happen, then the chances that one is right are extremely small.

D. Open Questions

Some moral problems can be considered open questions in the Church insofar as the hierarchy has given no clear teaching and there is no consensus in the Church on the point. Under what conditions, if any, may health care workers go on strike? On this issue there is no attempt by the hierarchy in general to give precise answers, though it has set forth certain general principles relevant to the problem. Nor is there a consensus in the Church on this issue.

Does this mean that Catholics are free to do as they like on this issue? Not at all. If on other issues Catholics feel bound by a Church teaching on morals it should be because they consider the teaching to be true. Fundamentally, it is by the truth that one is bound. Whether or not there is a clear teaching by the Church, there are other ways in which one can seek the truth on such ethical issues. One is bound to pursue these ways and one is bound by the truth as one discovers it.

E. Statements by Individual Bishops

The bishop who is the ordinary of a diocese has the responsibility for the teaching of Christian doctrine in that diocese. One way in which this responsibility is exercised is by issuing statements, either as pastoral letters or in some other form. To what extent are such statements binding on the Catholics in the diocese?

One must first consider the context and form of the statement. In a talk to the priests of a diocese, the ordinary in passing may make a particular point. No doubt he hopes that his listeners will take the remark seriously, but he is not giving it the full weight of his authority. Later in the talk, concerning another point, the bishop clearly and explicitly states that in this diocese a certain doctrine is to be taught and is not to be contradicted. Such a teaching has more authority behind it than does the first.

One should also relate any statement by a local ordinary to the teaching of the universal Church. Some statements by local ordinaries simply repeat positions already taken by Popes and the hierarchy generally. Of course such statements have great authority, even apart from their expression by this particular bishop. In other cases a local ordinary may make a pronouncement concerning which there is no definite papal teaching and no general agreement of the Church hierarchy. It seems that such statements cannot by themselves command the full assent of Catholics in the diocese. It would be strange if the fact of living in a particular diocese would make it obligatory for a person to accept as true some doctrine which he would be free to reject were he in another diocese. Bishops can, of course, make disciplinary rules which are to be obeyed even if one does not agree with them. The ordinary is responsible for the teaching of doctrine in his diocese. He can exercise this responsibility only if he has authority. If one is convinced that a bishop is mistaken, the normal response will be not to disregard his authority, but to try, if possible, to change his mind, or to have recourse to others who have a better chance of changing his mind. This does not mean that statements by ordinaries can have authority only as disciplinary rules. They can have authority also as statements of doctrine, but in this they have an authority which must be seen within the context of the whole teaching Church.

F. Papal Teaching without Consensus

Popes have taught consistently, over a considerable period of time, that artificial contraception is immoral.[5] This teaching was strongly reasserted by Pope Pius XI in 1930 in the encyclical letter *Casti Connubii*, and again by Pope Paul VI in 1968 in the encyclical letter *Humanae Vitae*. Through much of this time the papal teaching was accepted in the Church without much dissent. Since about 1960, however, a considerable number of Catholics, including many priests and theologians, have disagreed with this teaching.

Is an individual Catholic obliged to follow a papal teaching which is not presented as infallible[6] and concerning which there is no consensus in the Church?

1. The Appeal to History

The weight to be given to papal teaching must depend on the likelihood of its being correct. Some have argued that we should appeal to history in order to assess this likelihood. If it can be shown that papal teaching on moral matters has erred in the past, this lessens the weight we should give to it in the present. The argument then concludes with several instances of papal errors. [7]

The general lines of this argument seem to be sound. The more errors one can find in past papal teachings, the greater the likelihood of papal errors in the present, other things being equal. Furthermore, instances can be given of errors in papal teaching, or, at the very least, instances in which papal teaching had to be modified because at first it did not take account of all of the relevant factors. In other words, non-infallible papal teaching is not infallible, and history shows this.

However, to make this historical argument a sound one is not easy. If our purpose is to discover the likelihood of papal error, a simple list of four or ten or twenty papal errors is almost meaningless. More significant is the ratio of papal errors to times when the dissenters were wrong. At this point the magnitude of the task begins to appear.

To get a true picture, one should study all, or nearly all, of the instances of past dissent against papal teaching. This hardly seems possible, given the number of instances, the lack of records and the absence of effort by historians to be comprehensive on this matter. The two options are to get a representative sample or a random sample. It seems impossible to devise a plan to get a representative sample unless we know more than we do about the total sample. There seems to be no way of going back in history to get a random sample. The cases selected for study by historians are already biased by the various purposes of historians in selecting some cases for study and ignoring others. Theologians using the works of historians will add their own bias to the selection process, papal apologists noting especially notorious cases of errors by dissenters, while those on the other side are more likely to attend to cases of papal error.

The next problem will be to assess accurately that a Pope has been wrong. In certain cases this is clear enough, because the teaching of one Pope has been reversed or at least substantially modified by another Pope, and the change is not a matter of a mere change in circumstances requiring different applications. Where this change in official teaching is not present, then the assessment of whether the Pope erred will be a fallible human judgment, sometimes one shared by people generally once the arguments are made, sometimes one appealing only to a particular group.

Suppose that we were able to get an accurate list of times when Popes have erred and times when dissenters have erred, and we figured out the ratio between them. This information would still constitute too rough an instrument for bringing history to bear on the question of the reliability of papal teaching. More precise information about the papal errors would be necessary. Were they often on the level of general moral principles, or were they nearly all concerned with more specific norms? In the latter case even a considerable number of papal errors would not undermine papal authority concerning general moral principles. Were papal errors usually a matter of leaving out part of the truth, or were they often positive false teachings? Were many of the errors in matters which Popes had taught over a long period of time? Was the error usually a matter of the theology of the time being insufficiently developed, so that it was difficult to see how several aspects could be maintained at the same time, with the error being easily corrected with the advent of deeper theological insight in the Church? Or were the errors often the result of failure to use existing theology? Were the errors usually a result of caution, a concern not to jump into a new way of acting before sufficient time to evaluate it? Another set of questions might be posed concerning the conditions under which dissenters erred.

In order to illustrate the difficulty of applying historical information to the problem at hand, we will consider several cases which are frequently cited as instances of papal error. One such case concerned usury. During the rise of capitalism the Popes insisted, to an increasingly unheeding public, that usury, charging interest on a loan beyond that justified by the risk, is immoral. Gradually this insistence by the Popes ceased, and the Catholic Church apparently no longer condemns usury. This is sometimes presented as evidence that the papal condemnation of usury was an error.

The case bears closer analysis. A good case can be made that the Popes did not properly comprehend the creative role of capital in the economy, and so they failed to grasp the full import of the arguments justifying usury. To that extent any papal error concerned not basic values but applications in a particular area. Did the papal teaching, in balance, mislead the laity? It can be plausibly argued that it did not. The Popes were defending a basic principle which the capitalists neglected, and this neglect caused grave injustice. One possible formulation of this principle is that paying people in direct proportion to the wealth they already possess is not a just general system of distribution of material goods. Karl Marx rediscovered a form of this principle when he maintained that dead capital should not dominate living human beings. Had the papal teaching been taken more seriously, grave injustice might have been avoided without resorting to the extremes of communism.

In short, it is not clear that papal teaching on usury is a valid example of an error which would convince right thinking people to give less weight to papal authority on moral matters.

Another case sometimes cited as a papal error is the condemnation of democracy by Pope Pius IX in his *Syllabus of Errors*. Bishop Dupanloup of Orleans in France wrote a *Catechism of the Syllabus of Errors* in which he related the condemnation of democracy (and other condemnations in the *Syllabus*) to events of the time. The bishop distinguishes two levels. On the level of theory, the condemnation makes perfect sense. Democracy, as Pope Pius IX used the term, made the will of the people supreme. This would mean that the will of the people is not subject to the moral law or to God. Such a view is rightly condemned. On the level of concrete reality, certain political movements in France called themselves democratic. However, they did not necessarily espouse the erroneous position condemned by the Pope, so these movements were not necessarily condemned by the Pope. The bishop sent a copy of his *Catechism* to Pope Pius IX, who thanked him for his help in applying the teaching of the *Syllabus*. The Pope and the bishop may not have agreed entirely in their evaluation of certain political movements which were identified as democratic. However, if the Pope allowed this interpretation of his condemnation of democracy, that condemnation ceases to be a convincing example of a papal error.

Another case sometimes cited as an example of papal error is not primarily in the area of morals, but it is worth considering because it is sometimes introduced into the discussion of papal authority in morals. It is the case of the condemnation of modernism by Pope Pius X. Among the modernist doctrines condemned by the Pope are some now accepted by many Catholic thinkers, and even by the magisterium, at least in some modified form.

This condemnation of modernism must be evaluated in relation to the stage of development of thought on certain subjects at that time. Many of the modernist ideas were new to the Catholic Church at the time of Pope Pius X. Among those ideas, some have been shown to have implications clearly at variance with the Catholic faith. It would be asking a great deal of papal teaching to expect it immediately to sort out the ideas which were compatible with Catholic faith and those which were not. The Church exists as an historical entity, and its understanding develops in time.

One might suggest that, in cases such as the modernist crisis, authorities should remain silent until scholars have clarified the matter further. Such a practice is probably correct in a debating society. It is not obvious that it is correct in a Church whose members live by a set of beliefs, on the basis of which they try to relate to God, to pray, to discover what God is calling them to do. At the time of Pope Pius X some of the basic beliefs were being challenged. It is not merely that the uneducated need to be protected from the excess of academic speculation. It is not unthinkable that academics themselves, both in their theology and in their lives, may profit from pastoral guidance.

No effort is being made here to prove that Pope Pius X's treatment of modernism was the best possible, or faultless. The point is simply that it would be difficult to show that it was an error which would make any reasonable person give less weight to papal authority in the future.

Given the difficulties in appealing to history in evaluating papal authority in moral matters, any conclusions must be impressionistic. This author's impression is that in the very large majority of cases, papal teaching has been right and dissenters have been wrong, and especially so in the area of general principles.

The appeal to history provides only a very vague indication of the weight to be given to papal authority on moral matters. We will attempt to find more precision by considering three possible positions that might be taken on the question. The first two positions discussed are not meant to represent the thinking of any particular thinker, but are hypotheses set up as a means of probing the question.

2. *A Position Emphasizing Papal Authority*

An emphasis on papal authority might be supported by the following argument: clearly, papal teachings which are not set forth as infallible may err; however, in any particular case the papal teaching is more likely to be correct than is the position of dissent from that teaching; therefore dissent from papal teaching is never legitimate. This position allows further scholarly research and discussion on points on which there has been official papal teaching and the presentation of the results of this research and discussion to the hierarchy. Because papal teaching can be uncertain, even if more likely than dissenting views, this research and discussion is useful to achieve greater certainty, either by showing that the official position has stood up under critical examination, or by leading to modification of the official teaching to take account of all valid arguments that are offered. There are reasons to believe that this discussion will be more rational and nuanced, as well as less confusing to the public, if it takes place in scholarly circles rather than in the media. This scholarly effort would still need to learn from the living experience of unscholarly people.

The argument just set forth may appear too general to be convincing. Some dissenters may admit that in a large majority of cases the Popes have been right and dissenters have been wrong, or at least that the Popes have been closer than the dissenters to the truth. Even if this be granted, however, it does not prove that in each and every particular case an individual should conclude that the papal teaching is more likely to be right than is a dissenting opinion. The fact that most dissent is illegitimate does not prove that it is never legitimate in a particular case.

This argument may call for a further position from the pro-papal side. Suppose one grants that in certain cases an individual dissents not because of ignorance or bias or selfishness, but because of sound reasoning. Let us suppose, further, that there are valid criteria by which individuals can know whether their dissent is justified or not. Suppose then that one concludes that in certain special cases one may dissent from official papal teaching on morals. This conclusion, however, does not lead only to a few cases of valid dissent. It leads to a lot of other people thinking they have a valid case for dissent when they do not. The problem is that the criteria for judging whether dissent is legitimate are vague and prone to subjectivist use, and so they do not present real, effective boundaries for dissent. Allowing any dissent, this argument states, leads to more harm than good. Therefore one should adopt the rule that no dissent is legitimate.

This conclusion is not easy to disprove in any definitive way, given the difficulty of accurately calculating the possible good or evil results of either allowing or disallowing dissent. For the same reason, it is difficult to prove the conclusion definitively. On three points, however, the argument requires further clarification. First, does the denial of the legitimacy of any dissent adequately allow for the different degrees of authority attached to different papal teachings? Second, while allowing that there are bad results of allowing dissent, what are the bad results of disallowing it? Third, granted that certain ways of formulating the criteria for dissent are so vague that subjectivism results, can a more satisfactory formulation of the criteria be found?

We will begin with the first point. It is generally agreed that different papal teachings carry different degrees of authority. Other things being equal, a teaching repeated many times by several Popes over a long period of time has more authority than a teaching stated only once or twice. A papal statement on some point which has arisen recently usually will not carry as much weight as a papal teaching held consistently over a long period of time during which the subject has received frequent consideration. A papal statement on a point which has recently arisen may well be cautionary rather than definitive. It indicates that at this stage of the development of thought on the point, the new ideas cannot be accepted in the form in which they have been presented. At some later stage in the development of thought on a point, further formulations may be found which allow the acceptance of what is good in the new ideas without the acceptance of error or the denial of truths arrived at in the past. If the issue has arisen recently, the papal teaching is more likely to be cautionary and admitting of development than if the issue has been discussed for several generations.

Other things being equal, a papal teaching which has not been repeated for several decades, in spite of some Catholics disregarding it, does not have as much authority as a teaching which is repeated by Popes who try to convince dissenters to accept it. Other things being equal, a papal teaching on some point central to Christian life has more authority than a papal teaching on some more peripheral point. For example, a papal statement on the need for repentance is more authoritative than a papal statement on the value of boy scout training. The format and context of a teaching also indicate its authoritative quality. Other things being equal, a papal teaching which is the central theme of an encyclical addressed to all Catholics has more authority than a remark to an audience of visiting delegates to a journalists' convention.

If one holds that papal teaching is not entirely independent of the resources of the rest of the Church and of other people for reaching the truth, then the difficulty and obscurity which the subject matter presents to other people will affect the degree of certainty, and therefore the authority, of papal teaching. Often moralists attain a high degree of certainty on some general principle but only a lesser degree of certitude concerning policies for applying the general principle in special kinds of situations. For example, all agree that world leaders and others are morally obliged to put forth strenuous efforts to avoid war. Not all agree on the precise steps to be taken to achieve this end. It seems that papal teaching on the general principle can be more certain, and have greater authority, than can papal statements on the tactics to be used. (Of course in some cases one can be very certain even about what is to be done in particular cases, and in these instances the papal teaching on the more particular level would be highly authoritative.)

Again, if one holds that papal teaching is not entirely independent of the resources of the rest of the Church and of other people for reaching the truth, then the degree and quality of dissent seems to give some indication of the certainty, and therefore the authority, of papal teaching. If the only dissenters are ignorant people who are obviously biased, such dissent says little about the authority of a teaching. If the dissenters are careful, well-informed and fair-minded people who usually strive earnestly to fulfill their moral obligations, the dissent would be more relevant in assessing the authority of a papal teaching.

Noting several factors which might lessen the authority of papal teaching does not necessarily imply that in any case the papal authority becomes negligible. Authority may be lessened but remain very strong. For example, a certain type of dissent may lessen the certainty of a papal teaching but still leave a very strong presumption that the teaching is right.

If all dissent from papal moral teaching is forbidden, then the different degrees of authority of different papal teachings become irrelevant for the formation of conscience, for deciding what I should do in a particular situation. All papal teachings are to be followed, and therefore, from this point of view, all would have equal authority.[8] There have been a number of respected Catholic moralists in the past, writers whose books had ecclesiastical approval, who have rejected such a view. They have discussed the possibility of, and the conditions for, dissent from official Church teaching, even papal teaching.[9] However, it would be impossible to get agreement about where one should draw the line. All, or nearly all, serious Catholic moralists would agree that a papal statement on a very peripheral matter, or a passing remark to an audience of tourists, does not have fully binding authority. They would admit that one could act against such teachings when very good reasons were available, due counsel was taken, etc. Many, but not all, serious Catholic moralists would hold that if a papal teaching has not been repeated for several decades, in spite of the fact that a considerable number of Catholics are ignoring it, such a teaching might be rejected under certain conditions. In general, however, differences of opinion are many concerning what types of papal teaching should be seen as binding in all situations on all Catholic consciences. One generally accepted conclusion is that different papal teachings have different degrees of authority, and that there are cases in which this degree of authority will allow disagreement with the papal teaching.

The second point to be considered concerns the bad effects of disallowing all dissent from papal teaching on morality. One possible bad effect is obvious. Non-infallible papal moral teaching can err. Those following mistaken papal opinions cause harm. If dissent were allowed, some of that harm would be averted because some people would adopt and follow a norm closer to the truth than is the papal teaching.

A further factor may be relevant here. Members of the hierarchy can have their own biases, narrowness and other limitations in judging ethical matters. For example, some may emphasize authority to the extent of using it as a substitute for giving adequate reasons for moral norms. Some may suspect that other people will nearly always use their freedom badly. Some will fail to appreciate situations which are strange to them, or which are new, or which arise in a foreign culture. Nor are members of the hierarchy immune to the class or nationalistic biases which distort the thinking of other people.

Ideally, these and any other shortcomings of members of the hierarchy in making moral judgments will be overcome by the grace of office and by the use of various resources in the Church to help make sound ethical judgments. There is no guarantee, however, that these shortcomings are always overcome.

It is rather commonly noted that there is a sort of "curial mentality" that sometimes arises among Vatican officials which may set them at odds with the thinking and attitudes of others in the Church. This curial mentality has certain strengths, but it also has certain weaknesses. The ways in which some curial officials have dealt with certain scholars in the past, scholars who later have been "rehabilitated" and have had great influence on official Church thinking, cause many to be suspicious of the mentality of Vatican congregations. Theologians like John Henry Newman in the last century, and Henri de Lubac and Yves Congar in this century, seem not always to have gotten a fair hearing at the Vatican.

Will the Pope always overcome the limitations to which other members of the hierarchy are subject in judging ethical matters? One must note that Popes are in several ways favorably situated to do so. They have a special grace of office. Usually they have been selected for the office because of their outstanding intellectual and spiritual qualities. Furthermore, the Pope is charged with a mission more universal than that of other officials in the Church. He is a reference point for the whole Church. He is forced to consider a broad range of factors, to receive submissions from widely different groups. Those with more limited charges are more likely to have a more limited perspective. It is also clear that Popes characteristically have felt strongly that they are charged with guarding the faith which has been handed down, and this has given them a healthy distance from enthusiasms which have temporarily focused too exclusively on one aspect of the truth and have obscured other aspects of it. These advantages give added authority to papal teaching. However, we are given no guarantee that Popes will always overcome the limitations normal to human beings in making ethical judgments.

If one suspects that a particular papal teaching has indeed been the result of some shortcoming or limitation of the Pope, one's first responses should be prayer and making effective representations to the proper authorities. It remains possible that even very lucid and thoroughly reasoned representations will not get a good hearing. If no dissent is allowed, it becomes too easy for the hierarchy to stifle all opinions but their own, without the Pope really having much hand in the matter. Dissent, therefore, could be a useful corrective for shortcomings of the hierarchy, including the Pope, in making ethical judgments. The possibility of dissent increases the likelihood of extensive interaction between the Pope and others knowledgeable in ethical questions. This can lead not only to an increased likelihood of modification of papal teaching when that is needed, but also to an increased likelihood that papal moral teaching will be accompanied with persuasive reasons which help people to appreciate the teaching more fully.

We have spoken of possible evil results of disallowing all dissent from papal moral teaching. It is difficult to get agreement as to the extent of these effects in the real world. Some would consider that Popes err extremely rarely, at least on substantive matters, and so they see only a minimum of evil effects from disallowing dissent. Others see papal errors as more frequent and more substantive, with correspondingly greater harm resulting from lack of dissent. Against the evil effects (however great they are) of disallowing dissent from papal moral teaching we must weigh the evil effects of allowing such dissent. If it is possible to formulate criteria for dissent which people will apply objectively, so that most dissent that actually occurs is legitimate, then the evil effects of allowing dissent are minimal. If it is not possible to formulate such criteria, then the evil effects of allowing dissent will be serious indeed. What will result will be not simply the mistaken judgment and action of this or that dissenter, but the erosion in society of people's appreciation for genuine values and moral norms.

We will turn now to one attempt to formulate criteria for dissent from papal moral teaching.

3. A Position Allowing Limited Dissent

This section will present a position allowing limited dissent from papal moral teachings. In theory at least, this position sees the possibility of legitimate dissent, in special circumstances, from any papal moral teaching which has not been set forth as infallible. This position attempts to provide several safeguards in order to minimize illegitimate dissent.

First, in deciding whether dissent is justified one must take account of the different degrees of authority attaching to different papal teachings. These differences have been set forth in the preceding section. Dissent against the most authoritative non-infallible papal moral teachings would be justified only rarely and for the strongest reasons. According as the papal teachings are less authoritative, dissent would be justified more frequently and for less grave reasons. In no case, however, might dissent against a papal teaching be justified for anything less than serious and convincing reasons.

Second, dissent from a papal moral teaching is not justified simply because one is not persuaded by the reasons given in support of the teaching. If one agrees with papal teaching only when one is persuaded by the reasons given, one gives to the Pope no more authority than one would give to one's bartender or hairdresser or anyone with whom one might discuss an ethical question. The Pope would become simply one more person in the debate. Without further authority he cannot function as an instrument of unity in the Church, as an agent challenging all parties in the Church to adopt a comprehensive view of each issue, and as a guardian against erosion of fundamental values.

It follows that one should approach any papal teaching with a presumption that it is correct, and with an especially strong presumption that the more authoritative teachings are correct. More than that, one should hope to find that papal teachings are correct. If one values the unity of the Church one will be disappointed if it appears that an important instrument of that unity has failed in its task.

Consequently, if one finds oneself in possible disagreement with papal moral teaching, one should suspect that one has made a mistake in one's thinking. One should carefully review the reasons which are leading one to a conclusion incompatible with papal teaching, to see if those reasons appear sound. One should review the reasons given by the hierarcy or by theologians in support of the papal teaching, to see if one has grasped their full implications.

One's examination of the case should extend not only to intellectual arguments but also to one's own attitude. Am I biased? Am I rationalizing a decision I have made on selfish grounds? Am I being honest, humble, and courageous in facing my own limitations? Does my life exhibit patience, kindness, and the other gifts and fruits of the Holy Spirit? Or is my thinking too much influenced by anger, or disdain, or hurt feelings, or arrogance?

Before deciding that dissent is legitimate one should look at one's own capacity for making moral judgments. Am I well qualified to judge in these matters? If I attempt to make up for my lack of qualifications by seeking expert advice, am I well qualified to choose good advisors? Do I choose advisors because they are likely to say what I want them to say?

One should take counsel not only to get the views of specialists but also to gain objectivity. The advice of objective counselors is an important means for overcoming one's own bias and tendency to subjectivism.

On any important moral judgment one should pray, not as a pious afterthought but as an essential step. Many moral decisions have consequences and implications beyond our ability to grasp. We must open ourselves to the Holy Spirit to guide us by a wisdom greater than our own. Prayer is especially important if one is considering dissent from a papal moral teaching.

In this chapter we will use the expression "tentative personal judgment" to refer to the moral judgment one would make if there were no papal teaching. One may make a tentative personal judgment when first confronted by a moral issue. Finding that this judgment conflicts with papal teaching, one may go through the process of conscientiously applying the safeguards discussed above. At the end of that process one's tentative personal judgment may have changed to conform to the papal teaching. That is, a careful examination of the matter may lead one to conclude that the papal position would be the most convincing one even if it were not taught by the Pope. In that case the conflict is resolved and we need discuss the situation no further. The other possible outcome of conscientiously applying safeguards is that there is still a conflict between one's tentative personal judgment and the papal teaching.

There are three possible general policies which one might adopt for such situations. The first policy is that, after conscientiously applying the proper safeguards, one always follows the papal teaching. The second policy is that, after conscientiously applying the proper safeguards, one always follows one's tentative personal judgment. The third policy is that, after conscientiously applying the proper safeguards, one should sometimes follow papal teaching and sometimes follow one's tentative personal judgment, depending upon the situation. We will consider each policy in turn.

The first policy is equivalent to the alternative discussed in the preceding section. If one does not allow dissent from papal teaching after applying the safeguards, certainly one should not allow them before applying the safeguards. In effect, then, the first policy implies that one should never dissent from any papal moral teaching. In discussing this position in the previous section we suggested that it is not self-evidently right, and before it could be accepted as correct, several further matters would have to be examined. This examination has led to our present discussion.

The second alternative policy supposes that one has taken sufficient account of papal authority if one has conscientiously applied the proper safeguards. Having done so, one may follow one's tentative personal judgment with no further need to consider authority.

The legitimate reason for following any moral judgment is that it is true. This second policy, accordingly, implies that whenever one has conscientiously applied the safeguards, one's tentative personal judgment is at least as likely to be true as is the papal teaching. Now, at least sometimes, Popes can be expected conscientiously to apply the proper safeguards, and, at least sometimes, Popes are better situated to know the truth than are those who differ with them. It is hardly plausible, then, that in all cases when persons conscientiously apply the proper safeguards concerning a controverted moral issue, they are as likely to be right as is the Pope.

The point can be illustrated. From Pope Leo XIII to the present, the general social doctrine of the Popes has been critical of some aspects of capitalism and also some aspects of socialism. Some people, including some Catholics, dissent from the papal teaching because it is too capitalistic. Others, including some Catholics, dissent from it because it is too socialistic. (The fact that the dissent often consists of ignoring the papal teaching rather than addressing it directly does not make it any the less a real disent.) It is not likely that if all these dissenters were to apply the proper safeguards to the best of their ability they would all end up agreeing with the papal teaching. Deep-seated bias, particular group interests and long-standing habits of thought do not so easily dissolve. According to the second policy, all of those on the left and all of those on the right who continue to disagree with the Pope are at least as likely to be correct as is the Pope. One does not need to be a papal loyalist to see that this is improbable.

Another illustration might be taken from what could easily happen in the future. It is quite possible that a Pope may wish to make a pronouncement on liberation theology. Whatever that pronouncement might be, almost certainly a number of Catholics, even after conscientiously applying the proper safeguards, will maintain tentative personal judgments in conflict with the papal pronouncement. The second policy implies that, whatever the papal pronouncement may be, these tentative personal judgments in all cases are at least as likely to be correct as is the papal pronouncement. This is hardly plausible.

The third alternative is a policy of sometimes following papal teaching and sometimes following one's own tentative personal judgment, when a conflict between the two remains even after the application of the proper safeguards. On what criteria will one decide which course to follow? One must consider the degree of authority of the papal teaching; the greater the degree of authority, the stronger is the supposition that the papal teaching is correct and the stronger must be the reasons to justify dissent. This leaves us with vague criteria. The degree of authority and the strength of the reasons are not matters which can be nicely calculated and then compared. This vagueness leaves the way open to subjectivism, individuals calculating according to their own bias, selfishness, or narrow point of view.

Some authors may try to escape this danger of subjectivism, while still allowing some dissent, by saying that dissent against highly authoritative papal teachings would be justified only in extremely rare cases in which extraordinarily strong reasons for dissent are present. Others would object that, in order to prevent abuse, these authors have overstated the case against dissent, making it practically impossible. The problem seems to be that in order to remove abuse of the vague criteria it seems necessary to overstate the case against dissent.

The problem is to find criteria for dissent which can be applied without serious danger of subjectivism. If one could formulate such criteria, and then subject them to public scrutiny and discussion, perhaps most of the controversy in the Catholic Church about dissent from papal moral teachings would disappear. It is this author's impression that most of those who want to disallow all dissent or severely restrict it would be willing to allow it in a few more cases if they thought it could be kept within objectively pre-determined limits. It is this author's impression also that most of those who argue for more tolerance for dissent are not at all interested in sponsoring the kind of widespread dissent which arises from subjectivist application of vague norms.

Can such criteria for dissent be formulated in a satisfactory way?

4. Proposed Additional Criteria

This section offers further criteria for dissent from papal moral teachings, criteria which, it is hoped, can be applied more objectively than those usually proposed. The criteria given here are not easily usable by people unaccustomed to critical and sophisticated ethical thinking. These are criteria to be used by moralists. They are presented with the awareness that further discussion may show the need for substantial revision, or at least for modifications, of the position here presented.

We will distinguish two categories of papal moral teaching. The first category consists of those teachings which are stated as important points in a papal encyclical to the whole Church, or which have been presented by a Pope in an equally authoritative way, and which have not become "dead letters" because of papal silence over several decades in the face of a contrary practice by a significant number of Catholics.[10] The second category consists of all other papal moral teachings.

It seems that dissent from a papal moral teaching in the second category is legitimate if both of two conditions are fulfilled. First, after conscientiously applying the safeguards discussed above, one's tentative personal judgment is that the papal teaching is wrong. Second, one's tentative personal judgment is shared by a considerable number of respected Catholic moralists. Both of these conditions need further explanation.

To fulfill the first condition it is not enough that, after one has conscientiously applied the safeguards, one's tentative personal judgment leans toward the belief that the papal teaching is wrong. One must be able to say: "After conscientiously applying the safeguards, there is no real doubt in my mind that, had the Popes not taught this doctrine, I would be convinced that it is wrong. In balance, the arguments from human reason, experience, Sacred Scripture, tradition and authority do not incline me to accept this doctrine. The only reason why I might accept it is the papal authority."

The second condition is that one's tentative personal judgment is shared by a considerable number of respected Catholic moralists. Respected Catholic moralists are those who, by the quality of their writings or by some other means, have come to be judged by their peers to be moralists of superior learning and soundness of judgment in moral matters. "A considerable number" is a vague term, but a very precise term here is not defensible. A considerable number is a large enough number to assure that the position of these moralists on a particular question is not a result of personal eccentricities, and that the moralists do not come primarily from one area, class or in-group which would allow their position to be the product of group narrowness and bias. If one were to do a rather extensive consultation and found that twenty percent of the moralists consulted hold a particular position, and the moralists who make up the twenty percent do not come mainly from any one group, this would seem to constitute "a considerable number."

Notice that we do not require that one find a considerable number of Catholic moralists who actually dissent from the papal teaching. There need only be a considerable number whose tentative judgment of conscience goes against papal teaching. Were one to require for legitimate dissent that one first find others who dissent, no dissent could ever get started in a legitimate way. According to our position, dissent could begin in a legitimate way if a sufficient number of moralists began to make tentative personal judgments at variance with the papal theology.

These criteria for dissent from papal teachings in the second category remain vague. It seems that this vagueness can be tolerated without great harm. It need not erode the ability of Popes to perform their role in moral teaching. If a Pope finds that a particular teaching is being neglected, he can move that teaching out of the second category and into the first by repeating the teaching in a suitably authoritative way.

Concerning dissent from papal moral teachings in the first category it is important to formulate more precise criteria. It seems that dissent in this case would be legitimate only if all of three conditions are fulfilled. First, after conscientiously applying the safeguards discussed above, one's tentative personal judgment is that the papal teaching is wrong. Second, there is convincing support within the Church for one's tentative personal judgment. Third, adequate account is taken of the need for papal authority in moral matters. The first condition here is the same as the first condition for dissent from papal moral teaching in the second category. It need not be explained further here. The other two conditions require further explanation.

The second condition for dissent from papal moral teachings in the first category involves several requirements. First, a very significant number of respected Catholic moralists, close to a majority of those who have studied the question thoroughly, must agree with one's tentative judgment of conscience. Furthermore, it is not enough that we simply ascertain the number of moralists who hold this view. One must also examine their arguments critically. Have they fairly represented and properly understood the arguments of those who oppose their position? Are their own arguments sound? We must also critically examine the attitude of these moralists in the debate itself. Do they generally show patience, intellectual humility, fairness, respect for their opponents' intelligence? Or are they generally disdainful, impatient or hurt or angry when people oppose them, unable to acknowledge weakness or lack of clarity in their own position? One must also examine the attitude these moralists take in their other writings. Are they habitually fair-minded, patient, etc.? One should ascertain whether these moralists belong predominantly to any one class, geographic area, political unit or any other in-group. If so, is it likely that their positions are influenced by in-group bias or narrowness?

Among those moralists who dissented from the papal teaching on artificial contraception there were some who did not contribute to any "convincing support within the Church" for the dissenting view, because they failed to meet some of the above requirements. For example, some seemed to be very sensitive to hardships that might result from the papal teaching, but passed over very lightly the danger of erosion of values. Some lashed out at the "tired old celibates" in the Vatican who presumed to speak on the ethics of marriage. Any calculation of the convincing support in the Church for one's position must discount these dissenters and look only at the more carefully reasoned and fair-minded dissent.

The third condition for legitimate dissent against papal moral teaching in the first category is that adequate account be taken of the need for papal authority in moral matters. This requires that we have a very strong presumption that papal teachings in this category are correct. Only the very strongest and most convincing reasons could justify the judgment that they are false. "Very strong presumption" and "very strongest and most convincing reasons" are vague expressions. We can have greater precision if we say that the presumption that the papal teaching is true must be strong enough to ensure that the Pope can function effectively as an instrument to unify moral teaching in the Church, can challenge all parties in the Church to accept a comprehensive view on any moral issue, and can guard against the erosion of basic Christian values by a too easy acceptance of the spirit of a particular age, of a social class, of a fashion, or of any particular group. Part Four has attempted to explain why the Church needs the Pope to function in this way, and the discussion need not be repeated. Here it is sufficient to say that if bias, rationalization, narrowness of outlook, and special interests are extremely difficult to overcome, then papal authority must be correspondingly strong.

As a test of one's attitude, one should widen one's consideration, beyond the issue on which one would like to dissent, to include another issue on which one wholeheartedly supports the papal teaching. Suppose one would like to dissent from papal teaching on artificial contraception, but one wholeheartedly supports papal teaching on the need for wealthy nations to give extensive aid to the third world. One should ask: On the question of artificial contraception have I given to papal teaching a limited authority which, if applied generally, would allow others to continue to ignore their duties to the third world? In advocating the freedom to dissent on one issue, have I introduced a standard which, if used generally, would prevent the Pope from functioning effectively as a moral teacher?

The criteria for dissent given here are intended to cover the most likely cases. There may be very exceptional cases in which other criteria are important. For example, a Pope may show by a series of erratic actions or statements that he has lost possession of his critical faculties. In other cases it may be not moralists but much of the hierarchy which dissents from a papal teaching. In another type of case, a papal statement might be mainly a word of caution on a new problem the implications of which are not yet clear to the Pope and his advisors, while another group has had much longer to study the implications of the question. These cases would involve criteria beyond those discussed above.

There is a sort of continuum of non-infallible papal moral teachings, from the most authoritative to the least authoritative. For the sake of simplicity we have divided the continuum into only two categories. To apply our conclusions to actual situations a final qualification must be added. Some papal teachings belong to the second category but are toward the more authoritative end of that category. The potential dissenter against such papal teachings should make some limited use of the criteria for dissent against papal teachings of the first category.

Even these criteria for dissent against papal moral teachings in the first category are still somewhat vague. Some may object that they are so vague that they will be applied subjectively, leading to mistaken moral judgments and the erosion of values.

To this objection, several responses may be made. First, the objection may be right. This is not a question on which certainty is easily obtained. Second, perhaps it is not so much that these criteria are vague as that they require time, effort and expertise to be applied properly. Third, perhaps we have tended to depend too much on papal authority to unify moral teaching, to challenge consciences, to guard the permanently valid moral principles. While keeping a strong papal authority, perhaps we need a much greater emphasis on a vital community of life, a life of prayer, and a life of faith, by which the Holy Spirit will produce an inner unity. Fourth, whether the criteria which are presented here are satisfactory or not, it remains clear that a core question concerning dissent is whether it is possible to formulate norms which can be applied objectively. If the criteria for dissent formulated here are not satisfactory, that is no reason to give up the attempt to formulate better ones.

The criteria given above are suitable for application by specialists. What of the ordinary "man in the street"? Perhaps there are no criteria for dissent which can be applied easily by the non-specialist. In morals, as in medicine, law or engineering, often the laymen can exercise responsibility only by choosing and following an expert.

The choice of an expert in Christian morals presents another problem. The normal procedure for the non-specialist in the Catholic Church is to turn to the hierarchy, by which one is in touch with the universal Church, and to those experts approved by the hierarchy. Can it ever be a responsible action for the non-specialist Catholic to choose to be guided by a particular moralist or moralists rather than by the hierarchy? Such a choice seems to imply one of two things. It may imply that the chooser is competent to make this choice. This would be equivalent to dropping the role of non-specialist and assuming the role of competent specialist. Then the question is whether the person really has this competence. The other possible implication is that moralists themselves constitute a sort of magisterium to which the non-specialist can turn with the same confidence as to the hierarchy. How such an implication can be reconciled with unity in the Church is a question that this author cannot answer. Working out the answer may be a work more of ecclesiology than of ethics.

On the question of dissent against papal teaching, this book has attempted to locate the problem properly and to outline some of the relevant factors. It must end, however, not so much with an answer as with an agenda for further work.

5. *A Final Note*

Controversy in the Church has one sad side-effect. It focuses attention on the controverted point, on what is least certain, often to the neglect of what is more certain and perhaps more important. However satisfying this may be as an academic procedure, it can be almost catastrophic for the Church, for the people of God, for the body of Christ. It can starve the soul and destroy the only possible basis for future unity.

The current controversy on artificial contraception has left many Catholics with the impression that the main thing the Catholic Church teaches about sex in marriage is that birth control should not be used. The encyclical *Humanae Vitae* contains splendid passages about the positive meaning of marriage. What most Catholics know about it is that it condemns artificial contraception. If that particular question is ever going to be resolved in the Church, it will be because people begin to live to the full those basic truths about which there is no controversy. Then they will develop the virtues, the appetites, the perceptions, which will show what is truly of value. This is how the Holy Spirit, if allowed, will bring unity to the issue.

NOTES

Introduction

1. Of course I don't mean that this basis for Christian ethics is one simple thing or concept. To a question concerning the weight of each ship in the U.S. Navy, the one correct answer would be multiple, giving the different ships with the weight of each. Concerning the basis for Christian ethics there is one fully correct and adequate explanation, though that explanation would be complex.

2. Jacques Ellul is a good example of such a thinker. See, for example, his *The Theological Foundation of Law*.

Chapter One:
Elements of the Moral Act

1. Here we use the term "objective elements" rather than "object" because the latter term is commonly used to denote only one of the elements with which we are concerned here.

Chapter Two:
Ethical Relativism

1. A well-known advocate of ethical relativism earlier in this century was Edward Westermarck. His book *Ethical Relativity*, published in London in 1932, was republished in Paterson, N.J., in 1960, by Littlefield, Adams. A useful explanation of ethical relativism is given by Richard B. Brandt in Chapter Eleven of *Ethical Theory*, Englewood Cliffs, N.J., Prentice-Hall, 1959. Our purpose here is not to give a complete exposition of ethical relativism in its various forms, but only to

applied to moral good and evil whereas the relativism mentioned here applies to good and evil generally.

Chapter Four:
Human Appetitive Potential

1. A development of appetite is accompanied by a development in knowledge, since the appetitive act depends upon a cognitive act. A development of one's appreciation for friendship involves some development in one's knowledge of persons.

2. Later parts of this book will touch upon some aspects of this problem of certitude concerning what is good. Part Three will discuss how we go from general principles, which often are known with a considerable degree of certitude, to practical applications, which often are held with less certainty. Part Four will discuss how the individual's fallible judgment is helped by the resources of the community in judging what is good.

Chapter Six:
Moral Good and Moral Evil

1. Notice that we are talking here about *objective* moral good. In this second case we should not confuse the objective moral good, the good which happens to the other person, with the subjective moral good, my free choice to do what I judge to be morally good.

2. Of course in real situations the alternatives may not be simple goods or evils but combinations of several goods and evils. So when we speak, for the sake of simplicity, of a good, it may be a combination of goods and evils which provides for a preponderance of good over evil. In speaking of an evil we may be referring to a combination of goods and evils which gives a preponderance of evil over good.

When we speak of the whole of what is good for the individual it must be understood that the moral agent normally will not have perfect knowledge of all of the many things which go together to make up this total good. It is a question of making judgments as well as one can with imperfect knowledge.

3. When morality is considered in connection with one's relationship with God this choice of a lesser moral good and exclusion of a greater good takes on a further significance. The choice of the lesser good may in some cases at least be seen as a rejection of God, and so takes on the character of sin.

4. To some, the term "reason" may suggest a primarily cognitive element, whereas "subjective reason" here refers to appetite, and is the equivalent of "motive" as that term is used in Chapter Three. The use of the term "reason" to refer to an appetite has some foundation in popular usage. Anger and hunger are spoken of as reasons why people do certain things.

5. If the inability to learn to appreciate a certain thing (e.g., a state of consciousness) is the result of an inability to achieve it, then this source of variation in moral judgment seems to be not very different from the difference in situation which was noted in the previous paragraph as a source of variation.

**Chapter Seven:
Toward Adult Morality**

1. This discussion attempts to describe the development of feelings of guilt and of self-approval without adopting and trying to prove a Freudian or any other psychological theory.

2. We are speaking here of one type of feeling of guilt and one type of feeling of self-approval, the types of feelings which are learned by the child in response to blame or praise by parents or others. Presumably there are other types of feelings of guilt and of self-approval to which the following discussion would not apply.

3. Some writers have made much of the fact that one experiences an "inner voice" which accuses or praises or points out what is to be done, and that this "voice" is experienced as something objective insofar as it imposes itself on the person rather than seeming to arise from the subjectivity of the person. Some even go so far as to see in this "voice" a more or less direct evidence of God speaking inwardly to the person. That is, the fact that the voice imposes itself upon the person, and so does not appear as the voice of the subject but rather as the voice of an absolute authority above the subject, is taken as evidence that it is the voice of

God. Caution is required before coming to such a conclusion. If the "inner voice" is in fact the kind of feeling of guilt or of self-approval whose genesis we have discussed, quite a different conclusion is possible. Perhaps it is experienced as objective and as the voice of an absolute authority above the subject simply because that is how the child first experienced the praise or blame by the parent. This is not to deny that there are other aspects of moral experience which open one to a religious dimension of life.

Part Two

1. Any serious discussion of Scripture is confronted by the often controversial conclusions of scholars using modern methods of exegesis. Part Two presumes some general positions on which modern scriptural scholars are agreed. For example, it presumes that the Pentateuch contains materials written at different times over a period of some centuries. Some parts can be dated with some precision and certainty; some cannot. An attempt has been made in Part Two to avoid positions which are controverted by modern scholars. For this reason no effort has been made to support positions by reference to the abundant scholarly material which is available.

Chapter Eight:
Law and Covenant in the Old Testament

1. A number of authors have discussed the significance of the relation of the Mosaic law to the covenant. Especially helpful is *La morale de l'Alliance* (Cahiers de la Revue Biblique) by Jean L'Hour, Paris, 1966. Eichrodt has developed the theme of covenant as the key to understanding the Old Testament generally. See Walter Eichrodt, *Theology of the Old Testament*, Volumes I and II (translated from the German), Philadelphia, Westminster Press, 1967.

2. Scriptural quotations in this book are from the Revised Standard Version.

Chapter Nine:
Old Testament Notions of Flesh and Spirit

1. The term "flesh" in this chapter refers to the Hebrew term "basar."

2. Some time spent with a concordance to the Old Testament will show that a number of examples could be given for most of the usages mentioned in this chapter.

3. No one English word translates all of the different meanings of the Hebrew *ruah*. The word "spirit" translates most of the meanings which are important for our purposes.

4. Note John 3, 8: "The wind (Greek = *pneuma*) blows where it wills, and you hear the sound of it, but you do not know whence it comes or whither it goes; so it is with every one who is born of the spirit (*pneuma*)." The term *pneuma*, translated alternatively "wind" and "spirit," is roughly equivalent to the Hebrew *ruah*.

5. Some passages, such as those picturing God as breathing his *ruah* into human beings, raise some interesting questions. Is the *ruah* God himself or a created reality in a human being? Supposing that there is both a *ruah* in God and a created *ruah* in the enlivened human being, what is the relation between the two? Is the created reality a participation in the divine reality? The Hebrew writer working with images of breath and wind is not posing questions in these terms; nor need we do so here. For our purposes it is sufficient to keep in mind what the Old Testament authors clearly assert.

Chapter Ten:
The New Testament: Fulfillment of Promise

1. For example, Genesis 3, 15 expresses the belief that in the continuing struggle between the seed of the woman (mankind) and the seed of the serpent (forces of evil) mankind will achieve some sort of advantage over the adversary, but the symbolic language gives no further information about what will happen.

2. In some cases it is difficult to know whether the Old Testament author has in mind a fulfillment close to his own time, perhaps even in some historical person he already knew. In some cases New Testament

authors apply to Jesus and events in the early Church some texts whose original authors had in mind a fulfillment in other circumstances closer to their own time. In such cases this New Testament application of the text provides a meaning, an interpretation, beyond that intended by the original author. For example, Matthew 1, 23 applies to the birth of Jesus a text from Isaiah 7, 14. In Matthew the text reads: "Behold, a virgin shall conceive and bear a son, and his name shall be called Emmanuel." In Isaiah the word *alma* means "young woman," not necessarily specifically a virgin. The Septuagint Greek translated it as "virgin," and this is the meaning taken up in Matthew. It seems that here Matthew gives a meaning to the prophecy beyond that which the original author had in mind. We are here interested primarily in understanding the minds of the New Testament authors, rather than with the question of whether their understanding of the promises and prophecies corresponds exactly with that of the original Old Testament writers.

3. E.g., Jn 1, 45; Acts 7, 52; 10, 43; 13, 23; 18, 28; Lk 2, 25–32.

4. E.g., Mt 1, 22–23; 2, 15; 4, 13–16; 8, 16–17; 12, 15–21; 21, 1–5.

5. See Acts 2, 24–28; 3, 18; 3, 22–26; 8, 26–35; 13, 27–29; 13, 32–37; 17, 2–3.

6. See Mt 26, 31; 26, 52–56; 27, 9; Lk 22, 37; Jn 13, 18 (Acts 1, 16–17); Jn 19, 24 and 28; 19, 36–37.

7. Within that tradition in Israel which favored the monarchy, David came to be seen as the ideal king, and it was expected that God's promises would be fulfilled through a king in the Davidic line. Nathan promises David that his line will last forever (2 Sam 7, 16). Isaiah sees a future king in the Davidic line (from the stump of Jesse, David's father)—on whom will rest God's spirit, who will judge fairly, rule with justice, bring peace, and triumph over God's enemies. See Is 9, 1–7; 11, 1–16. Cf Jer 23, 5–6.

8. The genealogies in Matthew 1, 1–16 and Luke 3, 23–38 identify Jesus as belonging to the line of David. Jesus is frequently called "son of David." See, for example, Mt 9, 27; 12, 23; 20, 31; 21, 9; 21, 15. Mt 15, 22 shows that some Jews at least were expecting this descendant of David to come. See also Lk 1, 32–33.

9. Lk 4, 16–21 presents Jesus as applying to himself a similar prophecy from the last part of the book of Isaiah.

10. Though he may state the matter most clearly, Jeremiah is not

the first to speak of a covenant establishing a new situation. See, for example, Hos 2, 18–23.

11. On the endurance of the new covenant see Jer 32, 37–40; Ez 16, 60–63.

12. The Epistle to the Hebrews, which is written for readers thoroughly familiar with the Old Testament, elaborates on the notion of the new covenant. See Heb 8, 1–13.

13. For example, Isaiah 11, 1–16 and Ezekiel 36, 24–28 associate the coming of the spirit with a gathering of the Jews from exile. It would be easy for a Jew to see this as fulfilled in the return of the Jews from exile in Babylon.

14. When the New Testament uses the term "Holy Spirit" it does not mean that the human author has in mind explicitly the third person of the Trinity according to the definitions of later Church councils. The New Testament authors in some of these texts may have in mind simply the life-giving presence of God, much as the Spirit of God is understood by Old Testament authors.

15. Of course modern Scripture scholars have shown how care must be taken before pronouncing on the precise historical quality of texts of the New Testament. For example, the discourses of Jesus as they appear in the Gospels are not exact stenographic records of what Jesus said. One discourse in a Gospel may combine different materials which Jesus pronounced at different times. It is often difficult to determine for a particular passage whether it contains the very words of Jesus or formulations of later writers who have attempted to catch the meaning of what Jesus said and applied it to a particular situation. Similar difficulties arise in determining the exact historical quality of discourses in Acts. It is not our purpose in this chapter to establish whether the texts used here convey the exact words spoken by Jesus, Peter or Paul. Our purpose is to show how the New Testament writers understand Jesus and events in the early Church in terms of promises found in the Old Testament. Of course it is implicit in our approach that this understanding by the New Testament authors is a valuable understanding, is in fact a product of the inspiration of the Holy Spirit.

Chapter Eleven:
The Life of the Spirit

1. By "Pauline writings" here we mean not only the epistles such as Romans, concerning which there is little or no dispute that Paul was the author, but also other epistles, such as Ephesians and the pastoral epistles, which many believe were not written by Paul. For our topic all of these epistles can safely be treated as a unit. For convenience sake we will use expressions such as "Paul says . . ." when referring even to epistles whose Pauline authorship is disputed.

2. The New Testament Greek word for flesh is *sarx*.

3. See 1 Cor 15, 50; 2 Cor 4, 10; 7, 5, for other passages in which *sarx* refers to the physical body. It can refer also to the bodies of animals, as in 1 Cor 15, 39.

4. Some Christians take a more drastic view of human sinfulness. They claim that fallen human nature can do nothing but sin. The Catholic view, followed in this chapter, is that though fallen human beings are prone to sin and unable by their own power to attain or earn salvation, yet they are not so corrupted as to be capable of no good whatsoever. The more drastic view is also that the Christian, even after being justified in this life, in a sense remains capable in himself only of sin. The Holy Spirit indeed produces good works in the justified Christian, but these good works in a sense are not attributable to the human being, but are works only of the Holy Spirit. The Catholic view is that the good works of the Christian are attributable both to the Holy Spirit and to the human person who has been transformed in his being by the Holy Spirit and made capable of good actions.

5. Paul uses three Greek terms whose meanings overlap with the Hebrew *ruah*; of the three, psyche, nous and pneuma, only the latter is directly relevant to our topic.

6. Concerning both the classical Greek and the New Testament uses of *pneuma*, see *Theological Dictionary of the New Testament*, Vol. VI, edited by G. Friedrich, Grand Rapids, Mich., Eerdmans, 1968, pp. 332–451.

7. In 2 Corinthians 1, 21–22 Paul says: "But it is God who establishes us with you in Christ and has commissioned us: he has put his seal upon us and given us his Spirit in our hearts as a guarantee." Again it is a question of God enabling Paul in some sense to establish his credentials

with the Corinthians. The fact that the Spirit is *in the heart* of Paul (and of Timothy?) suggests some inner working of the Spirit. However, this might serve as a guarantee to Paul, in whom the Spirit was acting, but the text seems to suggest that the guarantee is to the Corinthians, since it is a matter of God establishing Paul with them. Perhaps then it means that the Spirit in Paul's heart manifests itself in some way observable by the Corinthians. Perhaps Paul's manner of life shows the presence of the Spirit in his heart.

8. For a further description of the qualities of *agape* see Rom 12, 19–21 and 1 Cor 13, 4–7.

9. See Mt 22, 37–39. Usually when Paul speaks about *agape* he is referring to love of neighbor. In relation to God, Paul speaks especially of human beings having faith, a disposition which includes more than mere intellectual assent and which can include what we would call love. Occasionally Paul speaks of *agape* which people have for God—e.g., Rom 8, 28; 1 Cor 2, 9; 8, 3; Eph 5, 24. Of course other New Testament authors frequently refer to *agape* humans have for God. Matthew 22, 37–39 and 1 John 4, 20–21 closely associate *agape* for God and *agape* for neighbor.

10. This explanation of how love of neighbor can be implicitly a love of God is offered as an attempt which may very well be too simple and may require modification or even more radical change to be acceptable.

Chapter Twelve:
The New Testament as Guide to Action

1. In using the term "moral good" in this chapter we are not trying to insinuate a particular philosophical or theological set of presuppositions in a hidden way into the interpretation of the New Testament. "Moral good" here is used insofar as possible without philosophical or theological presuppositions to denote that good which human beings should attempt to achieve and which has priority over other goods in the particular situation. The goods which the Christian is called to achieve can be called moral goods in this wide sense. This chapter will make use of certain philosophical elements elaborated in Part One. These elements

will be introduced explicitly when they are used, and the critical reader may judge at that point whether their introduction is legitimate.

2. Passages too numerous to mention could be cited. See, for example, Mt 25, 31–46; 1 Jn 4, 17; Jas 1, 26–27.

3. As will become clear in Part Three, in making moral judgments about particular cases the normative and the factual elements are not so clearly distinct from each other as this explanation suggests. The role of the Spirit in such judgments is not so easily isolated to the normative as distinct from the factual knowledge. Nonetheless, the explanation here, though overly simple, is substantially accurate.

4. The problem of determining to whom New Testament norms apply is further complicated by the fact that cultural factors affect whether or not people accept norms.

5. Besides the three steps here outlined there is another possibility to be taken into account in using New Testament statements as guides to action. Certain rules in the New Testament should perhaps be interpreted not as moral norms but as human laws made to organize a particular area of life for a certain period of time. For example, Paul gives directions concerning conduct at the gatherings of the faithful (1 Cor 14, 26–36). Not all of these directions need be thought of as in themselves moral norms. Some, or perhaps all, of them may be rules made by Paul to govern the assembly, one particular way of doing things but not necessarily the only possible correct way. These man-made rules have a moral aspect. There is some moral obligation that effective rules be made so that the assemblies will achieve the good for which they are intended. Also, once the rules are made by a legitimate authority there is some moral obligation to follow them, in order that the assemblies achieve their proper good. However, these rules may not be, in themselves, moral norms, and it may be a mistake to treat them as such.

6. Part Four will discuss problems involved both in the second and third steps.

7. For this interpretation I am indebted to Chapter Three of C.H. Dodd's *Gospel and Law*. I have not, however, tried to follow Dodd's interpretation exactly.

8. This presupposition is based on the Roman Catholic belief in the inerrancy of Scripture. The inerrancy of Scripture should, of course, be understood in relation to literary form. For example, in saying that the first three chapters of the Book of Genesis do not err, we are understand-

ing them as expressions of religious truth, not as scientific astronomy, geology or biology.

9. In claiming that these characteristics are present in Christian moral life we are not implying that they are never present in the moral thought and practice of non-Christians.

10. Paul speaks of the ability to discern spirits as itself a gift of the Spirit (1 Cor 12, 10). It is difficult to know for certain whether Paul is thinking of discernment in the wide sense in which we are using the term, i.e., as applying to moral judgment generally. Paul might be thinking of discernment in certain more explicitly religious matters. However, Paul thinks of the Christian moral life generally as a product of the Holy Spirit. It seems likely, therefore, that this gift of discernment of which he speaks applies to moral judgment generally.

11. Discernment of what is in accord with the Holy Spirit can take place on either of two levels: on the level of discovering moral norms, and on the level of applying those norms in making moral judgments concerning particular cases. This chapter has focused on discernment on the level of discovering norms.

12. Of course a moral norm may be presented as in accord with the Gospel but may not truly be so. Naturally, dissatisfaction with such a norm need not indicate a lack of the proper interior life.

Chapter Thirteen:
The Relation of Scriptural Ethics to Non-Scriptural Ethics

1. Unless one gives rather unusual definitions of "natural" and "supernatural" it seems that the problem of the relation between natural ethics and supernatural ethics is not exactly the same as the problem of the relation between non-scriptural ethics and Scripture-based ethics. Presumably the Holy Spirit works supernatural effects in the lives of persons who have not accepted, nor even heard of, the Christian Scriptures. Such effects could cause the person to accept certain values, and an ethics based partially on such values would contain some elements of the supernatural. On the other hand, unless one uses a rather unusual definition of "natural," there seems to be no convincing reason to suppose that God has not allowed any truths of natural ethics to be taught in the Christian Scriptures.

2. This separation of the level of norms from the level of application is somewhat artificial and imperfect, because in some cases the perception of a moral norm takes place in such a concrete form that one is not aware of it as a distinct step from the application of the norm to the particular case.

3. On what we mean by "true absolutely" see Chapter Two.

4. In some implicit way people without Scripture may have some knowledge of redemption and a redeemer and of God's salvific intervention. We are not discussing this implicit sort of knowledge here. The examples are of matters in which, without Scripture, there would be no explicit knowledge.

5. The *agape* of those who do not accept Sacred Scripture may take an imperfect form, insofar as it may not involve any explicit love of God.

6. Recall that here we have been speculating on the possible agreements and disagreements of those who are in agreement in accepting the moral theory in this book. Of course differences in moral theory constitute another great area for disagreement.

7. This willingness to use human resources to discover what is morally good is tied to a Roman Catholic belief that while human beings are wounded by sin, yet they are not fundamentally corrupted. Therefore God can still reveal what is morally good through the operation of human intelligence and appetites.

Chapter Fourteen:
Ethical Particularism

1. There is some difficulty finding a commonly acceptable term to denote the position discussed in this chapter. Joseph Fletcher in the book *Situation Ethics* uses the term "antinomianism" to denote a position more or less like the one discussed here, but that term already has a theological meaning of a different sort—i.e., it is the name of a particular school of thought which holds that faith alone, not obedience to the moral law, is necessary for salvation. The term we have chosen, while it may have some disadvantages, at least has the advantage of being sufficiently vague that readers may wait to see what meaning is given to it rather than assume that they know what it means.

2. Our descriptions of ethical particularism and of situation ethics

are not intended to represent adequately the positions of any particular thinkers. These descriptions are simplified in order to focus discussion on one or two crucial points.

3. In the terminology used here, general rules may admit of exceptions, but universal rules are rules which do not admit of exceptions.

4. "Pre-moral good" here corresponds to good in general as it is defined in Part One prior to the discussion of the specifically moral good in Chapter Six. "Pre-moral evil" here corresponds to evil in general as it is defined in Part One prior to the discussion of specifically moral evil in Chapter Six.

5. As the next chapter will make clear, these two phases do not give a comprehensive account of the process of making judgments of conscience.

Chapter Fifteen:
The Judgment of Conscience

1. Situation ethicists sometimes speak of making exceptions to general rules when the situation demands it. Strictly speaking, a situation, considered as factual, does not make moral demands. The "demand" requires the input of moral norms.

2. An examination of Jacques Maritain's *The Degrees of Knowledge*, or of Bernard Lonergan's *Insight* or of Hans-Georg Gadamer's *Truth and Method*, will give some idea of the complexity of the problem of how facts are understood. Furthermore, some types of "understanding" of the facts involve relating the facts to human needs, likes, dislikes, and values. Such an understanding involves elements which, according to our terminology, come under knowledge of norms rather than knowledge of facts.

3. Part Four will give some discussion of how we can recognize whose judgment is to be trusted in cases in which our own judgment is not sound.

4. When an individual's judgment of conscience differs from that of the consensus of people there is a special problem of discerning whether this judgment corresponds with the movement of the Holy Spirit. This constitutes the problem of distinguishing true from false prophets, a topic taken up in Part Four.

5. This book is concerned primarily with questions of objective good and evil. However, to prevent misunderstanding it seems useful here to introduce briefly the subjective elements of responsibility and attitude toward God.

6. Here we will not go into the further distinction between mortal and venial sin, since this would take us far into an analysis of the subjective aspects of morality.

7. In distinguishing these second and third states we are not pretending that there is a clear borderline so that all individual moral acts can be easily classified in one or other category.

Chapter Sixteen:
Situation Ethics

1. Even the enthusiastic situation ethicist Joseph Fletcher in *Situation Ethics* insists that one moral rule admits of no exceptions, i.e., the rule of love of neighbor.

2. Mr. Smith is not an ethical relativist if he is merely expressing his own or a general ignorance about certain cases. Many people (including this author) who reject ethical relativism also admit that although there is an objective reality which determines what is morally good or evil in any situation, yet in some cases one does not know this reality sufficiently well to make a certain judgment of conscience.

3. See Roland H. Bainton, *Christian Attitudes toward War and Peace: A Historical Survey and Critical Evaluation*, New York, Abingdon Press, 1960.

4. Insistence on following general laws in every case often is associated with other undesirable characteristics of legalism. It can shift people's focus to the negative side of morals, because most laws which people hold to be universal state what should not be done. People may lose sight of the positive good, the accomplishments which are the real goals of moral life. They may fail to grasp that fullness of life which cannot be depicted in any law, much less in a negative law. Universal laws are intended to apply to people generally, so they do not adequately express the special things to which particular people are invited by God at particular times. Finally, emphasis on observing the law may leave Christians feeling that if they observe certain laws they are justified by

their actions. They may forget that they are justified by God's free gift through faith in Jesus Christ.

5. It is possible that a moral judgment not be publicly defensible but be correct. One might judge on the basis of a private and incommunicable insight or on a special revelation by God which cannot be authenticated by any evidence one can share with others. Such judgments fall outside of direct guidance by ethics as a science, which must work with materials which in some way are publicly defensible. Ethics may give some indirect guidance concerning moral judgments which are not publicly defensible. It may offer criteria to help one know whether one is being deluded by a supposed insight or special revelation.

6. It is not a matter of depending on majority opinion and the ability to convince a majority in public debate as the main basis for accepting moral views. Some people are intellectually better equipped than others to follow rational arguments. Some people are less biased and more objective than others. Some people have the type of appetitive development which makes them especially able to appreciate various goods. It is the ability to convince the more expert type of moral thinker which makes a moral judgment defensible in a proper sense.

7. Notice that an evil may be caused indirectly in a physical sense but yet be done directly in the sense used here. Suppose that I ask my employee to tell a third party to burn down the property of a fourth party in order to convince the latter of the wisdom of paying my organization a certain amount in order to protect the rest of his property from similar accidents in the future. Although I do not do the damage directly in a physical sense, yet I do it directly in the sense intended here, because I intend it as a means to some further effect.

8. See F.J. Connell, "Double effect, principle of," *New Catholic Encyclopedia*, Vol. IV, pp. 1020–1022.

9. "Solid evidence" here means that when all reasonable means have been used to arrive at the truth, it appears that the good which is intended is greater or more important than the evil means employed. Full certainty is not required. "Solid evidence" means that reasons in favor of the conclusion are more convincing than are the reasons to the contrary. Of course in all these cases, if the good can be attained without causing evil, the evil should not be used as a means.

10. Here when we speak of the lack of solid evidence that the good intended is greater or less than the evil used as a means, we are considering

that evil more or less in its immediate context. As we shall see later, once we consider that evil in other contexts, it becomes clear that a further evil is involved.

11. The point here is similar to the one made by Germain Grisez when he insists that in many cases when one begins to make exceptions one pretends to measure against each other goods and evils which are incommensurable. See *A Grisez Reader for Beyond the New Morality*, edited by Joseph H. Casey S.J., Washington University Press of America, 1982, pp. 115ff. The passage here cited is taken originally from *Life and Death with Liberty and Justice*, by Germain Grisez and Joseph Boyle, Jr. I would not extend this notion of incommensurability as widely as Grisez does. He seems to conclude in a somewhat a priori basis that certain classes of goods or evils are incommensurable. I would prefer to look at particular cases where a particular good or evil is compared to another particular good or evil, with a view always to discovering whether publicly defensible criteria for comparison are available. From the examination of typical cases one can begin to generalize about what kinds of goods or evils are incommensurable in relation to what other kinds of goods or evils.

12. This brief discussion of truth-telling is not presented as an adequate demonstration that no lie may ever be told. It is presented as a reflection on the difficulty of elaborating a situation ethics of truth-telling which can be supported by publicly defensible arguments.

13. Of course by special divine revelation one might know this, and so these rules must be considered as universal unless one knows by special divine revelation that an exception may be made.

14. This rule does not cover cases in which a person might be killed for some reason other than for his own good.

15. While agreeing with the manualists that many of the rules which they class as universal, allowing of no exceptions, are indeed universal, I do not always concur in the reasons they give for this classification.

16. Mention should be made of another category, which may look like an exception to a general moral norm but which is not. Cases of this type are exceptions to moral norms materially considered but are not exceptions when one properly understands the meaning of the norm. For example, the Roman Catholic Church teaches officially that artificial contraception is morally wrong. If we understand this rule materially, it would not allow a woman to use contraceptive measures to prevent preg-

nancy. However, a less materialistic view of the rule would say that what is condemned is artificial contraception which is used in order to be able to engage in voluntary sexual relations without becoming pregnant. In this view, the evil of contraception is in wanting and deliberately engaging in sexual activity while excluding children. To exclude pregnancy resulting from involuntary sexual activity is not morally wrong. Therefore a woman who uses artificial contraception to avoid pregnancy which results from rape is justified not because this is a legitimate exception to the rule forbidding artificial contraception, but because the rule, properly understood, does not apply in her case. This is the line of thought pursued by Fr. M. Zalba in an article in *Rassegna di Teologia* 9 (1968) 225–27. I am dependent upon an unpublished translation of this article by Fr. Edward J. Bayer, S.T.D. with the English title: "The meaning of the principle of totality in the doctrine of Pius XI and Pius XII and its application to cases of sexual violence."

Chapter Eighteen:
Society and the Limits of Individual Conscience

1. Part Three focused mainly on judgments of conscience. Part Four is concerned with judgments of conscience and also with other kinds of moral judgments, in their relationship to the community. Part Three contained a discussion of how ignorance of norms, ignorance of facts, and bias can cause subjectivism in one's judgments of conscience. These three factors can cause subjectivism in other moral judgments, e.g., in one's formulation of intermediate maxims.

2. The fact that one's thought, emotions and attitudes are profoundly influenced by society need not be an argument in favor of relativism in knowledge. The fact that one lives in a particular age or century has much to do with one's belief that the earth is not flat, but this does not mean that the belief that the world is a sphere is no more objective than the belief that it is flat.

3. This chapter has discussed the relation of the individual to society, to other people generally. The next chapter speaks not of society but of community. The term "community" rather than "society" is applied to the Church to indicate that in the Church a *common* life is fostered, based on a deliberately formulated *common* belief.

Chapter Nineteen:
The Catholic Church and Moral Teaching

1. It seems to this author that some recent appeals to the tradition of probabilism are arguments in favor of this illegitimate type of pluralism. Examples might be the article by Carol Tauer, ''The tradition of probabilism and the moral status of the early embryo,'' *Theological Studies* 45 (1984) 3–33, and several articles to which she refers.

2. In some cases several different moral positions all seem to lead to relatively good results, and there seems to be little hope of pushing different parties beyond their particular views toward one commonly held position. In such cases it may be the case that the good accomplished by following any one opinion is not significantly greater or less than the good accomplished by following another opinion. Resting in such a pluralism would cause no signficiant harm.

3. The term ''magisterium'' has meant different things in the history of theology, as Fr. Yves M. Congar shows in the article ''A semantic history of the term 'magisterium' '' in *Readings in Moral Theology No. 3, The Magisterium and Morality*, edited by Charles E. Curran and Richard A. McCormick, New York, Paulist Press, 1982, pp. 297–313. This is a translation of an article in *Revue des sciences philosophiques et théologiques* 60 (1970) 85–98. Here by ''magisterium'' we mean the teaching office of the ecclesiastical hierarchy. This is the usual meaning of the term in current writings. The volume *Readings in Morality No. 3* contains a good selection of articles on the topics in Part IV of this book.

4. In calling this view democratic we do not imply that it is democratic in the same way as are certain forms of national government. We mean simply that in this view of the magisterium a very great emphasis is placed on popular opinion as a norm for teaching.

5. See 1 Cor 1, 18ff.

6. By this statement we do not deny that the hierarchy enjoys a special grace of office for teaching. We mean that members of the hierarchy must *also* use the other means for discovering the truth.

7. The term ''counter-culture'' arose in the 1960's among some people who were very opposed to the status quo in the U.S. and other Western nations. They realized that it is difficult, if not impossible, to be part of a culture and yet maintain enough independence to criticize and change it fundamentally. Some advocates of the creation of a counter-

culture were naive about the difficulty of the task, and most experiments in that direction were short-lived. Christians embarking on the creation of a counter-culture can point to some reasonably successful attempts in their own tradition, notably several of the great religious orders.

8. Of course the community life is not sought as an end in itself apart from union with God.

Chapter Twenty:
The Magisterium and Dissent on Moral Questions

1. We will not discuss here what kinds of moral truths might be defined (explicitly revealed, implicitly revealed, necessary to protect revealed truths, etc.). Nor will we discuss all of the different theological "notes" (*proxima fidei*, etc.) that can be attached to different propositions. For our particular purpose a simpler set of categories seems to be adequate.

2. See G. Ford and Germain Grisez, "Contraception and the infallibility of the ordinary magisterium," *Theological Studies* 39 (1978) 258–312.

3. Apparently this is an example of a New Testament teaching which the Church has not felt the need of defining solemnly because it has not been challenged by any significant group of Christians.

4. Some might argue that the Church teaches infallibly by its ordinary magisterium that slavery is wrong. This seems unlikely. As late as the middle of the last century there was slavery in the U.S. without, to my knowledge, a full consensus by the whole Catholic hierarchy that Catholics were morally bound in every situation to free their slaves. It would be interesting to speculate about the position of a slave owner in a primitive tribe today who converted to Catholicism. Were he to refuse to free his slaves he would be going against a rather solid consensus of Catholic thought, but would he be going against something that is of the Catholic faith? I believe not. A plausible case might be made that in the short term in particular situations it would be better to treat one's slaves humanely than to abolish slavery before other economic structures were available to assure a livelihood for all of the working class.

5. See John T. Noonan, *Contraception: A History of the Treat-*

ment by the Catholic Theologians and Canonists, Cambridge, Mass., Harvard University Press, 1965.

6. In using the Church's teaching on artificial contraception as an example in this section we are presuming that it is not an infallible teaching of the ordinary magisterium, contrary to the position of Ford and Grisez, *op. cit.*

7. A clear presentation of this argument is presented by Bruno Schüller, ''Remarks on the authentic teaching of the magisterium of the Church,'' in *Readings in Moral Theology, No. 3: The Magisterium and Morality*, pp. 14–33. This article is a translation of an article in *Théologie und Philosophie* 42 (1967) 534–551.

8. If all dissent from papal moral teachings were forbidden, the different degrees of authority of different papal moral teachings would remain relevant to scholars and Popes when they considered the possibility or advisability of changing the official teaching, but it would not be relevant in making a judgment of conscience while the teaching is in force.

9. Joseph A. Komonchak discusses the positions of several ''traditional'' moralists on dissent from papal teachings in ''Ordinary papal magisterium and religious assent,'' *Readings in Moral Theology, No. 3: The Magisterium and Morality*, pp. 67–90. This article originally appeared in *Contraception: Authority and Dissent*, edited by Charles Curran, New York, Herder and Herder, 1969, 101–126.

10. The conditions given below for dissent from papal teachings in the first category would apply to certain non-infallible teachings of ecumenical councils and to teachings of the whole Catholic hierarchy, because some of these teachings would possess a degree of authority similar to papal teachings in the first category.

BIBLIOGRAPHY

Aristotle, *The Nicomachean Ethics*, London, Allen and Unwin, 1953.

Curran, Charles E., and McCormick, Richard, Editors, *Moral Norms and Catholic Tradition* (Readings in Moral Theology, No. 1), New York, Paulist Press, 1979.

————. *The Distinctiveness of Christian Ethics* (Readings in Moral Theology, No. 2), New York, Paulist Press, 1980.

————. *The Magisterium and Morality* (Readings in Moral Theology, No. 3), New York, Paulist Press, 1982.

Deidun, Thomas, *New Covenant Morality in Paul*, Rome, Pontifical Biblical Institute, Analecta Biblica, 1981.

Deman, Thomas, *Aux origines de la théologie morale*, Montréal, Institut d'Études Médiévales Albert-le-Grand, 1951.

Dodd, Charles Harold, *Gospel and Law*, New York, Columbia University Press, 1951.

Ellul, Jacques, *The Ethics of Freedom*, Grand Rapids, Eerdmans, 1976.

Fuchs, Josef, *Human Values and Christian Morality*, Dublin, Gill and Macmillan, 1970.

Gilleman, Gerard, *The Primacy of Charity in Moral Theology*, Westminster, Md., Newman Press, 1959.

Häring, Bernard, *Free and Faithful in Christ: Moral Theology for Clergy and Laity*, 3 volumes, New York, Seabury Press, 1978.

Hiers, Richard H., *Jesus and Ethics*, Philadelphia, Westminster Press, 1968.

Leclercq, Jacques, *Christ and the Modern Conscience*, London, G. Chapman, 1962.

L'Hour, Jean, *La morale de l'alliance,* Paris, Cahiers de la Revue Biblique, 1966.

Lottin, Odo, *Au couer de la morale chrétienne: bible, tradition, philosophie,* Tournai, Desclée, 1957.

McDonagh, Enda, *Invitation and Response, Essays in Christian Moral Theology,* Dublin, Gill and Macmillan, 1972.

Schnackenburg, Rudolf, *The Moral Teaching of the New Testament,* Freiburg, Herder, 1965.

Pieper, Josef, *Prudence,* New York, Pantheon, 1959.

Vann, Gerald, *Morals and Man,* New York, Sheed and Ward, 1960.

von Hildebrand, Dietrich, *Christian Ethics,* New York, David McKay Co., 1953.

INDEX